D1383772

School, Home, Community

You and Your Health
Teacher's Edition

Julius B. Richmond, M.D.
Elenore T. Pounds, M.A.
Gladys Gardner Jenkins, M.A.
Dieter H. Sussdorf, Ph.D.

In consultation with
Orvis A. Harrelson, M.D., M.P.H.
Wallace Ann Wesley, Hs.D.

Scott, Foresman and Company
Glenview, Illinois

Dallas, Texas Palo Alto, California
Oakland, New Jersey Tucker, Georgia

Highlights of *You and Your Health*

A deeply human approach	Opening chapter in each text centers on mental health. Program emphasizes building of positive self-concepts; helps students understand themselves and others.
Easy for students to read and use	High-interest content, effective writing styles, and powerful visuals enhance readability. Readability is at or below grade level according to Fry and Dale-Chall formulas. Anatomical drawings are accurately done by a professional medical illustrator.
Easy to teach	Chapters organized for easy teaching and learning. Helpful "Teacher's Notes" printed on pupil's pages in *Teacher's Edition*. Chapters can be taught in any order. Books can be used with large or small groups or by individuals. Behavioral objectives are posed directly to students. Testing program is built into books. End-of-Book test is action-oriented.
Learner verified	Scott, Foresman health materials have been widely used in the classroom. This new Program has evolved out of 30 years of interaction among learners, teachers, and the publisher. New materials have been classroom tested. Classroom teachers have served as advisors on the Program.
Unique provisions for school-home communication	School and Home feature at the end of each chapter. Supplementary school/home *Activity Booklets* with parents' message on the back of each Activity Sheet.
Age-appropriate content written by health science experts	Content based on research about children's health and safety needs and concerns. Double-checked for accuracy by experts in all areas of the health sciences.

ISBN: 0-673-11015-X

12345678910-RRC-858483828180797877 76

Criteria for Selection of a Health Textbook*

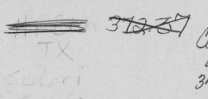

Does Level Six cover concepts in those aspects of a complete health education program that are appropriate to eleven- to twelve-year-olds?

Mental Health, Human Relations, and Values Awareness	*Pages 10-41, 173-174*
Personal Health, Fitness, and Dental Health	*Pages 98-147*
The Body, Human Growth and Development	*Pages 42-97*
Nutrition	*Pages 118-129*
Family Health	*Pages 41, 67, 97, 147, 197, 231, 249-252, 267*
Prevention and Control of Disease, Health Services	*Pages 62, 77, 130-141, 198-231*
Drugs (Including Alcohol and Tobacco)	*Pages 170-197, 224-225*
Community and Environmental Health (Human Ecology)	*Pages 232-267*
Consumer Health	*Pages 128, 173-174*
Safety and First Aid	*Pages 148-169*
Health Career Awareness	*Pages 141, 224-225*

A guide to the Scope and Teaching Sequence of YOU AND YOUR HEALTH K-8 is available on request from Scott, Foresman and Company. This guide includes concepts and selected behavioral objectives.

Does it motivate children to apply what they are learning in health to their daily lives at school, at home, and in the community?
Pages 21-32, 101-103, 115, 124-128, 148-169, 231, 249-252, 260-261, 267

Does it present materials and approaches that include the family in the health education program?
Pages 41, 67, 97, 147, 148-169, 197, 231, 249-252, 267

Does it use the problem-solving approach to develop critical thinking and decision-making skills on the part of children?
Pages 21-32, 159-162, 173-174

Does it build positive mental-health attitudes in children by enhancing their self-images and fostering appreciation of individual differences?
Pages 10-41, 71-76, 90-91, 101-103

---

*Based on Joint Committee on Health Problems in Education of the NEA and the AMA, *Why Health Education in Your School?* and *Suggested School Health Policies*, 5th ed., AMA.

Authors

Consultants

Julius B. Richmond, M.D. Professor of Child Psychiatry and Human Development and Professor and Chairman, Department of Social and Preventive Medicine, Harvard Medical School; Director, Judge Baker Guidance Center; Chief of Psychiatric Service, Children's Hospital Medical Center, Boston, Massachusetts.

Orvis A. Harrelson, M.D., M.P.H. Corporate Medical Director, Weyerhauser Company, Tacoma, Washington; former Administrative Director of Health, Tacoma Public Schools, Tacoma, Washington.

Elenore T. Pounds, M.A. Writer; lecturer; former Directing Editor of the Health and Personal Development Program; classroom teacher; coauthor of the *Health and Growth* Program; author of *Drugs and Your Safety* and other *Health Enrichment Booklets*.

Wallace Ann Wesley, Hs.D. Director, Department of Health Education, American Medical Association, Chicago, Illinois; former teacher at primary through college levels.

Gladys Gardner Jenkins, M.A. Lecturer in Parent-Child-Teacher Relationships, University of Iowa, Iowa City, Iowa; former member, National Advisory Council on Child Growth and Human Development; author of *Helping Children Reach Their Potential;* coauthor of *These Are Your Children.*

Learner Feedback

Dieter H. Sussdorf, Ph.D. Associate Professor of Microbiology, Cornell University Graduate School of Medical Sciences, New York, New York; coauthor of *Methods in Immunology*.

Experimental versions of many of the lessons in YOU AND YOUR HEALTH for grade six were used during the 1975–1976 school year with students at Jane Addams School, Lawndale, California; Jacksonville Beach Elementary School 144, Jacksonville Beach, Florida; and Public School 276, Brooklyn, New York. The authors and editors of the program are grateful to the students and to the teachers in these schools for their comments and their suggestions.

Content Specialists

Richard H. Blum, Ph.D. Consulting Professor, Department of Psychology and Director, Joint Program in Drugs, Crime, and Community Studies, Center for Interdisciplinary Research, Stanford University, Stanford, California.

Norman H. Olsen, D.D.S. Chairman of the Department of Pedodontics and Dean of The Dental School, Northwestern University, Chicago, Illinois.

Willie D. Ford, Ph.D. Professor, Nutrition and Home Economics, Grambling State University, Grambling, Louisiana; former Nutrition Specialist, U.S. Department of Agriculture, University of Nebraska, Lincoln, Nebraska.

Marguerite Robinson, M.A. Consumer Specialist, Department of Health, Education, Welfare, Food and Drug Administration, Chicago, Illinois; President, Chicago Nutrition Society, Chicago, Illinois.

Lucia Guzman, B.S. Assistant to the Dean for Student Affairs, University of Texas School of Allied Health Sciences, University of Texas Medical Branch, Galveston, Texas.

Joan Tillotson, Ph.D. Consultant in Movement Education, The University of North Carolina at Charlotte, Charlotte, North Carolina.

Barbara J. Kohuth, B.S. Environmental Health Educator; Head, Office of Environmental Education and Public Information, Cleveland Department of Public Health and Welfare, Cleveland, Ohio.

Wilma Yee, B.S., R.N. Public Health Nurse and School Nurse, Oakland Public Schools, Oakland, California.

Boyd T. Marsh, M.A., Deputy Health Commissioner for Environmental Health, Cleveland Department of Public Health and Welfare, Cleveland, Ohio.

The assistance of the National Safety Council, Chicago, Illinois, in reviewing the safety advice in this material is gratefully acknowledged.

Contents

Components of Level Six

Program Materials

Pupil's Text
Centers around the special health and safety needs and interests of the eleven- to twelve-year-old child.

The amount of written material and the reading level, grade 6 according to the Fry and Dale-Chall formulas, are appropriate to sixth-grade readers.

Heavily illustrated including full color photographs, original art, and reproductions of famous masterpieces.

Teacher's Edition
This *Teacher's Edition* contains the following aids:

Teacher's Supplement containing brief, professional "refresher" articles (T11–T23); enrichment suggestions for teaching each lesson (T24–T39); and reference materials for teachers, parents, and pupils (T40–T45). The complete contents are listed on page T6.

Instant-help "Teacher's Notes" in blue in the upper margins of the pupil's pages plus answers to test questions inserted in place.

Supplementary Materials

Activity Booklet
Perforated sheets in this 32-page, consumable booklet have health activities for *school use* on one side, health activities for *home use* and a special health message for parents on the other.

Features of Level Six

Chapter Openers

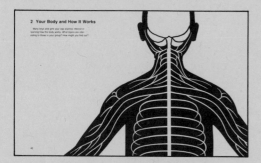

Each chapter begins with a distinctive introduction which conveys the meaning of the content and poses questions designed to lead the student into the chapter.

Photographic Essays

Picture essays are used to provide students with a look inside the Transparent Woman, to show them what the doctor sees in their throats, eyes, and ears, and to look at some environmental health problems and solutions.

Decision-Making Pages

Students are given the opportunity to make decisions about the right thing to do in the areas of mental health and safety. A problem situation is shown in an illustration. Students are asked what they should do in that situation. Then they are told to turn the page. When they turn the page, students find the correct things to do in the situation shown.

Enrichment Activities

Health- and safety-related enrichment activities are used throughout the text. "Enjoy It" pages expose the student to health-related poetry and fine art. "Tell It," "Write It," and "Investigate It" pages provide students with a pleasant way to express themselves, as well as with an opportunity to do some research to expand their understanding of the subject matter.

Health Around Us

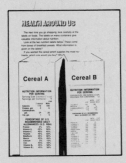

The "Health Around Us" page appears throughout the book. It is used to make students aware of intriguing aspects of health and safety in the world around them and to highlight new developments in the field of health.

Chapter Tests

End-of-chapter test is based on the content of the chapter. The test requires the student to define terms, choose the correct answer, supply the word to fill in a blank, and/or to correct false statements on a true-false test. End-of-book test is action-oriented.

Can You Show What You Know?

This is one of several evaluative techniques used in YOU AND YOUR HEALTH. Have behavioral objectives in the cognitive area are posed to students in simple terms. Students, in turn, give evidence of what they have learned by *observable behavior.*

School and Home

The "School and Home" page is the last page of each chapter in the pupil's text. This page suggests ways the child can bring home newly acquired health knowledge in order to share that knowledge with family members and to incorporate it in daily life.

Learner Feedback

YOU AND YOUR HEALTH has been developed as a result of reactions and suggestions from students and teachers who used the popular HEALTH AND GROWTH Program. Feedback from students and teachers was obtained through questionnaires, correspondence, prepublication testing, and classroom observation.

Level Six of YOU AND YOUR HEALTH contains less written material than level six of the preceding series. The reading level of the new text is on target for the grade level and an especially readable type face has been used.

The content of this text has been reorganized to emphasize cooperation between the school, the home, and the community. The opening chapter is oriented toward building positive self-images and improving students' relationships with each other and with the members of their families. The closing chapter of the text brings the student in contact with community and environmental health problems.

A "School and Home" page at the end of each chapter in YOU AND YOUR HEALTH suggests ways for the child to *bring home* the health knowledge that he or she has gained in that chapter. In addition, a new product—a *School/Home Activity Booklet*—has been made available for use with the text. This consumable booklet is designed to reinforce concepts taught in the text. Each lesson consists of an activity to be done in school, an activity to be done at home, and a health message for parents.

Other features have been included to increase student involvement and awareness of health and safety in their daily living and in the world around them. These include health poems, famous works of art pertaining to some aspect of the subject matter, short oral and written reports, simple investigations, and articles on interesting health and safety topics.

Finally, the teachability of the Program has been enhanced. A "Preview It" page at the beginning of each chapter introduces the students to the content and organization of the material to follow. And a "Review It" page at the end of each chapter provides students with an opportunity to test their understanding of the material presented. Behavioral objectives, stated in terms the students can understand, are presented as part of each chapter in YOU AND YOUR HEALTH. End-of-chapter tests are designed to test these objectives.

In order to continue Scott, Foresman's practice of making our programs responsive to the needs of students and teachers, we have included learner-feedback questionnaires in the Teacher's Supplement. *We would appreciate your completing the teacher's questionnaire on pages T47 and T48 and returning it to us after you have taught YOU AND YOUR HEALTH for most of the school year. If you would be willing to have your students fill out questionnaires, please make enough copies of the student questionnaire on page T46 for them. Then return the completed questionnaires to Scott, Foresman.*

A Healthful Classroom Environment

If health education is to be effective, it is important that it take place in a classroom environment that is physically and mentally healthy. Here are some things you can do to create a favorable *physical environment* for children.

To create a favorable physical environment

Turn on lights on dark days and try to have chairs and desks or tables arranged so no one faces a strong light or glare.

See that children have chairs and desks that are properly adjusted to their heights.

Allow plenty of time for, and give reminders about washing hands *before* eating and *after* using the toilet.

Alternate periods of concentrated work with periods of relaxing activities; alternate periods of strenuous play with quiet ones.

See that playtimes are a mixture of undirected play and of supervised activity during which pupils may explore and practice such skills as climbing, running, and jumping.

Be aware of the needs of some children for more sleep and adequate food. Tired, hungry children do not learn.

Be alert to signs and complaints of illness— watch for change in skin color (which may indicate fever), skin eruptions, dull or watery eyes, general or unusual listleness, irritability, signs of a cold. (See "Signs and Symptoms of Illness" on page T13.)

Cooperate with others in the school system in setting up a plan for health examinations and for keeping cumulative health records.

Pay attention to the environment in general —including aesthetics—as influencing the learning process.

The classroom environment which promotes mental health is one in which each child is helped to develop a strong, positive self-image; a feeling of belonging; and a sense of worth. Here are some things you can do to create such an environment.

To foster a strong, positive self-image

Make a point of learning children's names as soon as possible; check with each child to see if there is a nickname he or she prefers.

Encourage the making of self-portraits. If possible, have pupils use hand mirrors to study carefully hair color, eye color, and so on.

Post *all* the children's self-portraits in the classroom. If there isn't room, display them in "shifts" in randomly chosen order or find room in the hall outside the classroom. Be sure portraits are labeled so the child's name can be seen.

Take time for youngsters to talk about the topic "What I Like About Myself." Let them draw pictures of themselves in activities they feel they do well.

Read poems, such as the one in Chapter One, that stress each child's uniqueness.

Look for opportunities to emphasize that each youngster is different in many ways from any other human being; that he or she is "special"; that differences among individuals are natural and to be expected.

Ask children to draw pictures and write simple stories about their homes, their families, their pets, the foods they like best, things they like to do, a time when they felt sad or happy or angry.

To foster a feeling of "belonging"

Make your classroom a warm, friendly place.

Make it a point to celebrate birthdays by establishing simple ceremonies such as singing to the birthday child.

Watch out for the friendless child; do what you can to seat him or her beside outgoing youngsters and to team him or her with friendly children on committees.

When children are absent for a time, call their homes to inquire about their health. Have the class or individuals prepare simple get-well messages. Welcome back the absentees and let pupils brief them on what has happened at school during their absence.

Make special efforts to help newcomers feel comfortable. Assign friendly children to be "Big Brothers" or "Big Sisters" until the newcomers feel at home.

Let boys and girls have a part in planning various class undertakings.

Encourage the children to talk over problems that arise in the classroom and try to work out better ways of doing things.

To foster a sense of worth

Treat children as you treat your own good friends: find kindly, personal things to say; notice and comment on the positive things a child does.

Try to convey to pupils that you like them, that you have faith in them, that when something goes wrong you will try to help and to see their side of the situation.

Be friendly to *all* children and go out of your way to give an extra dose of friendliness to those who need it most—the noisy ones; the slow ones; the shy ones; the ones with problems such as divorce, illness, or unemployment in the family.

See that each child has a chance to taste success in some area—reading, singing, drawing, pantomiming, playing, caring for a classroom pet, or cleaning the chalkboard.

Build on a child's strengths, then help the child master his or her difficulties.

Keep in mind that praise for what a child has done, or tried hard to do, is a tonic that inspires greater efforts.

Evaluate a child's own progress rather than comparing him or her with others.

Help children learn to accept mistakes and to profit from them. But try to see that pupils have a variety of opportunities for successful experiences too.

Assume that a child having difficulty *wants* to learn but for some reason or other is not doing so; then try to seek the causes for the difficulty. Make use of personnel on the school staff—counselors, nurse, speech therapists, learning-disability specialists, psychologists, and so on—in seeking solutions.

Plan classroom activities to fit the abilities of each child in your room. Set goals for a child that are possible for him or her to achieve. Do not ask a child to achieve what is impossible.

Remember that the child's achievement can often be facilitated if you, the teacher, utilize all the helps at hand—supervisory bulletins, teacher's guides and resource books, courses of study, multimedia aids, an individualized curriculum, as well as sound, appealing instructional aids for pupils.

Signs and Symptoms of Illness[1]

Point of Observation	Physical Signs	Behavior	Complaint
General Appearance and Behavior	Excessive thinness or excessive overweight; very small or very large in body build for age; pallor; weary expression; fatigue; poor posture; dark circles or puffiness under eyes.	Acts tired or apathetic; is easily irritated; makes frequent trips to toilet; has persistent nervous habits, such as muscular twitching or biting of nails or lips; is subject to spasms (fits), fainting spells, or frequent nosebleeds; gets short of breath after mild exertion and climbing stairs; lacks appetite; vomits frequently.	Feels tired or is apathetic; doesn't want to play; has aches or pains; feels sick to stomach; feels dizzy.
Ears	Discharge from ear; cotton in ear; tired, strained expression long before day is over; watchful, bewildered expression.	Is persistently inattentive; asks to have questions repeated; habitually fails to respond when questioned; mispronounces common words; cocks one ear toward speaker.	Has earache; has buzzing or ringing in ears; ears feel stuffy; hears noises in head; feels dizzy.
Eyes	Inflamed (reddened) or watery eyes; frequent sties; crusted lids; cross-eye.	Holds book too close to eyes; squints at book or chalkboard; persistently rubs or blinks eyes; reads poorly.	Headache; eyes ache or smart; cannot see well (blurred vision).
Nose and Throat (Upper Respiratory Tract)	Frequent or long-continued colds; persistent nasal discharge.	Is frequently absent from school because of a cold; constantly clears throat or has frequent coughing or sneezing spells; is always sniffling or blowing nose; breathes persistently through mouth.	Throat feels sore or scratchy; has difficulty in swallowing; nose feels stuffy or sore.
Skin	Rashes or inflamed skin areas; scales and crusts; persistent sores; pimples and blackheads on face; boils; hives; persistent warts; accidental injuries, such as cuts.	Is always scratching himself; is subject to skin irritations (hives, eczema, puzzling rashes, etc.) which suggest sensitivity to one or more substances (allergic manifestations); is easily bruised.	Skin itches or burns.

[1] Courtesy of the Metropolitan Life Insurance Company.

A Developmental Profile of Eleven- to Twelve-Year-Olds

Health education, if it is to be effective, must be appropriate to the developmental level of the learner. The combined knowledge and talents of the author-consultant-advisor team (see pages T4 and T5) brought together to aid in creating this Program have yielded a highly useful profile of eleven- to twelve-year-olds. This profile was used as background for developing the pupil's book and related materials. While it is true that there is no typical child, certain characteristics which seem to be predominant in this age group are described below.

Emotional and social maturity fluctuates

Eleven- to twelve-year-olds want to be independent, but they are not ready to give up their dependence on parents and other adults. They seem surprisingly mature one day and quite dependent another day.

This is a transition year. Many of the children who are not approaching puberty are a bit steadier, a bit more responsible than they were a year ago. Boys and girls at this level of development are alert and energetic. They want to do things well and master new skills. For these youngsters, this is a good year for learning.

For others, the rapidly developing youngsters who are going through the bodily and emotional changes of approaching puberty, there may be some difficulties. They may be full of eagerness in the morning and uninterested in what is going on in the afternoon. They often become overcritical of parents and teachers, but they also develop crushes on adults to whom they are particularly attracted. And while these children frequently expect or want help from adults, they resent being told what to do.

A best friend is needed

The eleven- to twelve-year-old needs a best friend to bolster him or her. This best friend will often be a comparatively new or recent friend. Many youngsters who have been close friends now find themselves drawing apart. One youngster may have matured more rapidly, leaving the pair with no interests in common.

Parents and teachers need to be aware of this problem. And children at this level need an explanation about the differences in the rates of maturing between boys and girls and between youngsters of the same sex. Such knowledge can spare many anxieties.

Awareness of others is increasing

Eleven- to twelve-year-olds are concerned about whether or not others like them and about how others feel about what they are doing. They try to understand the behavior of others instead of complaining about it.

The group is very important

Being a member of a group gives all children of this age the feeling of belonging and being like the others. However, for those nearing puberty, the nature of the group is changing. Some misunderstandings are likely to develop among youngsters of differing maturity levels. Quarreling, dropping out, being left out—with all the resulting heartaches—are not uncommon.

Physical development varies considerably

Before the onset of puberty, there may be a period of six months or a year during which little gain in height or weight is made. This resting period is usually followed by a period of rapid growth which may last one or two years. For most girls, this growth spurt is at eleven or twelve—although it may come at any time between eight and fourteen. And it is usually from one to two years later for boys.

After the growth in height, there is a weight spurt. As the weight gains are made, the hips of girls begin to broaden and the breasts start to develop. The shoulders of boys begin to widen. Pubic hair begins to appear and girls begin to menstruate. Many girls are taller and heavier than the boys in their classes. This is a frequent cause of embarrassment and discomfort.

Awkwardness is common

Boys and girls undergoing rapid growth may be awkward and out of proportion for a time. Their legs grow first, then the trunk, and then in girls the chest and hips, and in boys, the chest and shoulders.

So-called laziness may have a real basis

The physical changes taking place often sap these youngsters' energies. Great spurts of energy may be followed by periods of laziness. Fatigue may be present, and what appears to be laziness may well be the result of the body's real need for rest. This tiredness of the rapidly-growing youngster is in sharp contrast to the energy of the same-aged child who is not nearing puberty.

Interest in the body continues

Even though they have studied about the body in earlier years, students want to know still more. Questions abound about all the body's organs, and especially about the brain and the heart. There is much interest in growth and some curiosity about heredity.

And there is a great desire to know ways to become and to remain physically fit.

Environmental health is a real concern

Eleven- to twelve-year-olds are worried about air, water, and food pollution, and about the effects of too much noise. These youngsters are often zealous in their efforts to assist in community recycling projects. They tend to be responsive to suggestions about conserving resources, avoiding littering, and trying to make the world around them a better place.

Curiosity about drugs poses a problem

Many eleven- to twelve-year-olds are experimenting with illicit substances. They are using or being tempted to use alcohol and tobacco. It is extremely important, therefore, that this age group have accurate and effective materials available to tell them what they want and need to know about drugs. Educational programs on drugs have their greatest impact on students in grades six to eight according to Dr. Richard Blum of the Joint Program on Drugs, Crime, and Community Studies at Stanford University.

Sports-related accidents are common

Eleven- to twelve-year-olds need to review and expand safety precautions in playing softball, in swimming, and in other sports. Falls and pedestrian accidents occur often enough among this age group that safety guides to prevent such accidents need to be discussed. And these youngsters should know what to do in the event of natural disasters such as tornadoes or in the event of emergency situations such as fires.

The Parent—Teacher Conference

A conference, for our purposes, means a face-to-face conversation between a teacher and a parent. The conference may be a part of the regularly scheduled school program or it may be called by the teacher to discuss a problem. Sometimes the parent initiates the conference because of a special concern.

Whether the goal is to become acquainted with parents, to report on how things are going in school subjects, or to work out a health problem or some other difficulty, teachers as well as parents can learn and profit from such an exchange of ideas.

A conference may last fifteen minutes or fifty. The teacher may have one or several conferences with a child's parents in the course of a school year. In any case, the pooling of information can result in a better understanding of the child and of ways in which the parents and the teacher can work together to help the youngster.

A conference calls for careful preparation. You will want to organize your thoughts in advance to be clear about what you wish to accomplish. And you may want to gather records and samples of the pupil's written work to go over with parents.

You may also want to collect information from the school nurse, the counselor, the speech therapist, and so on to have available as you explain referrals for medical or other attention.

Much that a teacher takes for granted about how children grow in the ability to share, to compromise, to take responsibility, to be self-reliant, and to be considerate of others is news to parents. You may need to explain that all children have basic emotional needs but that these needs show up in entirely different ways in different children.

What Do Parents Want to Know?

Parents want to know what and how their children are being taught. A comment such as "George is doing well" doesn't mean much to parents. More helpful is an explanation such as "George likes health. He uses some of his free time to read books about health. He reports on the books to the class, and that shows he's getting the sense of what he is reading."

Many parents want to know if there is anything they can do at home to help their child with schoolwork. You can suggest word games and number games to play at home that will augment skills without putting parents in the role of tutors.

Parents want, and should be able to get, an accurate interpretation of group-testing results given in laymen's terms. One cannot take for granted that parents know the nature of tests used.

In addition to information on academic achievement, parents often need and appreciate help on special health problems of their youngsters. Along with the school nurse, the teacher can help parents locate the community resources available for vision, speech, and hearing difficulties; dental care; immunizations; chest X rays; and emergency attention.

Ending the Conference

Close the conference on an optimistic note in order to send parents on the way with a good feeling about the conference and about their child. A minute's summary and a word about a future meeting is often useful. If that is not a sufficient signal that good-bys are in order, you can always stand up, mention that someone is waiting, and thank the parents for coming.

Movement Exploration and Games

Young people grow in physical well-being as they participate in vigorous muscular activity, although there are individual differences in the amount of activity required. All the body systems benefit and endurance is improved as a result of a program of guided exercise.

Youngsters grow in self-confidence and emotional maturity as they improve in fitness, gain skills, and apply the skills to such activities as games, sports, stunts, and dance. Moreover, they learn to understand and accept their own—and others' strengths and weaknesses.

Movement Exploration in Physical Education

Perhaps your pupils have had experience in movement exploration in preceding years. Even so, you may want to allow some time for further exploration. Remember, though, that while young children find joy merely in experimenting with different movements, middle-graders like to know *why* they are doing so. Thus they might experiment with *changing direction*, as they will need to do in playing basketball. Or they might experiment with *dodging movements*, such as they often use in team games.

Many variations and combinations are possible, such as skipping, sliding, or galloping; changing direction of movement; changing speed from fast to slow. The following characteristics might be explored:[1]

1. Size of movement (large, small)
2. Speed of movement (fast, slow)
3. Direction of movement (forward, backward, sideward)
4. Level of movement (high, medium, low)
5. Force of movement (strong, weak, heavy, light)
6. Path of movement (straight, curving, spiraling, zigzagging)
7. Design or shape of movement (changing position of the parts of the body; for example, legs, arms, head).

In their booklet *A Guide to Movement Exploration*,[2] Hackett and Jenson comment: ". . . By experiencing multitudinous movement patterns and physical challenges, the child . . . realizes that he is neither best nor worst in every activity; rather these extreme positions are shared by everyone at one time or another."

If you want to investigate more fully the many valuable activities that can be carried out in movement exploration, you will find suggested references on page T19.

Some Favorite Games

Eleven- to twelve-year-olds enjoy the team games that use the basic skills of the major sports. Movement exploration problems that use the skill of a particular game can be presented before the game is played. The following games, often called lead-up games, offer valuable practice in the skills of more highly organized games enjoyed later.

Corner Ball
Skills to be explored: Throwing, catching, taking one step with ball
Equipment: Soccer ball, volleyball, or playground ball
Players: 12 to 16 in a group or total class

---

[1] From page 8, *Exploration of Basic Movements in Physical Education*, copyright 1960 by the Detroit Board of Education. Used by permission.

[2] From *A Guide to Movement Exploration* by Hackett and Jenson, Rev. 1973. Reprinted by permission of Peek Publications, Palo Alto, Ca.

Place: Playground 15 m × 30 m or gymnasium

Draw a line across the center of the playing field to divide it in half. At each of the four corners of the field draw a square approximately two meters on each side.

Each team is assigned half the playing field. Players should be scattered so that all parts of the field are covered. Two players from each team take positions, one in each corner square of the opposing team's territory, with the opposing team between them and their own teammates. The corner players are goalkeepers or goalies.

The object of the game is to throw the ball over the heads of the opposing team to one of the goalies. A point is scored each time a goalie receives the ball from a member of his or her team.

The game is started by tossing the ball up between two opposing players in the center of the playing field. Each tries to tip it back to a member of his or her own team. Except at the beginning toss-ups, no player may step over the center line. Goalies may not step out of their boxes, and opposing players may not step into them. A player may take only one step with the ball and must play it within three seconds. Whenever a goalie receives the ball, he or she must return it to his or her own team. As the goalie returns the ball, the opposing team may intercept it.

Circle Soccer
Skills to be explored: Kicking, blocking, trapping, dribbling with feet, passing
Equipment: Soccer ball
Players: 12 to 16 in a group or total class
Place: Playground, playroom, gymnasium

Mark off a circle 6 to 7.5 meters in diameter, depending on the number of children playing, and divide the circle in half. Divide the class evenly and line up each team around its half of the circle.

The object of the game is to kick the ball out of the circle through the opposing team's area at shoulder level or below, thus scoring a point. If a player kicks the ball above shoulder level, or if the player kicks it outside his or her own half-circle, a point is scored for the opposing team. The first team to score ten points wins.

The ball may be blocked with the body or the legs, or it may be trapped with the foot or the knees. Hands and arms cannot be used. Students should fold arms across chest to avoid using them.

If a player touches the ball with his or her hands, a point is scored for the opposing team. If the ball goes out-of-bounds or dies, it should be dribbled back into position with the feet, not carried. The ball should be stopped momentarily before it is kicked back across the circle.

Capture the Flag
Skills to be explored: Running, tagging, dodging
Equipment: Two cloths
Players: 12 to 16 in a group or entire class
Place: Playground at least 15 m × 15 m

Mark off limits of the field and draw a line across the center. Divide the class into two teams. Each team has as its "country" one half of the playing area. Draw one by two meter rectangles at opposite corners of the playing area.

Each team places their flag along the end line of their own country. The object of the game is to capture the enemy's flag by snatching it and running back with it across the boundary line without being tagged or without running outside the playing area.

If a player is tagged while in enemy territory or if he or she steps outside the playing area, the player goes to "prison." The prison is the rectangle at the back of enemy territory. The prisoner may be rescued by a teammate who takes the prisoner's hand and runs across the boundary line without either of them being tagged. Only one prisoner at a time may be rescued. The enemy flag cannot be captured during a rescue.

Variation: Have several flags for each side. The game is won when all the opponent's flags are captured.

Dance in the Physical Education Program

With middle-graders, teachers often use folk and square dancing as vehicles for rhythmic development. Performing specific dances *well* is a challenge to these youngsters; also folk dancing offers an opportunity for development of wholesome boy-girl relationships at this level of physical-social development.

Creative rhythmic activities can be rewarding too. Once pupils have experimented with locomotor movements with partners, and as a total class, the outcome of their experimentation can be refined to produce a dance of their own making. Such is the case in the film *Movement Education: The Problem-Solving Technique* (Audio-Visual Center, University of Iowa).

Many specific references are available on folk and square dancing appropriate for this level. Some are included in the list at the right.

Physical Education References

American Alliance for Health, Physical Education, and Recreation. *AAHPER Youth Fitness Test Manual.* rev. ed. NEA, 1974.

Anderson, Marian H., et al. *Play with a Purpose: Elementary School Physical Education.* 2d ed. Harper, 1972.

Association for Childhood Education International. *Physical Education for Children's Healthful Living.* ACEI, 1968.

Dauer, Victor P. *Dynamic Physical Education for Elementary School Children.* 5th ed. Burgess, 1975.

Fabricius, Helen. *Physical Education for the Classroom Teacher.* 2d ed. W. C. Brown, 1972.

Fait, Hollis F. *Physical Education for the Elementary School Child.* 3d ed. Saunders, 1976.

Hackett, Layne C., and Jenson, Robert G. *A Guide to Movement Exploration.* rev. ed. Peek Publications, 1973.

Murray, Ruth L. *Dance in Elementary Education.* 3d ed. Harper, 1975.

Vannier, Maryhelen. *Teaching Physical Education in Elementary Schools.* 5th ed. Saunders, 1973.

Films

Learning Through Movement (S-L Productions).

Series of four films: *Movement Education: Guided Exploration; Movement Education in Physical Education; Movement Education: The Problem-Solving Technique; Movement Education: Time and Space Awareness* (University of Iowa).

Family-Life Education

Ideally, family-life education should be given in the home from the time a child first asks questions about how babies are born. The part that the home should play in this area is indeed important. But in recent years, parents in many communities have welcomed the aid of the schools in supplementing their efforts.

The Scott, Foresman HEALTH Program provides assistance to schools that wish to develop programs in education for human sexuality. Such schools should inform parents about what is being done and seek their cooperation and interest.

A strong strand devoted to various aspects of sex education is included in each level of the Program. This strand centers around building wholesome attitudes about the body. It emphasizes the importance of learning to understand oneself and to live in harmony and responsibly with others, and it includes an explanation of the growth patterns of preadolescents and young adolescents. But it does not include information on the "facts of life." This material has been placed in a separate booklet to enable the schools to take into account parents' viewpoints and to seek parents' help if a detailed program is to be presented.

A supplementary booklet, *The Human Story: Facts on Birth, Growth, and Reproduction*, is available for schools that wish to use it in connection with their own family-life courses at middle-grade levels. This booklet, designed for pupils aged ten to fourteen, was written by Sadie Hofstein in consultation with Julius B. Richmond, M.D. It answers some of the questions that students this age ask about their growing bodies, about reproduction and how babies are born, and about the way heredity affects their lives. It is suitable for classroom use and might also be sent home for pupils to share with parents.

Cooperation with Parents

Parents who realize that their children need guidance, but feel inadequate to give it, often turn to the school for help and advice. The well-informed teacher can do much to help these parents, both through individual conferences and through initiating PTA programs that focus on helping children to understand their sexuality.

In planning a PTA program, it might be wise to have a guest speaker. Good resource persons for such a program include a psychiatrist or psychologist, the school nurse, and the teacher responsible for courses on human relations, family life, or human sexuality.

Three films on birth, growth, and reproduction that might be useful for parent-teacher study sessions are *Human Reproduction*, Second Edition (McGraw-Hill); *Boy to Man* and *Girl to Woman* (Churchill). It is recommended that a skillful discussion leader be available to answer questions when films of this kind are shown.

In some schools, pamphlets about menstruation are made available to parents of fourth- to sixth-grade girls. The teacher can obtain, without charge, as many copies as he or she needs of the pamphlets produced by Kimberly-Clark Corporation, Neenah, Wisconsin 54956 or Personal Products Company, Milltown, New Jersey 08850. The latter company will also make available free to teachers one educational kit of materials on menstrual hygiene.

Parents might also be interested in viewing films on menstruation, such as the ones listed at the right, which are available for showing to parents or to mother-and-daughter groups. It is advisable to have a discussion leader present to answer questions after the showing of any such films. And better success is always achieved when such films are used as part of a series of group discussions about understanding ourselves.

Because many parents find it difficult to talk to their children about sex problems or to answer questions in this area, they appreciate knowing about books or booklets that can be of help. You might recommend some of those listed below. It is wise to suggest that parents read a book before giving it to their child. Children of this age vary in their maturity and parents' points of view vary also.

For Children

Gruenberg, Sidonie M., and Gruenberg, Benjamin. *The Wonderful Story of You.* Doubleday, 1960. For middle grades.

Hofstein, Sadie. *The Human Story: Facts on Birth, Growth, and Reproduction.* Rev. ed. Scott, Foresman, 1977. For upper grades.

Johnson, Eric W., and Johnson, Corinne B. *Love and Sex and Growing Up.* Lippincott, 1970. Specific sex information within a family context.

NEA-AMA Joint Committee on Health Problems in Education. *A Story About You.* Rev. ed. AMA and NEA, 1975. For middle grades.

Pomeroy, Wardell B. *Boys and Sex.* Delacorte, 1968.

———. *Girls and Sex.* Delacorte, 1969

Power, Jules. *How Life Begins.* Simon & Schuster, 1965. For middle grades.

For Parents and Teachers

Anderson, Wayne J. *How to Explain Sex to Children.* Denison, 1971.

Child Study Association of America. *What to Tell Your Child About Sex.* Rev. ed. Pocket Books, 1974.

Hofstein, Sadie. *Talking to Preteenagers About Sex.* Pamphlet No. 476. Public Affairs Committee, 1972.

Hoover, Mary B. *The Responsive Parent.* Parents' Magazine Press, 1972.

Mogal, Doris P. *Character in the Making.* Parents' Magazine Press, 1972.

NEA-AMA Joint Committee on Health Problems in Education. *Parents' Responsibility.* Rev. ed. NEA and AMA, 1970.

U.S. Department of Health, Education, and Welfare. *Moving into Adolescence: Your Child in His Preteens.* Children's Bureau Publication. U.S. Government Printing Office.

———. *Your Child from Six to Twelve.* Children's Bureau Publication. U.S. Government Printing Office.

Films and Filmstrips for Classroom Use

Boy to Man (Churchill).

Especially for Boys (Perennial, produced by Wexler). Filmstrip.

Girl to Woman (Churchill).

The Human Body: Reproductive System (Coronet).

Human Reproduction, 2d ed. (McGraw-Hill).

Films About Menstruation

Naturally . . . A Girl (Association—Sterling, produced by Personal Products Co.).

The Story of Menstruation (The Life-Cycle Center, Kimberly-Clark Corp., produced by Walt Disney Productions).

If Children Ask About Death[1]

By Gladys Gardner Jenkins

Children are curious about the beginnings of life. They are also curious about death. As teachers, we may be called upon to answer children's questions about death, to comfort a bereaved child, or on rare occasion to tell of the death of a classmate. At such times, we need to remember that the child's capacity to understand death will depend upon cognitive development plus experience.

One factor involved in understanding death is the cognitive knowledge of the facts of death as the end of life in the body. These facts can be given by a sensitive teacher as a child comes upon death—the flowers that die, the dead bird found on a walk, the death of a classroom gerbil. Later, as children gradually come to understand and appreciate the life cycle as it affects all living things, death will be put in perspective.

But understanding death also involves deep feelings. By the careful choice of stories children can be drawn into some of the feelings and concerns we all have about the death of a person for whom we care. Children have responded for many years to E. B. White's book *Charlotte's Web* (Harper).

However, some books today are presented with such realism that they may precipitate anxiety in children instead of developing understanding. For instance, a realistic presentation of the death of a grandparent may arouse anxiety in a child who had never thought of the death of a loved grandparent as imminent. A picture of the end of all living things might be a forceful lesson in ecology but a devastating thought for a young child.

Learning to accept reality is important. But the readiness of a child to be faced with reality which does not come from experience must be carefully weighed. It may be harmful rather than useful to stimulate imagination and provoke thoughts before the child has the resources to cope with them.

It is difficult to know what children are actually feeling, what their concerns, interpretations, and thoughts about death may be. This is why it is important to provide an atmosphere in the classroom in which children will feel free to ask questions and share ideas if the subject of death occurs.

Teachers may also be called upon to help children in their classrooms when the experience of death touches them through the loss of a parent, grandparent, sibling, friend, or classmate. This occasion may also call for facts, but the facts will now be interspersed with deep emotional feelings.

Death of one who has been close becomes a painful separation. Some children feel angry: "Why did my father leave me?" Many children, and many adults, have a feeling of guilt: "What did I do?" This feeling can be very strong and add anxiety to the grief of separation. A child should be reassured by being told the real cause of the death. There is also a fear that others whom the child loves may die, leaving the child with no one to care for him or her. Again, reassurance is needed.

Many children cannot express these feelings in words but show them in behavior. A child may become more demanding of attention or may cling to an adult. Older children may be so full of their thoughts that they can no longer focus on their schoolwork. Some children may not want to play with

[1] This article has been added to the *Teacher's Supplement* at the request of many teachers who have used previously published health materials by Scott, Foresman and Company.

their friends or take part in activities which they previously had enjoyed. Others cover their feelings by being aggressive or by acting as if nothing had happened. These are clues that the children need our help.

Grief in a child must have an outlet. The child who seems so brave, who does not cry, who goes about life as usual may be bottling up a deep grief that may cause difficulty at a later time. It does not help children to tell them to be brave, not to cry, to be a big boy or girl. Children need to grieve for a time. Neither does it help for adults to hide their grief, although hysterical grief can be deeply disturbing to children.

It is not wise to arouse thoughts of extra responsibilities such as: "You will be the man of the house" or "You will be the little mother now." Neither is it helpful to use the memory of the person who has died to encourage effort or better behavior. These are burdens a child is not able to carry. Such suggestions only build anxiety. In addition, it is better to talk about memories of a real person rather than a glorified one.

The most helpful support we can give as teachers is to let the child know that we do understand the mixed-up feelings, that we are ready to listen if talk would help, and that we will answer questions as honestly as we can. Often, too, the physical comfort of an arm around the child, or a shoulder on which to cry, can bring great relief.

If a child in the class dies, the other children will be tense and anxious. They can more easily accept death for old people than for another child whom they have known. The death of a classmate may arouse fear of death for oneself. The children should be told the truth about their classmate's death. It is wise to help them talk about it and to help them share their feelings and concerns. Discuss what they would like to remember about their classmate and what could be done as a special remembrance.

Such an open discussion may lead to questions about death. Some children may want to talk about the funeral, about burial, or about cremation. It can be explained that different groups of people have different customs or their own special ways of saying good-by. The most difficult questions to answer will be those that might be raised about life after death. The children will come from homes of many religious faiths. What they have been taught at home will influence what they believe to be true. Each religious faith explains what happens according to its own beliefs. A teacher should neither contradict the religious teaching of the home nor express his or her own religious beliefs.

Here are some books that can help a teacher meet situations involving death.

Grollman, Earl A. *Explaining Death to Children.* Beacon Press, 1967.

Harris, Audrey. *Why Did He Die?* Lerner, 1971.

Jackson, Edgar N. *Telling a Child About Death.* Hawthorn Books, 1965.

Kübler-Ross, Elisabeth. *Questions and Answers on Death and Dying.* Macmillan, 1974.

Mitchell, Marjorie Editha. *The Child's Attitude to Death.* Schocken, 1967.

Stein, Sara Bonnett. *About Dying.* Walker, 1974.

Overview

Chapter One focuses on mental health defined as the ability to feel comfortable about oneself, to feel kindly toward others, and to meet the demands of life. Students learn more about themselves, then consider ways they are like and different from others. Students then look at qualities that help them get along with others, and learn to deal with their emotions. They also look at things that help establish values and consider how to treat handicapped people.

Important Ideas Developed in the Chapter

The person you must live with all your life is *you.*

You can get to know yourself better by thinking about your interests, your values, your strengths and weaknesses, your problems, and your friends.

Each individual is unique in many ways, but is also like others in many ways.

Some basic human needs are to be wanted, to feel successful in at least some things, and to have companionship.

There are helpful ways of learning to deal with mistakes and failures.

Every person feels angry at times, especially when treated unfairly.

It helps to discuss with parents, or others who may help, any problem or emotion that you cannot work through alone.

Everyone feels fearful at times; fear is an emotion that you must be willing to recognize and then try to deal with wisely.

Some fears can be helpful. Most fears are learned from others who have them or from unpleasant experiences.

[1] See page T40 for Reference Materials related to this chapter.

Some important influences that help people form values are family, church, friends, school, people they admire, sports activities, and membership in groups with ethical codes such as 4-H or the scouts.

Handicapped people should be treated like anyone else insofar as possible.

People often express feelings through pictures they draw or paint or things they model from clay.

Getting along with others does not mean doing things others do that you think are "out of line."

Behavioral Objectives

See page 38 in the pupil's book where behavioral objectives in the cognitive area are posed directly to pupils in simple terms.

See also some hoped-for objectives, mainly in the affective area, set forth in the "Teacher's Notes" for page 38.

10–11 *You and Others* (Chapter-Opening Pages)

The questions on this page are ones students this age do ask and are interested in discussing. You might list other questions your pupils raise and check to see if they are answered in the chapter. If not, refer pupils to classroom reference shelf.

12 *Preview It*

A committee might be formed to get references from the school or public library. See the list suggested on page T40.

13–15 *What Are You Like?*

The "Newspaper of the Self" as illustrated here is based on an activity suggested in *Developing Individual Values in the*

Classroom by Richard and Geri Curwin (Education Today). Encourage pupils to make such newspapers or magazines. They can be simple or elaborate, written in first or third person.

16 *Enjoy It*
Students may enjoy making self-portraits or personal collages. Such collages could feature pictures from magazines that complete such ideas as: Favorite things I own are . . . . I want to become . . . .

17–19 *What Is Your Group Like?*
Students might graph the different ways group members get to school. Who comes on foot? On the school bus? By family car? In a car pool? On a bicycle?

20 *Enjoy It*
Continue the discussion by having volunteers tell *who* they would like to change places with for a week and why.

21–22 *How Can You Keep Your Friends?*
Students might compose a group code of suggestions on how to be a good friend.

23–24 *What Can Help When You Make Mistakes?*
Students should be allowed to sign or not sign their papers on "Once I made a mistake when . . . ." You might read aloud some of the papers and let the group discuss how the mistake might be dealt with.

25–26 *What Can Help When You Are Angry?*
Students might complete the starter "Once I felt angry when . . . ." You might read

aloud some responses. It reassures pupils to know that everyone gets angry at times.

27–28 *Why Are You Sometimes Afraid of Things?*
Students might graph some of the things members of the group are afraid of. It is comforting to know that everyone has fears of one sort or another.

29–30 *How Do You Build Your Own Values?*
Pupils might write about "A Person I Admire." Have them clearly describe the things about this person that they might like to emulate.

31–32 *How Do You Treat Someone Who Is Handicapped?*
Students might act out some things David might do once Max has arrived.

33 *Health Around Us*
Volunteers might find out what is done in their school to help the handicapped and report back to the class.

34–35 *Art and Feelings* (Picture Essay)

36 *Enjoy It*
Discuss ways to handle a situation where someone says, "Don't you agree?" and you *don't* agree. You might pleasantly say, "I see what you mean, but I don't agree."

37 *Things to Do*
Volunteers might pantomime such emotions as joy, surprise, fear, worry, and anger.

38–41 *Reviews, Tests, School and Home*

Enrichment Suggestions for Chapter 2
Your Body and How It Works[1]

Overview

Chapter Two offers students an opportunity to review and expand their knowledge about the body and its workings. Information is set forth in an adaptation of the recorded script spoken by the Transparent Talking Woman at the Robert Crown Center for Health Instruction in Hinsdale, Illinois. The chapter is enriched by photographs of the Transparent Woman in action as well as by many anatomical drawings.

Important Ideas Developed in the Chapter

The brain is the central exchange of the nervous system. Messages of sensation are carried to the spinal cord and brain over sensory nerves; orders for action are sent from the brain to the muscles over motor nerves.

The skeleton supports the body. Along with the skeletal muscles, the bones make it possible for the body to move about.

The endocrine glands produce many hormones. Among the hormones are the growth hormone from the pituitary gland and a hormone from the thyroid gland that regulates the pace at which you live.

The skin covers the outside of the body; it keeps out dirt and harmful bacteria.

A life-giving exchange takes place in the lungs: the red blood cells receive oxygen in exchange for waste carbon dioxide.

The heart propels blood throughout the body; the blood carries nutrients and oxygen to body cells and carries away carbon dioxide and other wastes from the cells.

The stomach and other organs of the digestive system change food into a form the body can use.

After food has been digested it passes through the thin walls of the small intestine and is carried by the blood to all parts of the body.

The food that was not completely digested passes into the large intestine where water from the undigested food passes into the bloodstream. The waste matter the body cannot use is expelled in a bowel movement.

The kidneys remove liquid waste products and water from the blood. The liquid wastes are stored in the urinary bladder until they are expelled from the body as urine.

The human body, like all living things, can reproduce.

Behavioral Objectives

See page 64 in the pupil's book where behavioral objectives in the cognitive area are posed directly to pupils.

See also some hoped-for objectives, mainly in the affective area, set forth in the "Teacher's Notes" for page 64.

42–43 *Your Body and How It Works* (Chapter-Opening Pages)

Keep initial discussion of the questions on these pages brief. You might have students look at the Contents page and express opinions as to which chapters hold the most interest for them.

44 *Preview It*

Volunteers might tell why they think that "of all wonders, the human body is itself most wonderful." They might even write

[1] See pages T40 and T41 for Reference Materials related to this chapter.

their responses. Then they could reevaluate the responses after completion of the chapter.

45 *What Is One Way to Learn About the Body?*

Discuss other sources of health information besides health museums. A committee might be formed to get reference books from the school or public library. Some suggested references are listed on pages T40 and T41. Another committee could clip newspaper articles and check listings or radio and TV programs giving health information.

46–56 *A Talk About the Human Body*

If Book Three of this series is available in your school, try to obtain a copy. Book Three features the transcribed talk given by this same Transparent Talking Woman to *primary-age children.* Your students might be interested in hearing the simpler version read aloud—and comparing it with the mature talk in their own texts.

Students might be interested in some of the following information about the body.

The skeletal muscles are not the only muscles in the body. Muscles are also found in the stomach, large and small intestines, and bladder. And special cardiac muscle is found in the heart.

The heart is really two pumps, side by side. They work at the same time. Each has an upper room, or chamber (the auricles). Each has a lower chamber (the ventricles). A wall of muscle separates the two pumps. Each pump has a separate job. The right pump sends blood with wastes to the lungs to get fresh oxygen; the left pump sends blood with fresh oxygen to all parts of the body.

The digestive process starts in the mouth. Teeth cut up the food; saliva moistens it. Chemicals in saliva start digesting the starch in such foods as bread and potatoes. The starch is changed into a form of sugar that can be dissolved. Everything in food must be dissolved in liquid before it can be used by the body.

57–61 *The Transparent Woman Exhibit* (Picture Essay)

This chapter would be even more meaningful to students if you could take them to see an exhibit similar to the one shown here.

62 *Health Around Us*

Other medical instruments that are used to see inside various parts of the body are:

The *otoscope* – used to look inside the ear.

The *ophthalmoscope* – used to look inside the eye.

The *gastroscope* – used to inspect the interior of the stomach.

The *cystoscope* – used to examine the urinary bladder.

63 *Things to Do*

You might have students who did special projects on the body and its functions open their exhibit to other classes. Each student might stand next to his or her project and try to answer any questions asked by the visitors.

64–67 *Reviews, Tests, School and Home*

Enrichment Suggestions for Chapter 3
Growth[1]

Overview

Chapter Three covers many aspects of growth. Students consider growth patterns of boys and girls during the preteen and teen years and review the fact that individuals have different rates of growing. They learn about the work of the endocrine glands and are introduced to growth of the body by cell division. Finally, students are provided with a simple explanation of heredity.

Important Ideas Developed in the Chapter

Each boy and each girl has his or her own way of growing and an individual timetable for growth.

Girls tend to grow taller sooner than boys their age do; but, boys usually overtake the girls before the growing years are over.

The endocrine glands play an important part in regulating growth.

The reproductive glands are endocrine glands that are different for boys and girls. They produce hormones that develop the sex characteristics.

The body is made up of tiny, living cells. Division of these cells makes growth possible. When cells divide, they make other cells just like the original ones.

New cells made by the body are also used for repair of worn-out or injured cells.

Important parts of the cell are the protoplasm, nucleus, chromosomes, and genes.

Heredity involves the passing along of traits from parents to their offspring.

When a sperm cell and an egg cell unite, each one brings exactly half of all the inherited traits the offspring will have.

It is extremely rare for any two mature egg cells or any two mature sperm cells to have the same chromosomes.

Identical twins develop from the equal division of a fertilized egg; fraternal twins develop when two egg cells are fertilized by two separate sperm cells. That is why no two individuals, except identical twins, have exactly the same heredity.

Genes are the carriers of heredity traits; some genes are dominant and some are recessive.

Men have two kinds of sex chromosomes, X and Y; women have one kind of sex chromosome, X. If the sperm cell containing an X chromosome unites with an egg cell, the baby will be a girl; if the sperm cell containing a Y chromosome unites with an egg cell, the baby will be a boy.

What a person is and becomes depends not only upon the traits he or she has inherited but also upon experiences and the use he or she makes of the heredity and the experiences.

Behavioral Objectives

See page 94 in the pupil's book where behavioral objectives in the cognitive area are posed directly to students.

See also some hoped-for objectives, mainly in the affective area, set forth in the "Teacher's Notes" for page 94.

68–69 *Growth* (Chapter-Opening Pages)

These pages offer an opportunity to explore what students already know about growth and to note what questions they have about the topic.

---

[1] See page T41 for Reference Materials related to this chapter.

70 *Preview It*

Pupils may attempt to answer the questions here. Do not allot much time for this as the questions' chief purpose is to arouse curiosity and an eagerness to learn.

71-73 *Are You Growing As You Should?*

Personal charts for boys' and girls' growth records can be obtained from the American Medical Association, 535 North Dearborn Street, Chicago, Illinois 60610.

74-75 *Each Individual Grows in His or Her Own Way* (Picture Essay)

Volunteers in your group might line up as those in the picture have done. The result will be a living example of individual differences in height, weight, and body build.

76 *Enjoy It*

Students might write essays on how they feel about their size. Topics could include "It's Tough to Be Short" or "It's No Fun to Be Taller than Everyone" or "I Like My Size." Writings should be kept anonymous. With permission of the writer, you might later read aloud some of the essays.

77 *Health Around Us*

The growing ends of different bones ossify at different ages. For example, the growing ends of the ankle bones become solid bone sometime between the ages of 13 and 18. The growing ends of the upper leg bones become solid bone sometime between the ages of 14 and 18 years.

78-80 *Why Do You Stop Growing Tall?*

You might ask students, "Which gland has most to do with height and growth?"

81-83 *What Happens When You Grow?*

You might explain that tissues form body organs, and organs form body systems such as the digestive system and the circulatory system. All of the systems together form the human body. The systems work together efficiently, and each one helps to sustain the body.

84-89 *Why Do Individuals Differ?*

A summary discussion of "What I Learned That I Didn't Know Before" might be used to end this section.

90-91 *Individual Differences That Are Inherited* (Picture Essay)

Students might make their own fingerprints by pressing their thumbs or forefingers on an ink pad and then on a sheet of paper. An exhibit of fingerprints might be placed on the bulletin board.

92 *Enjoy It*

Remind students to check the pronunciation of the artist's name with that given in the Glossary. Another painting by Renoir that shows family resemblances is of the two sisters in "Two Little Circus Girls."

93 *Things to Do*

Students may want to talk about dwarfs or "The World's Tallest Man" or "The Bearded Lady" or other abnormalities they have seen or heard about. Be sure to stress that these peculiarities are most unusual and do not occur very often.

94-97 *Reviews, Tests, School and Home*

Enrichment Suggestions for Chapter 4
Health Questions Answered[1]

Overview

Chapter Four answers some frequently-asked questions of eleven- to twelve-year-olds. The questions cover emotions and body functions, sleep and dreams, physical fitness, care of teeth, good nutrition, and the periodic health checkup. Information students need to know is given as well as information to satisfy their curiosity.

Important Ideas Developed in the Chapter

Emotions can affect body functioning.

Sleep-deprived people become irritable.

During sleep many changes take place in the body. Breathing and the heartbeat slow down; the senses are dulled; parts of the brain are less active than usual and other parts remain quite active.

Sleep refreshes the mind and body.

There are two kinds of sleep, sleep with dreams and sleep without dreams. Everyone dreams; most people dream three or four times a night; most dreams contain color.

To be physically fit means to be in the best possible physical condition for you.

Plaque is a sticky, colorless film of bacteria that constantly forms on the teeth.

In the presence of sugar, bacteria in plaque form acids that attack the teeth and form cavities. To help prevent cavities, cut down on how often you eat sweet foods.

Daily flossing and brushing are necessary to remove plaque.

Periodontal diseases affect the tissues around the teeth.

Nutrients are nourishing substances in foods. To be sure you get the nutrients you need each day, follow a Food Guide.

[1] See page T42 for Reference Materials related to this chapter.

Important nutrients missed by skipping breakfast may not be made up in other meals.

An essential step in good preventive health is having periodic health checkups.

Behavioral Objectives

See page 144 in the pupil's book where behavioral objectives in the cognitive area are posed directly to pupils.

See also some hoped-for objectives, mainly in the affective area, set forth in the "Teacher's Notes" for page 144.

98–99 *Health Questions Answered* (Chapter-Opening Pages)

You might ask students to bring in health columns from the local newspapers. Have them select only those with questions pertinent to needs and interests of their age group. You might also discuss other ways they can get answers to their health questions

100 *Preview It*

Volunteers might assemble reference books from the school and public libraries. See the suggested list on page T42.

101–103 *Can Emotions Affect How Your Body Works?*

You might use dramatic skits to review helpful ways of dealing with strong emotions. After class discussion of ways to manage strong feelings, students might give skits showing helpful and not-so-helpful ways of coping with fear, anger, and worry.

104–107 *What Is Known About Sleep and Dreams?*

A special effort to remember dreams often aids people who think they don't dream.

Students might write about a dream they tried to remember. Later you could tabulate the different kinds of things students dreamed about.

108-111 *How Can You Be Physically Fit?*
Volunteers might try demonstrating the complete workout pictured on page 109, doing all the exercises at one time.

An article on "Movement Exploration and Games" can be found on page T17.

112-113 *Enjoy It*
Volunteers might draw pictures of a variety of athletes "in action." Other volunteers might write descriptions using the four-line pattern of Walt Whitman's "The Runner."

114-117 *How Should You Take Care of Your Teeth?* and *Tell It*
Here are some flossing hints from the American Dental Association. Divide your mouth into four sections; floss half the upper teeth, then the other half; do the same for the lower teeth. Some bleeding and soreness may occur the first few times you floss. As the plaque is broken up and the bacteria are removed, healing of the gums begins and bleeding usually will stop. Remember to be gentle when inserting floss between your teeth and under the gum line.

118-122 *What Are Nutrients?*
Explain that while we may not think of water as a food, it is usually grouped with the main kinds of nutrients. Water is needed to carry nutrients to the cells, to carry products away, to build tissue, to help regulate body temperature, to help in digesting food, to replace daily water loss, and to maintain the health of all body cells.

123-125 *How Can You Get All the Nutrients You Need?*
Booklets and display materials on nutrition are available from such sources as: American Dietetic Association, 620 North Michigan Avenue, Chicago, Illinois 60611; Cereal Institute, Inc., 135 South LaSalle Street, Chicago, Illinois 60603; and National Dairy Council, 111 North Canal Street, Chicago, Illinois 60606.

126-127 *Does It Matter If You Skip Breakfast?*
Volunteers might tell about foods they like for breakfast as well as foods they can prepare on their own.

128-129 *Health Around Us* and *Write It*
This is a good place to discuss such benefits of good nutrition as better resistance to disease, firm muscles, straight spine, high vitality, good appetite, good digestion, ability to reach growth potential, a sense of well-being.

130-140 *What Happens in a Health Checkup?*
You might have students discuss the behavior of those who hesitate to visit a doctor for fear the doctor will find something wrong.

141-143 *Tell It* and *Things to Do*
Students might like to know that doctors ask about the health of one's relatives so they can watch for hereditary illnesses.

144-147 *Reviews, Tests, School and Home*

Enrichment Suggestions for Chapter 5
First Aid and Safety[1]

Overview

Chapter Five presents correct first-aid procedures for such major emergencies as choking, breathing stoppage, fainting, severe bleeding, a child's swallowing poison, and a broken bone. Students also learn first-aid procedures for such minor problems as small cuts and scratches, mild burns without blisters, blisters that have not broken, and nosebleed.

Students cover safety rules for such activities as softball and swimming because sports account for many accidents in this age group. Students also learn what to do in the event of a tornado warning, and they review safety procedures that can help prevent falls and pedestrian accidents.

Important Ideas Developed in the Chapter

In case of choking, encourage the person to cough up the object; suggest deep, slow breathing. If the object is not coughed up at once, try the Heimlich Maneuver. If that fails, rush the victim to a doctor or a hospital emergency room.

In case of breathing stoppage, use Mouth-to-Mouth Rescue Breathing to get air in and out of the victim's lungs.

In case of fainting, keep the person lying down with head lowered; if the victim does not regain consciousness within a minute or two, call a doctor.

To stop severe bleeding, exert downward pressure on the wound.

In case of poisoning by mouth, call the local poison control center, a doctor, or the hospital emergency room at once. If possible, have an adult make the call.

In case of a broken bone or suspected break, keep the victim quiet; do not move the person. Get medical help.

Softball players should know appropriate safety guides before they play the game.

Safety guides for swimmers include never swimming alone, swimming only in protected areas, avoiding horseplay in the water, staying in shallow water unless one is a good swimmer, diving only in deep water and in places where a lifeguard is on duty.

Behavioral Objectives

See page 166 in the pupil's book where behavioral objectives in the cognitive area are posed directly to pupils.

See also some hoped-for objectives, mainly in the affective area, set forth in the "Teacher's Notes" for page 166.

148–149 *First Aid and Safety*
(Chapter-Opening Pages)

Students might discuss situations they know about, have read about, or have seen on TV in which prompt first-aid procedures were needed and successfully used. Volunteers might tell of first-aid instruction they may have received. Others could report on the availability of first-aid instruction in their community.

150 *Preview It*

This is a good time to arrange for films and filmstrips to be shown with this chapter, and to assemble a classroom library of books on first aid. See the suggested list on pages T43 and T44.

---

[1] See pages T42 and T43 for Reference Materials related to this chapter.

151-157 *How Much Do You Know About Emergency Situations?*

Enrich discussion of each of the first-aid situations given on pages 151-157 by such activities as these:

1) Stress the *reasons* for the first-aid procedures suggested.

2) Encourage skits in which correct first-aid procedures are portrayed. Such skits help "fix" the procedures in students' minds.

3) Invite discussion of true incidents in which bystanders were able to give proper first aid in emergencies.

4) Have students check the newspapers for accounts of accidents in which first aid was given until medical help arrived.

5) Show films that reinforce correct first-aid steps.

6) Encourage pupils' suggestions about ways to avoid accidents leading to such emergencies as broken bones, severe bleeding, and poison by mouth.

7) Invite volunteers to make posters with appropriate first-aid messages on them.

158 *Tell It*

Students might discuss this safety message which is on a National Safety Council poster: *Germs can hatch in a scratch.* Ask, "Why should a cut or scratch be covered with a sterile bandage?" (To help keep germs out of the wound.)

If pupils are making first-aid notebooks, have them add the minor first-aid items on this page.

159-162 *How Can You Play Softball Safely? and How Can You Keep Safe When You Swim?*

Here are some activities that might be used

during the study of these pages:

1) Students might compile a list of words often associated with rough play; for instance, pushing, shoving, slapping, punching, and tripping.

2) Discuss why safety is often called a "Do It Yourself" project.

3) Keep a record of accidents that happen to students in the group—in the gym, on the playground, in unsupervised games and sports at home (in yards or nearby play places). Consider how each accident might have been prevented.

4) Invite volunteers to compose safety slogans or couplets; for example, "Call fly balls, or risk bumps and falls."

163 *Safety Around Us*

Volunteers might prepare safety skits centering around what to do in the event of a tornado warning (a) if one is indoors and (b) if one is out in the open and unable to seek shelter indoors.

Committees might be appointed to study and then report on what to do in electric storms, in the event of a hurricane warning, and in the event of a flood.

164-165 *Things to Do*

Students might make a survey of the school playground to check for things that might cause accidents—old tin cans, pieces of glass, small pits that could cause a person to turn an ankle or fall. Insofar as possible, the hazards should be eliminated.

166-169 *Reviews, Tests, School and Home*

Enrichment Suggestions for Chapter 6
Drugs and You[1]

Overview

Chapter Six acquaints students with what drugs are, why they should be used cautiously, what is meant by the risk factor in taking any drug, and why labels on drugs should be followed exactly. Students learn about stimulants, depressants, tranquilizers, LSD, marijuana, narcotics, and sprays and solvents that may be used in unintended ways. The effects of alcohol and cigarette smoking on the body are also discussed.

Important Ideas Developed in the Chapter

Drugs are prepared substances that if taken into the body cause changes.

Medicines are a kind of drug that can help prevent or treat an illness or deaden pain.

Individuals react in different ways to drugs. There is always some risk in taking any drug; there may be unwanted side effects.

Directions on drug labels should be followed exactly.

People sometimes use drugs in disapproved, unsupervised ways; this can be dangerous.

Mixing of drugs can be hazardous; for example, people have died after mixing alcohol and sleeping pills.

Stimulants increase the activity of the brain and other parts of the nervous system.

Depressants can be medically useful in quieting the nerves and encouraging sleep.

Tranquilizers may relieve nervousness or help people who often feel under stress.

Depressants, stimulants, and tranquilizers should be used under medical supervision.

All narcotics must be used with utmost care.

Hallucinogens produce changes in sensations; LSD can be a highly dangerous hallucinogen.

Marijuana is a mild hallucinogen; much more research is needed on the long-time physical effects of marijuana; meanwhile it should be noted that use of this drug is illegal in many states.

Deliberate inhaling of certain solvents and sprays can produce harmful effects in the body; damage may occur to the nose, throat, lungs, brain, liver, kidneys, or other organs.

Alcohol is a depressant drug; the more alcohol a person drinks, the greater its effects will be.

Alcoholics are heavy drinkers who cannot control their use of alcohol; they need medical help or help from others who understand the problem.

Too much alcohol at one time can be a poison.

The drug in cigarettes and cigarette smoke is nicotine.

The greatest danger in cigarette smoking is that it can cause lung cancer.

Cigarette smoking can be a factor in causing heart disease and emphysema.

Cigarette smoke can be annoying and at times harmful to those who breathe it "second hand."

Behavioral Objectives

See page 194 in the pupil's book where behavioral objectives in the cognitive area are posed directly to pupils.

See also some hoped-for objectives, mainly in the affective area, set forth in the "Teacher's Notes" for page 194.

---

[1] See pages T43 and T44 for Reference Materials related to this chapter.

170-171 *Drugs and You*
     (Chapter-Opening Pages)
   The questions here are open-ended. Their purpose is to encourage preliminary discussion and to stimulate curiosity.

172 *Preview It*
   You might appoint a committee to start collecting reference materials on drugs. See the list suggested on page T43.

173-177 *What Should You Know About Drug Safety?*
   You might point out that advertising for OTC drugs on radio, TV, or in newspapers sometimes exaggerates the need for a drug or suggests a need that doesn't really exist. Or the ad may promise more than can reasonably be expected. Thus no OTC drug can melt fat away, create instant popularity, or even cure a headache in an instant. People must learn how to evaluate ads cautiously. They must be sure they are not being persuaded to buy something they don't need.

178-182 *What Are Some Drugs That May Be Misused?*
   You may want to stress the dangers in using several drugs at the same time. Each drug (or medicine) acts on the body, but each one may also alter the effects of any other drug being taken. Sometimes this can cause dangerous—even fatal—reactions. People may forget that alcohol is a drug. And alcohol may increase the effects of another drug that is being taken. Before using any combination of drugs—prescription drugs with OTC drugs, or several OTC drugs together—it is important that a person consult a doctor about the combinations.

183-185 *What Should You Know About Alcohol?*
   It may come as a surprise, but many eleven- and twelve-year-olds are using alcoholic beverages. And some do foolish and dangerous things such as having drinking contests. It is very important to stress that too much alcohol at one time can be a poison.
   You may want to discuss things that can make life pleasurable for people so they won't have to find their joys in misuse of drugs. Some things that may be suggested are sports, hobbies, and satisfying friendships. You might mention that many people who become "hooked" on drugs are very lonely. One reason Alcoholics Anonymous has been so successful is that it offers troubled and sometimes lonely alcoholics contacts with friendly people who care about them and want to help them.

186-189 *What Is Harmful About Smoking?* and *Health Around Us*
   Volunteers might write to the local branch of the American Lung Association for free pamphlets on smoking. Students might also tell what they know about stop smoking clinics in their community.

190-191 *A Smoking Demonstration*
   You might contact the local branch of the American Cancer Society about borrowing a set of the "Smoking Lungs" for this demonstration.

192-193 *Things to Do*
   Note that *menthol* is an additive that merely changes the taste of the smoke.

194-197 *Reviews, Tests, School and Home*

Enrichment Suggestions for Chapter 7
The Long Struggle Against Communicable Diseases[1]

Overview

Chapter Seven documents the long struggle against communicable diseases with the action that took place from the 1600's to the drug discoveries of the 1900's. Students get an idea of how scientists today have built on the work of health pioneers of the past. And students learn much about communicable diseases—how they are caught, how immunization can be used to prevent some of them, how they are spread, and how germ-killing drugs can help in the conquest of certain diseases.

Important Ideas Developed in the Chapter

At one time, epidemics of communicable diseases were common throughout the world.

Before there could be any success in fighting communicable diseases, their causes and methods of spreading had to be understood.

The first breakthrough in understanding communicable diseases came with the discovery of the microscope, and the discovery by Leeuwenhoek of microbes as seen under the microscope.

Jenner's discovery of vaccination against smallpox was the beginning of real progress in preventive medicine.

Pasteur gave the world a great store of knowledge about the cause and control of communicable disease, including the "germ theory" of disease and a way to vaccinate sheep against anthrax and people and animals against rabies.

Lister accepted the germ theory of infection and introduced antiseptic methods in surgery.

[1] See page T44 for Reference Materials related to this chapter.

Walter Reed discovered how yellow fever is spread, thereby helping to conquer it.

Disease germs may be spread by direct contact; by indirect contact; by air, by water, by food; and by various animals.

Truly effective germ-killing drugs were first developed in the early 1900's; the search for such drugs continues today.

Behavioral Objectives

See page 226 in the pupil's book where behavioral objectives in the cognitive area are posed directly to pupils.

See also some hoped-for objectives, mainly in the affective area, set forth in the "Teacher's Notes" for page 226.

198-199 *The Long Struggle Against Communicable Diseases* (Chapter-Opening Pages)

The questions here are designed to stimulate preliminary discussion, to create curiosity, and to find out how much pupils know.

200 *Preview It*

You might review the main groups of disease germs: bacteria, protozoans, and viruses. Disease-causing bacteria are mainly round, rod-shaped, and spiral-shaped. Protozoans are microscopic animals, most of which are harmless. But some protozoans cause amoebic dysentery, malaria, and sleeping sickness.

Viruses are so tiny that it takes an electron microscope to see them.

201-203 *What Were Health Conditions in Early Days?*

Students might compare health conditions in their community with those of the early communities described here.

204-205 *What Did Leeuwenhoek Discover?*
Students might make a series of shoebox dioramas featuring famous health pioneers.

206 *What Did Spallanzani Learn About Microbes?*
Students might figure out how many microbes grow from one microbe in a day.

207-209 *What Did Jenner Contribute to Disease Prevention?*
Students might like to know that the final victory against smallpox is almost won. In a few years smallpox may be wiped out. This has been done by years and years of tracking down people all over the world and immunizing them against smallpox. The last case of smallpox in the United States was in 1949.

210-215 *How Did Pasteur Help in the War Against Disease?*
Review Pasteur's work by asking students what interesting stories these words bring to mind: *silkworms, fermenting, 50 sheep, Joseph Meister.*

216-217 *How Did Joseph Lister Fight Infection?*
Discuss some of the antiseptic methods pupils use to fight infection. They may wash out a small cut or scratch with soap and water (soap is a germ killer). Or they may put an antiseptic such as peroxide, alcohol, or iodine on a small wound.

218 *How Did Walter Reed Help Conquer Yellow Fever?*
Explain that Dr. Reed had volunteers sleep in contaminated pajamas and with contaminated bedclothes to see if yellow fever germs were passed indirectly from these contaminated materials to the volunteers.

219 *Enjoy It*
Some students may want to draw pictures of Walter Reed's experiments. Others may want to include Reed in their dioramas.

220-223 *How Are Disease Germs Spread?*
Some diseases are spread by *human carriers.* A few people have germs of diseases such as diphtheria or typhoid fever in their bodies and can spread the disease to others. But they themselves look and feel well and are not ill. When located, carriers can be medically treated, but they should not work with food preparation or serving.

224-225 *Health Around Us*
You might mention some other familiar antibiotic drugs. In 1948, after screening soil samples for three years, Dr. Benjamin Duggar developed *Aureomycin* from a mold-like substance in soil. Later the antibiotic *Terramycin* was made from a soil microorganism. In laboratories today, scientists are examining packets of soil from all over the earth. They hope to find other useful drugs. Scientists are also exploring algae and other products of the sea for effective disease-germ killers.

226-227 *Things to Do*
You might check with your Community Health Department about how to safely dispose of the potato slices on which microbes are growing.

228-231 *Reviews, Tests, School and Home*

Enrichment Suggestions for Chapter 8
A Healthy Environment[1]

Overview

Chapter Eight focuses on things that are involved in working for a healthy environment—concern for the environment; conservation of resources; safeguarding of the water, air, and food supplies; proper disposal of solid wastes. Students are led to think about what they can do to make the environment of their community more healthy.

Important Ideas Developed in the Chapter

A healthy environment is one in which people have safe water to drink, clean air to breathe, pure food to eat, and sanitary ways to get rid of solid wastes.

People need to live and work where there is not too much noise.

A healthy community provides parks, playgrounds, and open spaces of green, growing things.

Newspapers, radios, TV, and magazines are sources for learning about environmental health matters.

Water sources may be polluted by household and industrial wastes and by soil, pesticides, and fertilizers draining off the land into the water.

To safeguard the community's water supply, modern communities use such means as water treatment plants to purify water and waste-treatment plants to take care of sewage in sanitary ways.

Many industries now remove polluting materials from wastes before dumping them into waterways.

Air may be polluted by burning, by exhaust gases from vehicles, by industrial pollutants, by pesticides.

Air pollution worsens when there is an upper layer of warm air to hold it down and very little wind.

Air pollution can be reduced by reducing the vehicles on the roads, by the production of cleaner cars, by greater use of public transportation (instead of private cars), by reducing burning and industrial pollutants, by reducing use of pesticides.

Food pollution can be reduced by following sanitary food handling guides.

Sanitarians are community health workers who help safeguard food handling and food processing.

Some means of disposing of solid wastes are open dumps, the sanitary landfill, and incinerators.

Open dumps are unsanitary and efforts to eliminate them should be made.

One way to reduce a community's solid wastes is for people to cut down on the garbage and trash they throw away.

Recycling is a valuable means of reclaiming resources and for saving trees that would be cut down to make new paper.

Behavioral Objectives

See page 264 in the pupil's book where behavioral objectives in the cognitive area are posed directly to pupils.

See also some hoped-for objectives, mainly in the affective area, set forth in the "Teacher's Notes" for page 264.

232-233 *A Healthy Environment*
         (Chapter-Opening Pages)

Use the questions here to create interest in the chapter and to briefly explore information students may have.

---

[1] See page T45 for Reference Materials related to this chapter.

234 *Preview It*

You might have volunteers write for some helpful materials on environmental health. Some sources are: *Water Pollution Control Federation*, 3900 Wisconsin Avenue, N.W., Washington, D.C. 20016; *Air Pollution Control Association*, 4400 5th Avenue, Pittsburgh, Pennsylvania 15213; *Friends of the Earth*, 32 East 42nd Street, New York, New York 10017; *Environmental Protection Agency*, Waterside Mall, 401 M Street, S.W., Washington, D.C. 20460; *National Solid Waste Management Association*, 1145 19th Street, N.W., Washington, D.C. 20036.

235–241 *How Can You Become Alert to Environmental Health Concerns?*

Students might take a brief walk around their community and jot down observations of air pollution, water pollution, smog, trash in streets or alleys, litter, noise, excessive traffic, and visual pollution. The class could then discuss the findings.

242–245 *How Is the Water Supply Safeguarded?* and *Investigate It*

Possible sources of information about the community's water sources and problems include parents, neighbors, and the city water department.

246–253 *What Is Known About Air Pollution?* and *Investigate It*

Use the replica of the scrapbook material on pages 249–252 to guide detailed discussion of what individuals and communities can do to reduce air pollution. Invite special comment on what students' own families and communities are doing.

254–255 *What Is Known About Food Pollution?*

Remind students that a great many bacteria die off by themselves and a great many do no harm. Otherwise we would be sick all the time. We are concerned about those bacteria that can, if proper precautions are not taken, bring on sickness.

You might mention that favorite "homes" of bacteria that pollute foods include milk, cooked eggs, meats, shellfish, poultry, and water.

256 *Health Around Us*

Students might investigate and report on the information given on a carton of milk—whether or not it is pasteurized, if vitamin D has been added, if fat has been skimmed off, if it is low-fat in content, if it is homogenized. Have students look up *homogenized* in the dictionary.

257–261 *What Should Be Done with Garbage and Trash?* and *Tell It*

Students might make a graph to dramatize this information: how many of the students' families participate in newspaper recycling activities, how many save old cans for recycling, how many save used glass containers for recycling? What does the information indicate?

262–263 *Things to Do*

Have students give examples of people who have worked to make their homes and yards visually pleasant.

264–271 *Reviews, Tests, School and Home, Bibliographies*

Reference Materials

Chapter One: You and Others

Books for Students

Alexander, Arthur. *The Hidden You: Psychology in Your Life.* Prentice-Hall, 1962. Good reference.

Hall, Elizabeth. *From Pigeons to People: A Look at Behavioral Shaping.* Houghton, 1975. Well-written book tells the story of behavior modification.

_____. *Why We Do What We Do: A Look at Psychology.* Houghton, 1973. A lively book that tells what modern psychology is and how it adds to our understanding of ourselves and others.

LeShan, Eda. *What Makes Me Feel This Way? Growing Up with Human Emotions.* Macmillan, 1972. A highly readable book that discusses the whole range of feelings, including those we don't always like or understand very well.

Rosenbaum, Jean. *What Is Fear?* Prentice-Hall, 1972. About children's fears and the angers that cause them.

Wolf, Bernard. *Don't Feel Sorry for Paul.* Lippincott, 1974. Several days in the life of a handicapped child.

Materials for Teachers and Parents[1]

Curwin, Richard L., and Curwin, Geri. *Developing Individual Values in the Classroom.* Education Today, 1974. An invaluable source of activities, teaching ideas, and approaches to help students clarify their values.

Erikson, Erik H., ed. *Youth: Change and Challenge.* Basic Books, 1963. Excellent material for helping understand children.

Hawley, Robert C. *Human Values in the Classroom.* Hart, 1974. Sets forth a basic approach to teaching and learning based on human needs.

Jenkins, Gladys Gardner, and Schacter, Helen S. *These Are Your Children.* 4th ed. Scott, Foresman, 1975. A definitive text on child growth and development.

Reid, Virginia M., ed. *Reading Ladders for Human Relations.* 5th ed. American Council on Education, 1972. Guide to books that help children build a positive self-image, grow in understanding of others, appreciate different cultures, and cope with change.

Films and Filmstrip[2] for Classroom Use

Am I Dependable? (Coronet).

At Your Age . . . (FilmFair Communications).

Consideration for Others (Society for Visual Education).

Courtesy at School (Coronet).

Developing Responsibility, 2d ed. (Coronet).

Family Teamwork and You (Aims).

I Am (Wombat).

Labels: If You Label It This, It Can't Be That (FilmFair Communications).

Learning from Disappointments (Coronet).

Let's Share with Others, 2d ed. (Coronet).

A Little Fable (American Educational Films).

Our Angry Feelings (Perennial, produced by Peshak-Raskin).

School Problems: Getting Along with Others (BFA Educational Media).

Steps Toward Maturity and Health (Walt Disney).

Values: The Right Thing to Do (BFA Educational Media).

Chapter Two: Your Body and How It Works

Books for Students

Bendick, Jeanne. *The Human Senses.* Watts, 1968. Very easy-to-read material.

Elgin, Kathleen. *The Muscles.* Watts, 1973. Part of a well-illustrated reference series, *The Human Body.* Some other books in the series are *The Heart, The Digestive System,* and *The Skin.*

---

[1] See also specialized reading lists on pages T19, T21, and T23.

[2] Filmstrip is marked with an asterisk.

Kalina, Sigmund. *Your Blood and Its Cargo.* Lothrop, 1974. Excellent presentation, written in simple terms.

Noel, Janet. *The Human Body.* New ed. Grosset & Dunlap, 1974. Students are fascinated by the illustrations. Includes material on heredity.

Ravielli, Anthony. *Wonders of the Human Body.* Viking, 1954. A long-time favorite. Accuracy of the text and drawings has been checked by specialists.

Riedman, Sarah. *How Man Discovered His Body.* Abelard-Schuman, 1966. Describes research and experiments that led to present knowledge.

Zim, Herbert S. *Your Brain and How It Works.* Morrow, 1972. Excellent reference by author of *Bones* and *Your Heart and How It Works.*

Materials for Teachers and Parents[1]
Byler, Ruth; Lewis, Gertrude; and Totman, Ruth. *Teach Us What We Want to Know.* Published for the Connecticut State Board of Health by the Mental Health Materials Center, 1969. Tells health interests and concerns of children of all ages.

Model
Human Skelton Model. A plastic model of the human skeleton. Model No. 5228 is available, assembled and mounted on a wire stand, from Ideal School Supply, 11000 S. Lavergne Avenue, Oak Lawn, Illinois 60453.

Films and Filmstrips[2] for Classroom Use
About the Human Body (Churchill).

Breathing Easy (American Lung Association).

Circulation and the Human Body, 2d ed. (Churchill).

Physical Fitness and Good Health (Walt Disney).

*Sensing, Learning, Remembering, and Thinking (BFA Educational Media).

The World's Most Important Feet (American Podiatry Association).

*You—The Human Animal (Walt Disney).

*You—The Living Machine (Walt Disney).

Your Nervous System (Coronet).

Chapter Three: Growth

Books for Students
Bedeschi, Giulio. *Science of Medicine.* Watts, 1975. Complex theories of genetics and role of nucleic acids handled simply and thoroughly in this reference for good readers.

Bendick, Jeanne. *How Heredity Works: Why Living Things Are As They Are.* Parents' Magazine Press, 1975. An extremely easy book suitable for reluctant readers.

Hofstein, Sadie. *The Human Story: Facts on Birth, Growth, and Reproduction.* Scott, Foresman, 1977. Sex-education booklet includes section on heredity.

Lerner, Marguerite Ruth. *Who Do You Think You Are: The Story of Heredity.* Prentice-Hall, 1963. A highly useful reference book.

Power, Jules. *How Life Begins.* Simon & Schuster, 1968. Describes how fish, birds, and mammals are born; concludes with material on development and birth of humans.

Randal, Judith. *All About Heredity.* Random House, 1963. One of the few available references on this subject written for this grade level.

Sullivan, Navin. *Controls in Your Body.* Lippincott, 1971. Students will find the chapter on "Weight and Growth" particularly interesting.

Zappler, Georg. *From One Cell to Many Cells.* Messner, 1970. Discusses the cell as a basic unit of life. Includes many diagrams.

Films and Transparencies for Classroom Use
Boy to Man (Churchill).

Exploring Your Growth (Churchill).

Genetics: Human Heredity (Coronet).

---

[1] See also specialized reading lists on pages T19, T21, and T23.
[2] Filmstrips are marked with an asterisk.

Girl to Woman (Churchill).

Human Heredity, 3d ed. (Perennial, produced by E. C. Brown Trust).

Inheriting Your Physical Traits (Coronet).

The Me I Want to Be (The Life Cycle Center, Kimberly-Clark Corp.) Transparency series for girls, including Teacher's Guide.

Naturally . . . A Girl (Association-Sterling Films, produced by Personal Products Co.).

Chapter Four: Health Questions Answered

Books for Students
Barr, George. *Young Scientist and the Doctor.* McGraw-Hill, 1969. Excellent reference on the examinations and tests a doctor makes during a health checkup. See also *Young Scientist and the Dentist* by Barr.

Cobb, Vicki. *How the Doctor Knows You're Fine.* Lippincott, 1973. Easy-to-read explanation of a health checkup.

Dunahoo, Terry. *Emily Dunning: A Portrait.* Reilly & Lee, 1970. Story of a woman who was determined to become a physician, and did.

Goodsell, Jane. *The Mayo Brothers.* T. Y. Crowell, 1972. Story of the two brothers who moved on from their father's small hospital to develop the renowned Mayo Clinic. Easy.

Knight, David C. *Your Body's Defenses.* McGraw-Hill, 1975. Fine reference on the body's immune system. For advanced students.

Silverstein, Alvin, and Silverstein, Virginia. *Sleep and Dreams.* Lippincott, 1974. Most helpful material that helps unravel some of the mysteries of what happens during sleep.

Materials for Teachers and Parents[1]
American Dental Association. *Cleaning Your Teeth and Gums* and *Happiness Is a Healthy Mouth.* ADA. Basic, up-to-date information on flossing and brushing provided in two booklets.

The Bureau of Dental Health Education of the American Dental Association has available, at low cost, many dental health teaching kits, pamphlets, and posters. Write to the Bureau at the ADA, 211 E. Chicago Avenue, Chicago, Illinois 60611 for a catalog.

Periodicals for the Teacher
Family Health. Family Health Magazine, Inc., 1271 Avenue of the Americas, New York, New York 10020.

Journal of Physical Education and Recreation. Published September to June by the American Association for Health, Physical Education, and Recreation (AAHPER).

The Journal of School Health. The American School Health Association, Kent, Ohio 44240.

Films and Filmstrips[2] for Classroom Use
Eat to Your Heart's Content (American Heart Association).

Food, Energy, and You; Vitamins from Food; and *What's Good to Eat?* (Perennial, produced by Wexler). Three films on nutrition.

Infectious Diseases and Man-Made Defenses (Coronet).

Nutritional Needs of Our Bodies (Coronet).

*The Road to Good Health (Curriculum Materials).

Save Those Teeth (Britannica Films).

*You—And Your Food (Walt Disney).

Chapter Five: First Aid and Safety

Books for Students
American Red Cross, ed. *Basic First Aid: Books 1, 2, 3, 4.* Doubleday. Series of four easy books of programmed first-aid instruction.

---

[1] See also specialized reading lists on pages T19, T21, and T23.
[2] Filmstrips are marked with an asterisk.

Bendick, Jeanne. *The Emergency Book.* Rand McNally, 1967. A self-help book for this age group. Emergencies discussed include household, fire, and weather emergencies.

Frey, Shaney. *The Complete Beginner's Guide to Swimming.* Doubleday, 1975. Good material on water safety, lifesaving techniques.

National Safety Council. Safety Education Data Sheets. *Bad Weather: Hazards, Precautions, Results; Baseball; Bicycles; Falls; Safety in Bad Weather Conditions; Safety in the Gymnasium; Safety in Sports: Basketball; Swimming.* NSC. A wealth of safety concepts on the topics listed.

Vandenburg, Mary Lou. *Help! Emergencies that could happen to you, and how to handle them.* Lerner, 1975. Easy-to-read instructions on what to do in several types of common emergencies.

Materials for Teachers and Parents[1]
American National Red Cross. *Advanced First Aid and Emergency Care.* Doubleday, 1973. A good reference for those versed in first aid.

————. *Standard First Aid and Personal Safety.* Doubleday, 1973. An invaluable reference. Every library should have a copy.

National Safety Council. Safety Education Data Sheets. Those listed for students are also valuable for teachers and parents.

————. *School Safety World.* NSC. A newsletter put out four times a year for teachers.

Thygerson, Alton L. *Safety: Principles, Instruction, and Readings.* Prentice-Hall, 1972. Complete discussion of all aspects of safety education.

Films and Filmstrips[2] for Classroom Use
A Chance to Save a Life (National Council of Boy Scouts of America).

First Aid Series (McGraw-Hill).

**Happy Hollow Makes the Honor Roll* (Society for Visual Education and National Safety Council).

[1] See also specialized reading lists on pages T19, T21, and T23.
[2] Filmstrips are marked with an asterisk.

How to Save a Choking Victim: The Heimlich Maneuver (Paramount Oxford Films).

Learn Not to Burn (National Fire Protection Association).

On Your Own (Sid Davis).

Safety with Fire (Coronet).

Chapter Six: Drugs and You

Books for Students
Englebardt, Stanley L. *Kids and Alcohol, the Deadliest Drug.* Lothrop, 1975. Really good book for advanced readers except for "preaching" tone of first chapter.

Gorodetzky, Charles W., and Christian, Samuel T. *What You Should Know About Drugs.* Harcourt, 1970. Gives straightforward answers to many of the questions students ask.

Lee, Essie E., and Israel, Elaine. *Alcohol and You.* Messner, 1975. Well-written, informative book on alcohol. Good data without preaching.

Madison, Arnold. *Smoking and You.* Messner, 1975. A highly readable and informative book for middle-grade students. Also see *Drugs and You* by the same author.

Zim, Herbert S. *Medicine.* Morrow, 1974. Objective approach to good and bad uses of medicine.

Materials for Teachers and Parents[1]
American Cancer Society. *Answering the Most-Often-Asked Questions About Cigarette Smoking and Lung Cancer.* ACS. For students too.

National Safety Council. Safety Education Data Sheet: *Alcohol and Traffic Accidents.* NSC. Students should also read this.

U.S. Department of Health, Education, and Welfare. Public Health Service. Alcohol, Drug Abuse, and Mental Health Administration. National Institute on Drug Abuse. *Marijuana and Health.* Third Annual Report to Congress from the Secretary of Health, Education, and Welfare. DHEW Publication No. (ADM) 75-132.

_____. Center for Disease Control, National Clearing House for Smoking and Health. *Listen Smokers.* DHEW Publication No. (CDC) 74–8731.

_____. National Institute on Alcohol Abuse and Alcoholism. *Alcohol and Health.* First Special Report to Congress from the Secretary of Health, Education, and Welfare. DHEW Publication No. (HSM) 72–9099.

Films for Classroom Use
Alcohol: A New Focus (American Educational Films).

Be Smart—Don't Start (Smoking) (Aims, produced by Films/West).

The Drag (McGraw-Hill, produced by National Film Board of Canada).

Drinking: How Will Charlie Handle It? (McGraw-Hill).

Drugs: The First Decision (BFA Educational Media).

The Huffless-Puffless Dragon (American Cancer Society).

Marijuana: The Great Escape (BFA Educational Media).

Smoking: A New Focus (American Educational Films).

Speedscene: The Problem of Amphetamine Abuse (BFA Educational Media).

Chapter Seven: The Long Struggle Against Communicable Diseases

Books for Students
Aylesworth, Thomas G. *The World of Microbes.* Watts, 1975. Good reference in area of microbiology. For good readers.

Dietz, David. *All About Great Medical Discoveries.* Random House, 1960. Covers the work of many medical pioneers.

Eberle, Irmengarde. *Modern Medical Discoveries.* 3d ed. T. Y. Crowell, 1968. Interesting and readable.

Epstein, Samuel, and Williams, Beryl. *Medicine from Microbes: The Story of Antibiotics.* Messner, 1965. For curious advanced readers.

Groh, Lynn. *Walter Reed: Pioneer in Medicine.* Garrard, 1971. Easy-to-read action-packed biography.

Lewis, Lucia Z. *The First Book of Microbes.* Rev. ed. Watts, 1972. Satisfying reference source for students. Don't miss chapter seven.

Lietz, Gerald S. *Junior Science Book of Bacteria.* Garrard, 1964. Useful reference for reluctant readers.

Phelan, Mary K. *Probing the Unknown: The Story of Dr. Florence Sabin.* T. Y. Crowell, 1969. Story of the doctor who did research on how the body defends itself against infections.

Villiard, Paul. *The Hidden World: The Story of Microscopic Life.* Four Winds, 1975. Beautiful photographs make the "invisible world" visible.

Materials for Teachers and Parents[1]
Donahue, Parnell, and Capellaro, Helen. *Germs Make Me Sick.* Knopf, 1975. Reference covers wide variety of diseases and their treatment.

Metropolitan Life Insurance Company. *Health Heroes.* Metropolitan Life. Free pamphlets are useful for both teachers and students.

Rosebury, Theodor. *Life on Man.* Viking, 1969. Fascinating reference.

Films and Filmstrip[2] for Classroom Use
*Bacteriology—Louis Pasteur and Robert Koch from *Great Discoveries in Science* series (Scott Education Division).

Flies and Mosquitoes—Their Life Cycle and Control (Britannica Films).

Health Heroes: The Battle Against Disease (Coronet).

Immunization, 2d ed. (Britannica Films).

_____

[1] See also specialized reading lists on pages T19, T21, and T23.
[2] Filmstrip is marked with an asterisk.

Infectious Diseases and Man-Made Defenses (Coronet).

Microbes and Their Control (BFA Educational Media).

Chapter Eight: A Healthy Environment

Books for Students
Adamson, Wendy Wriston. *Saving Lake Superior, A Story of Environmental Action.* Dillon Press, 1974. Fascinating account of ways people are working to protect Lake Superior. For advanced readers.

Aylesworth, Thomas G. *This Vital Air, This Vital Water: Man's Environment Crisis.* Rev. ed. Rand McNally, 1974. Presents facts about air, water, and noise pollution throughout the world in a clear, effective way. For good readers.

Beame, Rona. *What Happens to Garbage?* Messner, 1975. Very easy book discusses methods used by New York City to collect and dispose of refuse.

Berger, Melvin. *The New Water Book.* T. Y. Crowell, 1973. Chapter of experiments on pollution in book that tells story of water.

Gabel, Margaret. *Sparrows Don't Drop Candy Wrappers.* Dodd, Mead, 1971. Simple *do's* and *don'ts* about small ways to make the world a better place to live.

Hilton, Suzanne. *How Do They Get Rid of It?* Westminster, 1970. Discusses not-so-good ways of getting rid of solid wastes along with hopeful trends for the future. For advanced readers.

Pringle, Laurence. *The Only Earth We Have.* Macmillan, 1969. Outstanding book for middle-graders effectively explains what can be done to protect and preserve the only earth we have.

Shuttlesworth, Dorothy E., and Cervasio, Thomas. *Litter—The Ugly Enemy.* Doubleday, 1973. Good emphasis on how the problem of solid wastes is being slowly conquered by scientists, technicians, and private citizens.

Materials for Teachers and Parents[1]
Miller, G. Tyler, Jr. *Living in the Environment: Concepts, Problems, and Alternatives.* Wadsworth, 1975. A good reference.

Sale, Larry L., and Lee, Ernest W. *Environmental Education in the Elementary School.* Holt, 1972. A helpful textbook to help teachers plan environmental-education experiences for students.

Tangen, Lillian, ed. *A Better Place to Be, A Guide to Environmental Learning in Your Classroom.* U.S. Department of the Interior, 1975. U.S. Department of the Interior, Washington, D.C. 20240.

Films for Classroom Use
Community Helpers—The Sanitation Department (Aims).

Conservation/A Job for Young America (McGraw-Hill).

Conservation: For the First Time (Contemporary—McGraw-Hill). A film made by children.

Conserving Our Natural Resources (BFA Educational Media).

Cycles (Association-Sterling Films). Deals with recycling.

Health—You and Your Helpers (Aims).

Noise (BFA Educational Media).

The Poisoned Air (Carousel, produced by CBSTV).

---

[1] See also specialized reading lists on pages T19, T21, and T23.

Student Questionnaire *You and Your Health*

How do you like your *Health* book?

I like it very much ☐1   It's O.K. ☐2   I don't like it ☐3

How easy is it for you to read?

Just right ☐1   Too easy ☐2   Too hard ☐3

What would you say about the pictures in the *Health* book?

Help me a lot ☐1   Help me sometimes ☐2   Don't help me ☐3

What parts of the *Health* book do you like?

☐1   The body and how it works   ☐8   Health careers

☐2   Care of the body   ☐9   How you grow

☐3   Diseases and germs   ☐10 Medical advances

☐4   Drugs including alcohol and tobacco   ☐11 Safety and first aid

☐5   Ecology and pollution   ☐12 Teeth

☐6   Exercise and sleep   ☐13 Understanding others

☐7   Foods   ☐14 Understanding yourself

What special sections of the *Health* book do you like?

☐1   Can You Show What You Know?   ☐5   School and Home

☐2   Enjoy It   ☐6   Tell It

☐3   Health Around Us   ☐7   Things to Do

☐4   Safety Around Us   ☐8   Write It

If there are any other parts of the *Health* book you liked, write them below.

Scott, Foresman and Company   1900 East Lake Avenue   Glenview, Illinois 60025

Teacher's Questionnaire *You and Your Health*

Please complete this questionnaire after you have finished teaching the **new** Scott, Foresman HEALTH Program for the school year. Remove the questionnaire from the book, fold it as shown, staple it, and place it in the nearest mailbox. No postage is required.

1. How would you identify the overall ability of the children in your class?

   EMH or TMH ☐   Below average ☐   Average ☐   Above average ☐   Gifted ☐

2. Was the text an effective teaching tool? Why or why not? _____

   _____

   _____

3. What is your opinion of the readability? _____

   _____

4. How useful are the illustrations in helping students learn? _____

   _____

5. Did any parts of the text cause learner difficulty? _____

   _____

   _____

6. What improvements would you suggest? _____

   _____

   _____

7. What health questions do your pupils ask most often? _____

   _____

   _____

8. Indicate which features of the text you like and which features you do not like.

Like	Don't Like		Like	Don't Like	
☐	☐	Chapter-Opening Pages	☐	☐	Things to Do
☐	☐	Preview It	☐	☐	Can You Show What You Know?
☐	☐	Enjoy It	☐	☐	Review It
☐	☐	Tell It	☐	☐	Chapter Test
☐	☐	Write It	☐	☐	School and Home
☐	☐	Health Around Us	☐	☐	Special Research

9. Indicate which features of the Teacher's Edition you like and which features you do not like.

Like	Don't Like		Like	Don't Like	
☐	☐	Teacher's Notes	☐	☐	A Healthful Classroom Environment
☐	☐	Family-Life Education	☐	☐	Signs and Symptoms of Illness
☐	☐	Enrichment Suggestions	☐	☐	The Parent-Teacher Conference
☐	☐	Reference Materials	☐	☐	If Children Ask About Death
☐	☐	A Developmental Profile of Eleven- to Twelve-Year-Olds	☐	☐	Movement Exploration and Games

If you would be willing to complete a questionnaire after teaching the program for another year, please fill in your return address.

Name _____

School _____

Address _____

City _____ State _____ Zip Code _____

Fold on dotted line so return address and mailing address are on outside of questionnaire.

FIRST CLASS
PERMIT No. 282
GLENVIEW, ILL

POSTAGE WILL BE PAID BY

SCOTT, FORESMAN AND COMPANY
1900 EAST LAKE AVENUE
GLENVIEW, ILLINOIS 60025

School, Home, Community **You and Your Health**

Julius B. Richmond, M.D.
Elenore T. Pounds, M.A.
Gladys Gardner Jenkins, M.A.
Dieter H. Sussdorf, Ph.D.

In consultation with
Orvis A. Harrelson, M.D., M.P.H.
Wallace Ann Wesley, Hs.D.

Scott, Foresman and Company
Glenview, Illinois

Dallas, Texas Palo Alto, California
Oakland, New Jersey Tucker, Georgia

Authors

Julius B. Richmond, M.D. Professor of Child Psychiatry and Human Development and Professor and Chairman, Department of Social and Preventive Medicine, Harvard Medical School; Director, Judge Baker Guidance Center; Chief of Psychiatric Service, Children's Hospital Medical Center, Boston, Massachusetts.

Elenore T. Pounds, M.A. Writer; lecturer; former Directing Editor of the Health and Personal Development Program; classroom teacher; coauthor of the *Health and Growth* Program; author of *Drugs and Your Safety* and other *Health Enrichment Booklets*.

Gladys Gardner Jenkins, M.A. Lecturer in Parent-Child-Teacher Relationships, University of Iowa, Iowa City, Iowa; former member, National Advisory Council on Child Growth and Human Development; author of *Helping Children Reach Their Potential;* coauthor of *These Are Your Children.*

Dieter H. Sussdorf, Ph.D. Associate Professor of Microbiology, Cornell University Graduate School of Medical Sciences, New York, New York; coauthor of *Methods in Immunology*

Consultants

Orvis A. Harrelson, M.D., M.P.H. Corporate Medical Director, Weyerhauser Company, Tacoma, Washington; former Administrative Director of Health, Tacoma Public Schools, Tacoma, Washington.

Wallace Ann Wesley, Hs.D. Director, Department of Health Education, American Medical Association, Chicago, Illinois; former teacher at primary through college levels.

ISBN: 0-673-11015-X

ISBN: 0-673-11007-9

12345678910-RRC-8584838281807978 7776

Content Specialists

Richard H. Blum, Ph.D. Consulting Professor, Department of Psychology and Director, Joint Program in Drugs, Crime, and Community Studies, Center for Interdisciplinary Research, Stanford University, Stanford, California.

Willie D. Ford, Ph.D. Professor, Nutrition and Home Economics, Grambling State University, Grambling, Louisiana; former Nutrition Specialist, U.S. Department of Agriculture, University of Nebraska, Lincoln, Nebraska.

Lucia Guzman, B.S. Assistant to the Dean for Student Affairs, University of Texas School of Allied Health Sciences, University of Texas Medical Branch, Galveston, Texas.

Barbara J. Kohuth, B.S. Environmental Health Educator; Head, Office of Environmental Education and Public Information, Cleveland Department of Public Health and Welfare, Cleveland, Ohio.

Boyd T. Marsh, M.A., B.S. Deputy Health Commissioner for Environmental Health, Cleveland Department of Public Health and Welfare, Cleveland, Ohio.

Norman H. Olsen, D.D.S. Chairman of the Department of Pedodontics and Dean of The Dental Schoool, Northwestern University, Chicago, Illinois.

Marguerite Robinson, M.A. Consumer Specialist, Department of Health, Education, Welfare, Food and Drug Administration, Chicago, Illinois; President, Chicago Nutrition Society, Chicago, Illinois.

Joan Tillotson, Ph.D. Consultant in Movement Education, The University of North Carolina at Charlotte, Charlotte, North Carolina.

Wilma Yee, B.S., R.N. Public Health Nurse and School Nurse, Oakland Public Schools, Oakland, California.

The assistance of the National Safety Council, Chicago, Illinois, in reviewing the safety advice in this material is gratefully acknowledged.

Learner Feedback

Experimental versions of many of the lessons in the YOU AND YOUR HEALTH Program for grade six were used during the 1975-1976 school year with students at Jane Addams School, Lawndale, California; Jacksonville Beach Elementary School 144, Jacksonville Beach, Florida; and Public School 276, Brooklyn, New York. The authors and editors of the program are grateful to the students and to the teachers in these schools for their comments and their suggestions.

Teacher's Notes

In this *Teacher's Edition*, "Teacher's Notes" are overprinted on the pupil's pages.
With the exception of specialized health and safety words, this book is written chiefly in the vocabulary of well-known vocabulary lists for fifth-grade and early sixth-grade levels.
The pupil's text has been kept easy so that all eleven- to twelve-year-olds can enjoy health and safety material "custom built" for their special health needs and interests.
Readability scores for this book are:
Fry, Grade 6; and Dale-Chall, Grade 6.

Contents

For the Teacher

1 You and Others

You probably have questions about yourself and about others. Some questions that others your age have asked are "How do I know myself?" and "How can I understand others better?" What are some other questions *you* have about yourself and about others?

Preview It

Who is the person that you must live with all your life? It is *you!*

In this chapter you will learn more about yourself. You will think about the kind of person you are, and the kind of person you may want to become.

For the rest of your life you will be involved with other people. How well you understand and get along with others will affect your happiness. It will affect your success in life too.

This chapter offers information to help you better understand yourself and understand others. Look quickly through the chapter. What are some questions that will be discussed in the chapter? Which of these topics is most important to you?

Are there other questions that you want answered? How might you find the answers to your own questions?

Start the chapter now. Begin by reading about how to get better acquainted with yourself.

What Are You Like?

"How do I know myself?" is a question often asked by boys and girls your age. Stop and think about yourself. What is important to you? What things are happening in your life right now? What do you do well and what don't you do well? What things do you care about most? Whom do you admire? What are your problems? Who are your friends?

To get your thoughts together you might make a newspaper about yourself. What would you write about?

What can you find out from the homemade newspapers on this page and the next few pages?

THE DEBBIE JONES MIRROR

Debbie Likes Math,
Has Trouble with Spelling

"There is one subject I do well in at school," said Debbie Jones. "I am good in math."

Then Debbie went on to talk about spelling.

"Spelling bugs me," she said. "I still have trouble spelling words like their and there, quiet and quite."

Debbie Jones Moves to Chapel Hill

Debbie Jones, age eleven, recently moved to Chapel Hill from Columbia, South Carolina.

Debbie has a mother, father, an older brother named Will, and a little sister, Fran.

When she was asked if she liked her new home and school, Debbie said, "I don't know yet. I am trying to make new friends. Maybe I will. Everybody seems to know everybody except me. I just wish someone would notice me."

Joe Janda's
Journal

News Story in Brief

Who: Joe Janda

Where: Chapel Hill,
North Carolina

When: September

What: Information
about myself

Why: To know
myself better

Missing: Boy from
Chapel Hill, Age 11

What is I should turn
up missing? How would
people describe me in
the missing persons
report?

I am eleven. On
December 26 I will be
twelve. That's really a
bad birthday. Instead
of two presents from
someone at Christmas, I
get one. It says "Merry
Christmas and Happy
Birthday."

I am short for my age
and I don't weigh
very much. I sure wish
I could start to grow
taller. I like basketball
and I play pretty well.
But how will I make the
team if I don't start
growing?

Joe's Friend Frank

I don't have a lot of
friends. But I am lucky.
I have one very good
friend. His name is Frank
Chinn. Frank likes me, and
I like him.

When we tried out for the
baseball league last summer,
I didn't have a good glove.
So Frank let me use his.

Frank and I usually
play together after school.
If it is raining, we play
Monopoly inside. We look
at TV too.

Frank says maybe his
family is going to move
soon. I hope not. I don't
like to think about not
having Frank around.

Something I Do Fairly Well

I like science and I do all right in it.

I am good in baseball and basketball.

I can cook. The family likes my scrambled eggs.

I shop for the family when I am needed.

Something I Have Trouble With

I have trouble keeping my temper. I hate to give oral reports and I often mess them up.

I don't think I'm very good as as actor in class plays.

You should see how I make my bed.

What about Brothers and Sisters

I don't have any brothers but I have an older sister named Judy. Some of the time she's OK. But some of the time we don't get along at all. I think it's because she's bossy. Or maybe I am jealous of her. Most of the time when I have to go to bed, she can stay up for a while. We have trouble with TV too. She says the programs I like are awful. And I know the ones she likes are terrible.

A Problem

Some kids I know are starting to smoke. They say I should do it. I don't think I should. My mother and dad would have a fit. But how do I get out of doing it?

ENJOY IT

Me Myself and I

Isn't it strange
That however I change,
I still keep on being me?

Though my clothes get worn out,
Though my toys are outgrown,
I never grow out of me.

Though I may taste a mango,
Or dance a fandango,
It's still *my* tongue and *my* feet.

Though I greet a plumber or tailor,
A sailor, a doctor, a parakeet—
Whomever I meet,
They meet *me*.

No matter what faces I make,
Though I wriggle or wiggle or shake;
Though I've learned subtraction and adding a sum:
I never can take away me,
And nobody else I become.
. . . .
If I say 'yes,' or if I say 'no';
If I go fast, or if I go slow;
When I'm at work, or when I'm at play:
Me I stay.

I may lose many things and frequently do.
I never lose me.
Does that happen to you?

You will keep on being "ME" all your life.
There is nobody in the world just like you.
What was unique about *you* in the newspaper or
journal you made about yourself?

Teacher's Notes
A special attempt is made in this
health series to enrich children's lives
by exposing them to poetry and to art
that is related to the lesson topics.
This page allows the students to enjoy
a poem about "Me". Give the students
a chance to share with others their
personal newspapers or journals.
Volunteers might read to the group
parts of their materials. If pupils ask
what the word *fandango* means, it is a
lively Spanish or Spanish-American
dance.
See page T25 for additional teaching
suggestions.

What Is Your Group Like?

Perhaps you are wondering about the large graph you see in the picture. It gives information about a group of eleven-year-olds. It shows that people are alike in many ways and unique in other ways.

On the next two pages you can study the graph in detail. Find out what things this group shared in common. What interesting information does the graph give?

Your group can make a graph like this one. It will help you know more about others in the group. You can see how you are alike and different from others.

Are there any other items that you would include in your graph?

All About Our Group

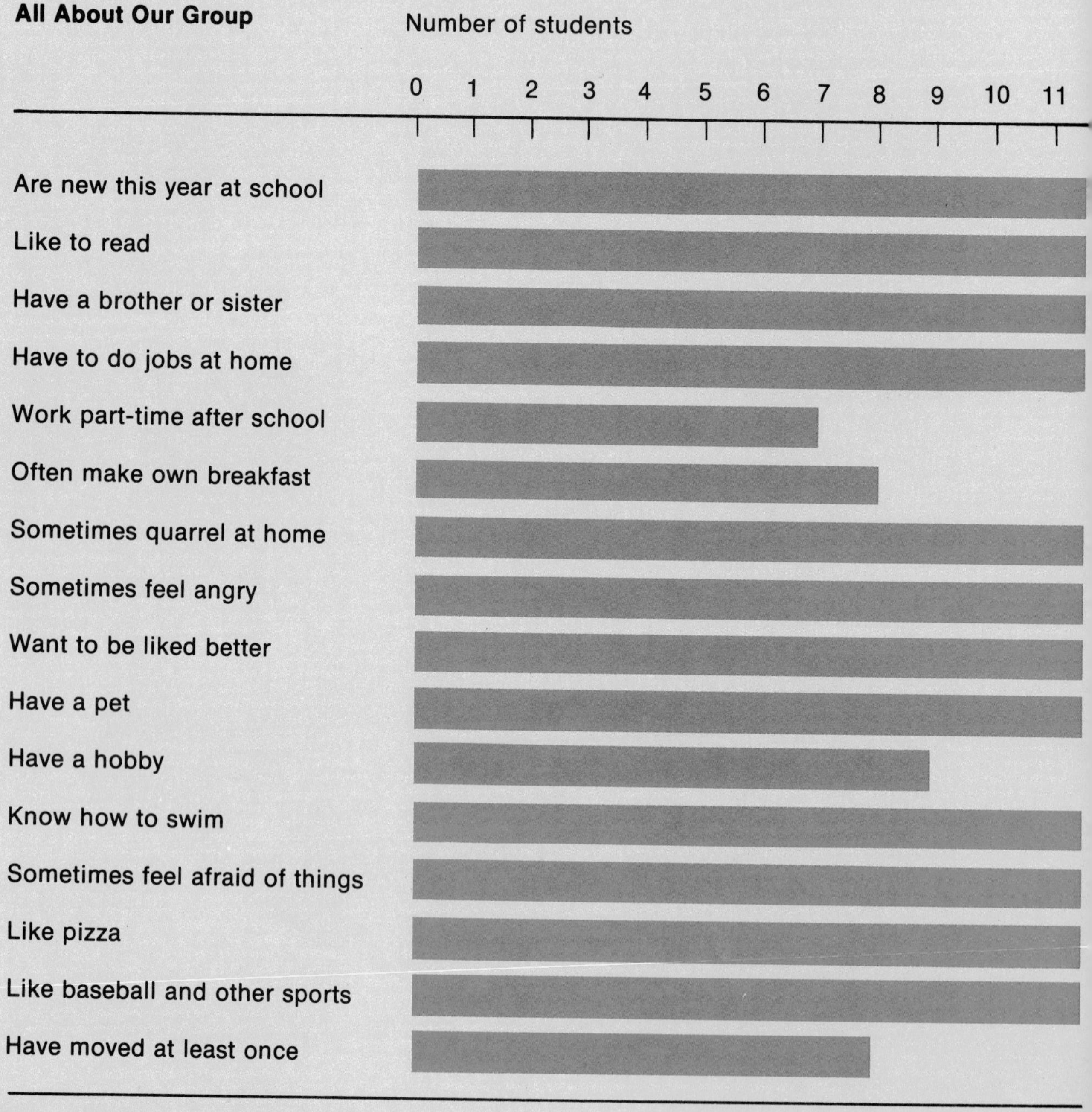

Number of students

	0	1	2	3	4	5	6	7	8	9	10	11

Are new this year at school

Like to read

Have a brother or sister

Have to do jobs at home

Work part-time after school

Often make own breakfast

Sometimes quarrel at home

Sometimes feel angry

Want to be liked better

Have a pet

Have a hobby

Know how to swim

Sometimes feel afraid of things

Like pizza

Like baseball and other sports

Have moved at least once

Teacher's Notes
An "About Our Group" graph offers
an effective way to show that while
each individual is unique, he or she
may also share experiences, likes, and
dislikes with others in his group.
See also page T25 for additional
teaching suggestions.

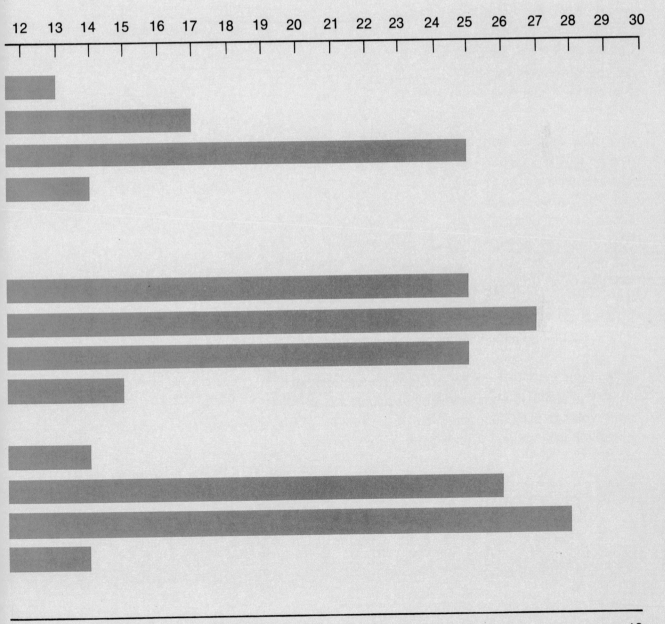

ENJOY IT

Wish

I know what *I* feel like;
I'd like to be *you*
And feel what *you* feel like
And do what *you* do.
I'd like to change places
For maybe a week
And look like your look-alike
And speak as you speak

And think what you're thinking
And go where you go
And feel what you're feeling
And know what you know.
I wish we could do it;
What fun it would be
If I could try *you* out
And you could try me.

Why might it be interesting to be someone else for a week?

You can't really do that. But you can do the next best thing. You can read about some other people's problems. You can think about their feelings. You can "put yourself in their shoes." That is what you will do next.

Teacher's Notes
A special attempt is made in this health series to enrich children's lives by exposing them to poetry and to art that is related to the lesson topics.
After reading the poem on this "Enjoy It" page, discuss the value of being able to "put yourself in someone else's shoes," or to see things from the other person's point of view.
Ask the students to pretend that they are a newcomer to school. This will give them the chance to think how the stranger feels.
See also page T25 for additional teaching suggestions.

How Can You Keep Your Friends?

After school one day Nan saw three girls going to the library together. They had not asked her to go along.

"I thought Jean, Terri, and Pam were my friends," she said to herself. "But I guess they really aren't. I wonder what's the matter with me. I make friends, but I can't seem to keep them."

How do you think Nan feels? What should she do?

Do you know how to keep friends? What are some suggestions you could give to Nan?

Now turn the page. Compare your ideas with the ones suggested.

Now look at some of the conversations Nan has had with her friends. What needs did she overlook?

Be ready to act out these situations. Show some friendly, thoughtful things Nan could say.

The chart demonstrates some basic human needs. What are they?

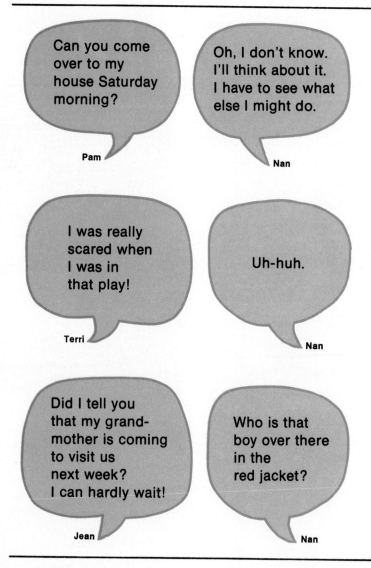

Pam: Can you come over to my house Saturday morning?

Nan: Oh, I don't know. I'll think about it. I have to see what else I might do.

Terri: I was really scared when I was in that play!

Nan: Uh-huh.

Jean: Did I tell you that my grandmother is coming to visit us next week? I can hardly wait!

Nan: Who is that boy over there in the red jacket?

Everyone Needs to Feel Wanted

If others feel from the way you look, act, and talk that you like them, they are most likely to enjoy being with you.

Everyone Needs to Feel Successful

We all thrive on achievement and on its recognition. Do you remember to notice achievement in others and to comment on it? If so, others will feel good about your approval.

Everyone Needs Companionship

When something great or something awful happens to you, you want to tell your friends. Are you equally interested in hearing what they have to say?

Do you enjoy sharing their experiences? To have friends, you must be a friend.

What Can Help When You Make Mistakes?

Ed really felt down. His test paper had ten mistakes on it.

All sorts of thoughts went through his mind. "It's Mr. Amano's fault," he muttered. "He makes the tests too hard."

"There's no use trying anymore," he decided for himself. "I'm just dumb."

His shoulders slumped and he had a funny feeling in his chest.

Have you ever felt like Ed? What can help you when you have done poorly and feel terrible about your mistakes?

Read on and see what ideas some boys and girls your age offer as suggestions.

TELL IT

Which idea given below do you think may be helpful to you? What other ideas do you have?

Can you predict how things might be if Ed continues to feel angry and dumb?

What might happen if he decides to ask for help?

Teacher's Notes

Another feature of this book and others in the series is the recurring use of reports by children. Exposure to these "Tell It" pages offers the students an opportunity to do some reporting of their own.

Here students might discuss whether all work at school should be so easy that no one makes mistakes.

Point out that mistakes and failures can be a spur to greater achievement. See page T25 for additional teaching suggestions.

It doesn't help to blame others for your mistakes. It is better to be honest with yourself, and admit your own mistakes.

I think it is natural to feel dumb and a bit angry when we make mistakes. But we shouldn't feel that way for long. We shouldn't let our mistakes get us down. I try to think, "Well, I'll see if I can do better next time."

Instead of quitting or of giving up hope of improving, ask for help. Teachers can help you when you don't understand. But you have to ask for help. Sometimes someone at home can help too. My older sister helps me.

Everyone makes mistakes. No one is perfect. But people can learn from their mistakes. If we do, maybe we won't make the same mistakes again.

Isabel

Leo

Paul

Nicola

What Can Help When You Are Angry?

Vicki was all ready for school one morning. She went to put on her green sweater. But it wasn't in the closet.

"Rita has borrowed it again!" she yelled. "She took it when I wasn't looking and went to school in it!"

While walking to school, Vicki became so angry that she threw her books down. She even kicked one of them.

"I'm so angry I don't know what to do," she thought. "Wait till I see that sister of mine!"

Have *you* ever felt like Vicki?

Some boys and girls think you should never get angry. What do you think?

What can help when someone feels very angry?

Now read on. See what ideas are given.

Teacher's Notes
Discuss situations that justifiably make
anyone feel angry, for example, if
someone is treated cruelly; if our
belongings are stolen, damaged, or
borrowed without permission; or if an
animal is mistreated.
Sometimes our anger can help to stop
behavior that should not occur.
See page T25 for additional teaching
suggestions.

We all feel angry when we think we have been treated unfairly. We feel angry when someone else is not being treated fairly.

We shouldn't hit or hurt someone because we are angry. It is important to learn to control our destructive kind of anger.

But we can't keep angry feelings locked up inside us for very long either. As long as we have such feelings locked up inside, we will be cross and unhappy.

Because we all do feel angry now and then, we need to know ways to deal with our anger.

Below are some helpful ideas on ways to deal with angry feelings.

What Can You Do When You Feel Angry?

1 Be willing to admit your feelings. Do not try to pretend that they do not exist.

2 When you are too angry or upset to know what to do, turn your attention to something else for awhile. Work on a hobby, watch TV, play a game, visit a friend, or ride your bike. Try to think about your problem when you have calmed down.

3 Remember some good can come out of angry feelings. Such feelings can lead to a discussion that "clears the air."

4 When you are angry for a long time, talk with someone. You might talk with a parent, an older brother or sister, or a friend. Talking things over helps you get your feelings into the open. Then you may be able to handle them better.

Why Are You Sometimes Afraid of Things?

"Now what am I going to do?" thought Dan as he saw a dog on the walk ahead.

"I'm scared to death of that dog, and I think he knows it. I guess I'll walk back to the corner and go home another way."

Dan felt foolish about his fear of dogs. He was glad his friends weren't along to see how scared he was. He was sure that he was the only one who ever felt afraid of things.

Do you think Dan is the only one who ever feels afraid of things?

What are *you* afraid of?

What can help you when you are scared or afraid?

Now turn the page and read on. Compare your ideas with the ones given there.

27

Teacher's Notes
Discuss Dan's fear of dogs. Remind the students that everyone should be careful with strange dogs. Ask these questions:

"Was Dan's fear useful?"

"What could Dan do about his fear?" (He could talk it over with someone he trusts. Then he could try to get the courage to put their advice into action.)

Stress that we all have fears at times. Many boys and girls are afraid of high places, darkness, spiders, lightning, and so on.

(*Note:* "Sum It Up" is a feature that occurs at intervals throughout each chapter of this book and in this health series. Pupils can use this study aid to review important ideas learned in the preceding pages.)

(*Note:* Special features in the margin such as "Books to Read" are designed to keep the pupils active, interested, and alert throughout each chapter.)

See page T25 for additional teaching suggestions.

It is natural to have fears. Everyone does at times. But not everyone is willing to admit it.

Fear, like anger, is an emotion. We must learn to admit it so we can deal with it.

Often a fear can be useful. Fear of being hit by a car helps make you alert when you cross the street. What is another useful fear?

Most fears are learned. You learn them through unpleasant experiences, or from others.

When you admit that you fear something, you are ready to work at overcoming the fear. Dan's fear of dogs can be traced to the time a big dog knocked him down when he was a toddler. What might Dan do to overcome his fear? What should he keep in mind about strange dogs?

Sometimes we fear things that are unknown to us. Gwen, for example, was afraid to get her teeth cleaned by the dentist. Afterward she was amazed at how easy it was. It didn't hurt at all.

At times we fear doing things we think we may not do well. Walt is fearful of giving a report. After Walt gave a few reports in front of his class, it became easier for him.

Some fears are not easily removed. If your fears are accompanied by a great deal of worry, you should tell someone. Talk over your fears with an adult you trust. How might that help?

Sum It Up

How are you unique? How are you like the others in your group?

What can you do to help get over angry feelings?

Why might you be afraid of something? What is the first step in overcoming a fear?

A Book to Read

Look in the school or public library for this book:

LeShan, Eda. *What Makes Me Feel This Way?* (Macmillan).

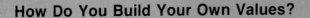

How Do You Build Your Own Values?

José, Bonnie, Amy, and some others found an interesting quiz in their weekly newspaper. The quiz was called "Would You Do It?"

One question was "Would you let a friend copy from your paper?" Another was "Would you call a newcomer names if your friends were doing it too?" Still another was "Would you tell one person you couldn't go to a movie and then go to it with someone else?"

"My answer to those questions is 'No,'" said Amy. "They aren't the right things to do."

"But how do we always know what is right?" asked José.

How *do* we know what is the right thing to do? How do we build a set of values to guide our thoughts and behavior?

Discuss your ideas. Then turn the page and compare your ideas with the information there.

In this chart you can see some of the sources responsible for helping you form your values. What are some of these sources?

In what ways have you been influenced by some of the sources shown below?

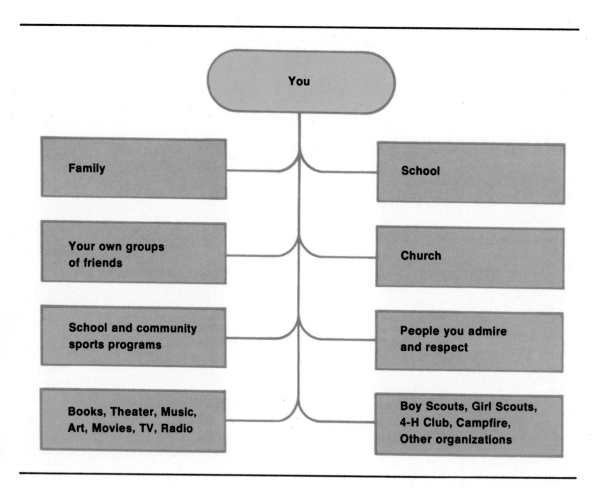

How Do You Treat Someone Who Is Handicapped?

Something unusual is going to happen at David's home. His mother has a friend whose son Max is blind. Max is about David's age. Max and his mother are coming to visit David for a few days.

David is worried. He knows he will be expected to help entertain Max. But he doesn't know how to treat a blind person.

"Will I have to help Max do everything?" he asked his mother. "What will I talk about? How do you treat a person who is handicapped?"

What ideas could you give David? How *do* you treat someone who is blind or deaf or handicapped in some other way?

After you discuss your ideas, turn the page and compare your ideas with the ones given there.

Teacher's Notes
Many youngsters are curious tb know
what it means to be mentally retarded
or mentally handicapped. These terms
apply to those who have limited
abilities to learn. But most mentally
retarded are capable of learning, at
their own rate, what they need to
know to become independent adults.
Stress that mentally retarded children
can be born to any parents. The
mentally retarded child has the same
basic human needs, and enjoys many
of the same activities, as other children.
They just learn things at a slower rate
and in a limited way.
See page T25 for additional teaching
suggestions.

If possible, a handicapped person should be treated just like anyone else. Treat the person as you would like to be treated.

What is it like to have a handicap? Is a handicapped person really so very different from people who are not handicapped? How could you find out?

David could try something that would help him change places with Max. He could try listening to his TV for a while without looking at the picture. He could try finding his way across the room with his eyes closed.

David would probably discover that even without seeing, he was still the same person. He still had the same feelings. He still was in touch with his surroundings.

Handicapped people often say, "Don't try to do everything for us. Let us do what we can on our own." David, for example, should wait to see what Max can do for himself. What do you think some of these things will be?

Handicapped people also may say, "Remember that we have feelings too." Often thoughtless people make remarks that are hurtful. In the presence of a handicapped person they may comment, "What's the matter with *him?*" or "Wouldn't you hate to be like *that?*"

Now what ideas do you have about how David should treat his blind guest.

Sum It Up

How do people build values?

What have you learned that can help you understand handicapped people better?

Books to Read

There are fine books at the library that can help you better understand handicapped people. Here are a few:

de Angeli, Marguerite. *Door in the Wall: Story of Medieval London* (Doubleday).

Friis-Baastad, Babbis. *Don't Take Teddy* (Scribner).

Wolf, Bernard. *Don't Feel Sorry for Paul* (Lippincott).

HEALTH AROUND US

It is hard for people in wheelchairs to get around. They have trouble getting in and out of some buildings.

Some new buildings are being built with the needs of people in wheelchairs in mind. Certain old buildings are being changed. These buildings now have ramps for wheelchairs to roll up and down. The doors swing in and out.

As a result, people in wheelchairs can visit, shop, and eat in many more places. They also can work in places where it is easy for them to get around.

The symbol below is often put on buildings that are planned for people in wheelchairs. Have you ever seen this symbol on any buildings? If so, where?

Teacher's Notes

"Health Around Us" is a recurring feature in this book and in this health series. It focuses on interesting and intriguing aspects of health in the world around us. At times new developments in the field of health will be highlighted.

Ask the pupils to suggest other things that can help handicapped people in wheelchairs. For example, ramps instead of curbs at street corners.

See page T25 for additional teaching suggestions.

ENJOY IT

Art and Feelings

Often you can express your feelings or emotions in pictures you draw or paint. Or you can express feelings in objects you make from clay.

"Mother is gentle and a child sleeps in her arms."

On these pages you see the work of some children who are
expressing their emotions through art. It may interest you to know
that this artwork was done by blind children. What emotions are
expressed in their artwork?

"Joy, Happiness"

"Can't you see that I am furious?"

ENJOY IT

Decision

Getting along with people is fine
But when the others want to do
Anything that is out of line
With the things I think are true
Though they heckle, tease, and flout me
I'll agree to disagree.
They can get along without me
But I must get along with me.

"Decision" by Jane Merchant. Copyright © 1958 by W. L. Jenkins as appearing in *Venture*. Used by permission of Abingdon Press.

Teacher's Notes
Have the students act out ways to "agree to disagree." Look back at Joe's Journal on pages 14–15. Note that Joe has a problem concerning smoking. Some of his friends want him to start. What can Joe say as he "agrees to disagree"?
See also page T25 for additional teaching suggestions.

Things to Do

Teacher's Notes
"Special Research" offers extra research or investigation activities for superior or highly motivated pupils. Ask students to write summaries or tell about books that they have read that help you "put yourself in someone else's shoes."
See page T25 for additional teaching suggestions.

1. Plan to give some skits to show helpful ways to deal with these problems:

   a girl is afraid to try out for a play her scout troup is giving.

   a boy is angry because he can't watch his TV program.

   a girl makes a mistake when weeding the garden and pulls up some flowering plants.

2. Think about a time when you were very angry. How did you handle your angry feelings? How would you deal with them now? Write about it.

3. Demonstrate some ways to convey your feelings without saying any words. For example, *winking, patting someone on the shoulder, waving.* What are some other ways?

4. Look for books at the library that will help you better understand other people's problems. You may enjoy these books: Little, Joan. *Mine for Keeps* (Little, Brown). Sal is a victim of cerebral palsy. She has been away in a special school. Now she is home to stay and has many adjustments to make.

Rich, Louise D. *Star Island Boy* (Watts). Larry is sent to live with another set of foster parents.

Robinson, Veronica. *David in Silence* (Lippincott). A deaf boy begins to take part in activities along with children who can hear.

Stolz, Mary. *A Wonderful, Terrible Time* (Harper). Two girls react in different ways to their first experience at camp.

Special Research

Here are some psychology books you may be interested in reading:

Hall, Elizabeth. *Why We Do What We Do, A Look at Psychology* (Houghton).

LeShan, Eda. *What Makes Me Feel This Way? Growing Up with Human Emotions* (Macmillan).

Can You Show What You Know?[1]

Teacher's Notes
Here behavioral objectives in the *cognitive* area are posed in childlike language directly to the students themselves. In turn, boys and girls give evidence by *observable behavior* of what they have learned.

Other hoped-for behavioral objectives lie chiefly in the less easily observed *affective* area— objectives that pertain to feelings, attitudes, and values. Some of them are:

Grows in self-understanding

Is sensitive to the needs and problems of others.

Appreciates and takes into account the basic human needs that all people have.

Page numbers show you where to look back in the chapter for information, if you need it.

1. Tell one way you are unique. (13-16)
2. Mention several ways in which you are not unique. (17-19)
3. List three basic human needs. (22)
4. Act out a courteous way to respond to an invitation. (22)
5. Suggest two or three ways to deal with upset feelings. (24)
6. Mention two helpful ways to deal with angry feelings. (26)
7. Discuss two ways in which people may acquire fears. (28)
8. Suggest a way to deal with the fear of doing something that you don't do well. (28)
9. Give an example of a fear that is helpful. (28)
10. List four sources that can influence a person's values. (30)
11. Suggest two helpful ways to treat handicapped people. (32)
12. Mention one thing that is being done to help handicapped people get around in wheelchairs. (33)

[1]Behavioral objectives in the cognitive area are stated here directly to students themselves.

Review It

Teacher's Notes

"Review It" is a feature that occurs at the end of each chapter in this book and in this health series. It gives children a chance to think over what they have learned, to summarize, and to store away important ideas. Page references after each item make this review a self-help one. However, group discussion can be a valuable aid.

Page numbers show you where to look back in the chapter for information, if you need it.

1. "If I only were the right kind of person, I'd never feel angry," thought Nora.

Do you agree with Nora? Why or why not? (25-26)

2. When Betty Halda gets a paper back with mistakes on it, she quickly throws it away. "I don't want to look at it," she thinks.

Do you agree with Betty? Why or why not? (24)

3. "I never give compliments," Bob says. "Compliments just make people 'stuck up'!"

Do you agree with Bob? Why or why not? (22)

4. "How do kids know what is right to do?" asked Ted. "Their parents aren't always around to tell them."

How *do* boys and girls get their ideas about what is right or wrong? (30)

5. Suppose that you were crippled and had to get around in a wheelchair. How would you like others to treat you? (32-33)

6. One day Ray saw some mentally retarded youngsters on the playground. Mentally retarded people are limited in their ability to learn. "Look at the dummies," shouted Ray. "Don't say that," said Linda. "Those children may hear you." "Oh, they won't care," said Ray.

Do you agree with Ray? What should you keep in mind about all handicapped people? (32)

7. "I'm scared to give my report on tornadoes," said Marsha. "Maybe I'll stay home tomorrow. The teacher may forget about me after that."

What do you think of Marsha's plan for dealing with her scared feelings? What might help her get over her feelings? (28)

Health Test for Chapter One

Teacher's Notes
After students have taken the test and their papers have been scored, the test items can serve as guides for a summary discussion. Volunteers can read aloud their rewording of the false statements.
"What Do You Think?" is a special feature that offers pupils a chance to evaluate some of their newly acquired knowledge.

Copy each number on a piece of paper. After each number write the correct answer, *true* or *false*. Rewrite each false statement to make it true.

T 1. You can learn from your mistakes.

F 2. When you make a mistake, it is helpful to blame the teacher.

T 3. Try to admit your mistakes and see what can be done about them.

T 4. We all need to feel successful in some of the things we do.

T 5. It helps to let others know that you like to be with them.

T 6. Talking over angry feelings may help you feel better.

T 7. Hitting or hurting others is a destructive kind of anger.

T 8. Most of our fears are ones we have learned.

T 9. We often tend to fear things that we don't know much about.

T 10. Only a few people ever have fears.

F 11. You are born knowing what is right and what is wrong.

F 12. You should be ashamed of having feelings of fear.

T 13. One of the influences in building your values is your family.

F 14. Handicapped people want you to help them in every way possible.

T 15. Handicapped people have feelings just as you do.

T 16. You get some of your values and standards from people you admire.

F 17. Try to hide all your angry feelings; pretend they don't exist.

T 18. In some ways you are different from everyone else in the world.

T 19. You are like others in some ways.

F 20. Getting along with people means doing everything that they do.

Number of Answers	20
Number Right	
Score (Number Right x 5)	

What Do You Think?

What did you learn in this chapter that can help you understand yourself or others better? Write about it on a piece of paper.

SCHOOL & HOME

You can use what you have learned in this chapter to help you be a better family member.

Maybe you have a little brother or sister that you consider a "pest." When he or she wants to show you something, you may be in the habit of saying "Get out of here!"

What have you learned about human needs that might help you change your way of behaving?

Perhaps you have thought that it is all right for *you* to get angry. But you may be upset if someone else in your family gets angry. What have you learned about angry feelings that can help you be more understanding?

There is one basic key to understanding others at home or elsewhere. Try to put yourself in their place. Ask "How would I feel in that situation? What would I want others to do to help me?"

Teacher's Notes
Special efforts are made in this book and in this health series to foster school-home communication. Understanding basic human needs and feelings is a concept expressed on this page.
(*Note:* Also available from Scott, Foresman to help further school-home communication is the consumable *Activity Booklet* for your class. See page T7 for a description of this booklet.)

2 Your Body and How It Works

Many boys and girls your age express interest in learning how the body works. What topics are interesting to those in your group? How might you find out?

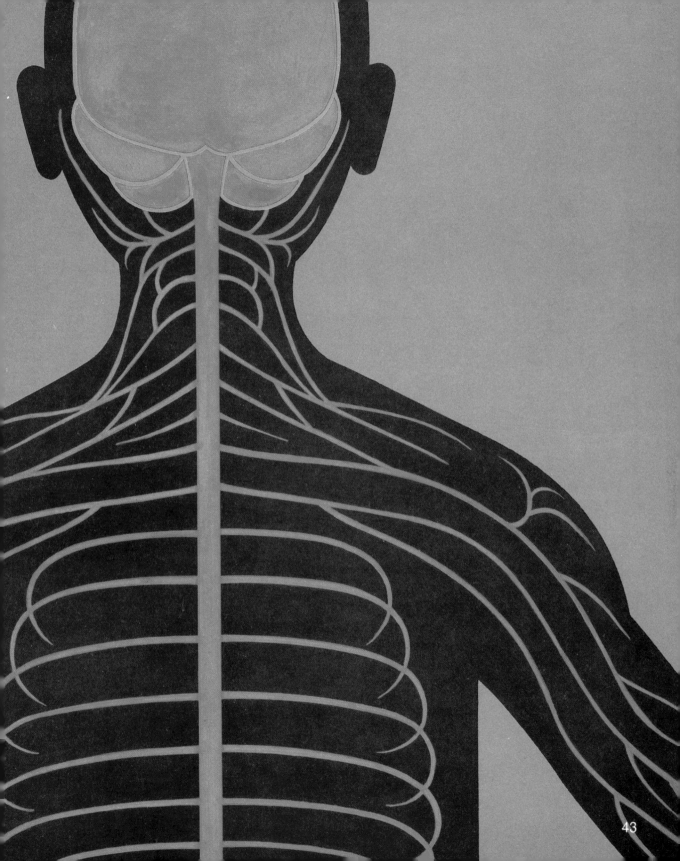

Teacher's Notes

"Preview It" is a special feature that occurs at the beginning of each chapter in this book and in the health series. Here students do some *anticipating*. They skim over the main headings in the chapter. Most of these headings are, by design, study questions. Curiosities are aroused, and pupils are given a framework for detailed information to follow.

Glossary words: *thyroid, insulin*
See page T26 for additional teaching suggestions.

Preview It

You may already know many things about the human body. This chapter may review what you know, but it will do so in an interesting way. You will read the script from a tape recording used in an exhibit at a health center. The script tells the story of the body and how it works.

No matter how much you already know, there is always more to learn. Do you know the answers to these questions?

Why will you stop growing?
Where is your thyroid gland and what does it do?
What form is food in when it leaves the stomach?
Where does it go from the stomach?
What is insulin? What happens if your body does not produce enough insulin?
What do the kidneys do?

You will find the answers to these questions in this chapter.

As you read, think about this statement: "Of all wonders, the human body is one of the most wonderful."

What Is One Way to Learn About the Body?

One interesting way to learn about the body is to go
to a health center. If you have never been to a health
center, you can do the next best thing. You can read
about it. That is what you will do in this chapter.

An exhibit that attracts much attention by students
your age is the plastic Transparent Woman. The plastic
woman is modeled after a living person. It is built so
that you can see inside the body. A recording describes
the different parts of the body. Each part lights up as
it is being described.

Teacher's Notes
Have the pupils look at the pictures on pages 57–61. They will want to see what this transparent figure looks like. Discuss why the transparent figure does not include the skeletal muscles. See page T27 for additional teaching suggestions.

The following discussion is the talk given by the Transparent Woman. This exhibit is found at the Robert Crown Center for Health Education in Hinsdale, Illinois.

Before you read what is said, glance at the pictures on pages 57–61. These pictures show the Transparent Woman from time to time as it "speaks."

A Talk About the Human Body[1]

Suppose you could see through your skin. What if your skin and skeletal muscles vanished? Inside, you would look like me, the Transparent Woman.

Keep in mind as I talk that all the parts of my body work together. This makes the human body a wonderful creation!

The Brain and Nerves

The *brain* is called the "central exchange" of the nervous system. It receives messages from all parts of the body. Then it directs the body to respond. The brain is the center for thinking, creating, reasoning, and remembering.

Messages from the eyes, ears, nose, tongue, and nerve endings in the skin travel over a network of *sensory nerves.* These messages go to the brain. The brain evaluates the messages. If action is needed, the brain sends messages by another network of nerves, the *motor nerves.* These messages go to certain muscles. Then the muscles move as directed.

Adaptation of the script "Valeda, the Transparent Woman, Speaks" (A Transcribed Talk). Reprinted by permission of Robert Crown Center for Health Education, Hinsdale, Illinois.

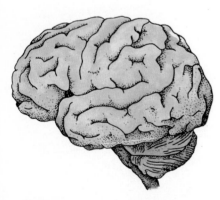

What do you know about the brain?

46

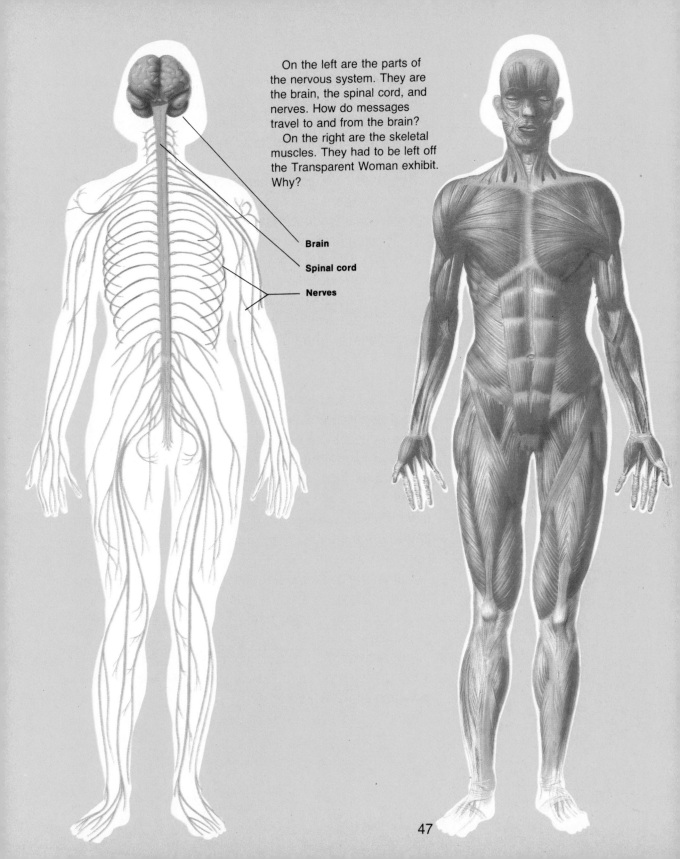

On the left are the parts of
the nervous system. They are
the brain, the spinal cord, and
nerves. How do messages
travel to and from the brain?

On the right are the skeletal
muscles. They had to be left off
the Transparent Woman exhibit.
Why?

Brain

Spinal cord

Nerves

47

Teacher's Notes
Discuss some of the functions of the bones and skeletal muscles. Also talk over the nature of the endocrine glands. You might ask:
"What have you learned about the pituitary? The thyroid? The adrenals? The pancreas? The reproductive glands?
Encourage the use of the Glossary for additional information and pronunciations.
Glossary words: *pituitary gland, endocrine gland, thyroid gland, adrenal gland, pancreas, cortisone, adrenaline, insulin, hormone*

Bones and Muscles

A framework of bones called the *skeleton* supports your body. There are more than 200 bones in your skeleton. And there are more than 600 skeletal muscles. Bones and skeletal muscles help you move.

Endocrine Glands

The endocrine glands manufacture substances called *hormones.* Hormones are sent directly into the bloodstream. They produce certain changes in the body. The "master gland" of the endocrine system, called the *pituitary gland,* is under the brain. It influences the way all the other endocrine glands work.

The pituitary gland produces several hormones. One of these, the growth hormone, is made only during the growing years. When growth hormone is no longer made, the body may grow heavier. But it will not grow taller.

Another endocrine gland, the *thyroid,* is found just below the voice box. The thyroid makes a hormone which regulates the pace of your body's processes. Too much of this hormone causes you to be overactive and excitable. Too little causes you to slow down.

The adrenal glands, located near the kidneys, produce the hormones *cortisone* and *adrenaline.* Each of these hormones has many important functions in the body.

The *pancreas* is another endocrine gland. It produces *insulin,* a hormone which regulates the use of sugar in the body. A lack of insulin results in a disease known as *diabetes.*

The *ovaries* and the *testes* are also endocrine glands. They produce hormones which give you either female or male characteristics.

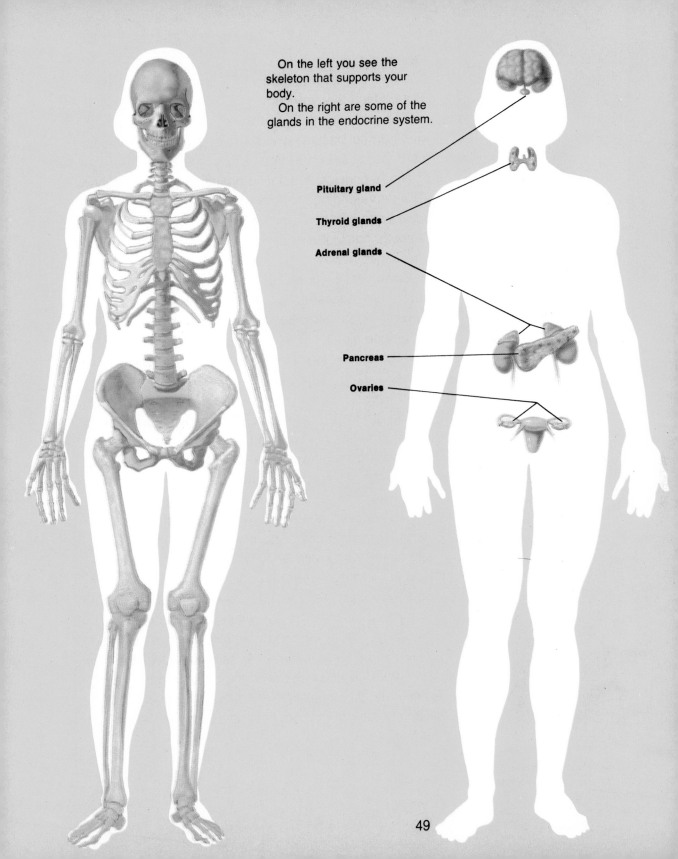

On the left you see the skeleton that supports your body.

On the right are some of the glands in the endocrine system.

Pituitary gland

Thyroid glands

Adrenal glands

Pancreas

Ovaries

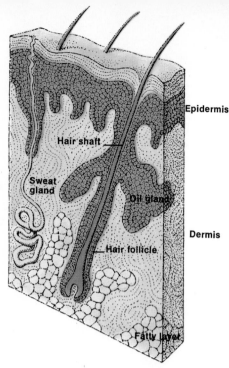

Here you see a cross section of the skin. What parts do you see in it?

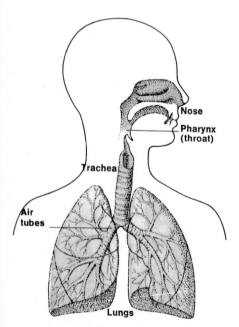

What parts of the respiratory system do you see? What happens in the lungs?

The Skin

In this transparent model you cannot see the skin. But pretend that you can.

The skin covers the outside of the body. It keeps dirt and harmful bacteria out of the body. Thus, it protects your muscles, bones, and cells.

Nerve endings in the skin provide the sense of touch. The nerve endings send messages to the brain. Then your brain tells you if things are hot, cold, rough, smooth, hard, or soft. Other special nerve endings send messages of pain.

Blood vessels in the skin help regulate body temperature. When these blood vessels contract, less blood flows through them. So less heat leaves the body. When the blood vessels expand, more blood flows through them. More heat leaves the body and it is cooled.

The Larynx

The *larynx* is the voice box. It contains the vocal cords. The vocal cords are two membranes which stretch across the windpipe. Air coming from the lungs makes the membranes vibrate and produce sounds.

The Lungs

The *lungs* are the major part of the respiratory system. They are made of hollow air tubes which branch into smaller and smaller air tubes. Finally the air tubes end in millions of clusters of tiny air sacs. The air sacs are surrounded by tiny blood vessels called *capillaries.*

When air is inhaled, it is drawn into the air sacs in the lungs. There the oxygen in the air moves into the blood in the capillaries. At the same time, wastes such as carbon dioxide pass from the blood into the air sacs. Then the air containing the wastes is exhaled. This is an important exchange that takes place in the lungs.

Heart and Blood Vessels

The heart, the blood, and a network of blood vessels form the *circulatory system.* The heart pumps blood throughout the body. The blood moves through blood vessels called *arteries, veins,* and *capillaries.*

Arteries carry blood rich with oxygen and nourishing substances, called *nutrients,* to all parts of the body. The main artery, the *aorta,* leads away from the *left* side of the heart. The aorta branches into many smaller arteries. These smaller arteries branch into tiny blood vessels called capillaries.

What happens when blood from the arteries enters the capillaries? Oxygen and nutrients pass through the thin walls of the capillaries into the surrounding cells. Wastes from the cells, such as carbon dioxide, are picked up by the blood in the capillaries.

The capillaries connect with larger blood vessels called veins. The veins carry blood with waste products back to the *right* side of the heart.

Next the blood is routed from the right side of the heart to the lungs. In the capillaries of the lungs, carbon dioxide leaves the blood and oxygen is picked up. The blood, which is now rich with oxygen, returns to the left side of the heart. Then it is pumped again through the arteries to the rest of the body. All of this happens with each heartbeat.

If you are about twelve years old, your heart probably beats about ninety times a minute. But the heartbeat can vary in people, and it can vary in different situations. Exercise and strong emotions can speed up the heartbeat.

Teacher's Notes

After the pupils have read about the skin, the larynx, the lungs, the heart, and blood vessels, ask these questions:

"What are the main functions of the skin?" (A body covering, a regulator of temperature, and a place containing nerve endings that give us our sense of touch.)

"How do you control the amount of sound you make?" (You regulate the amount of air passing through the larynx. To shout you take a deep breath. To whisper, you hold your breath.)

"What is the life-giving exchange that takes place in the lungs?"

"What happens when blood from the arteries enters the capillaries?"

Glossary words: *larynx, trachea, capillary, bacteria*

See page T27 for additional teaching suggestions.

How does blood get from the arteries to the veins?

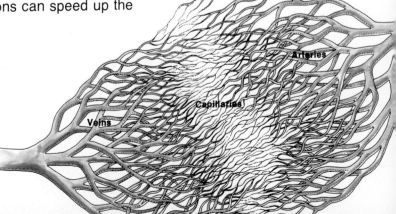

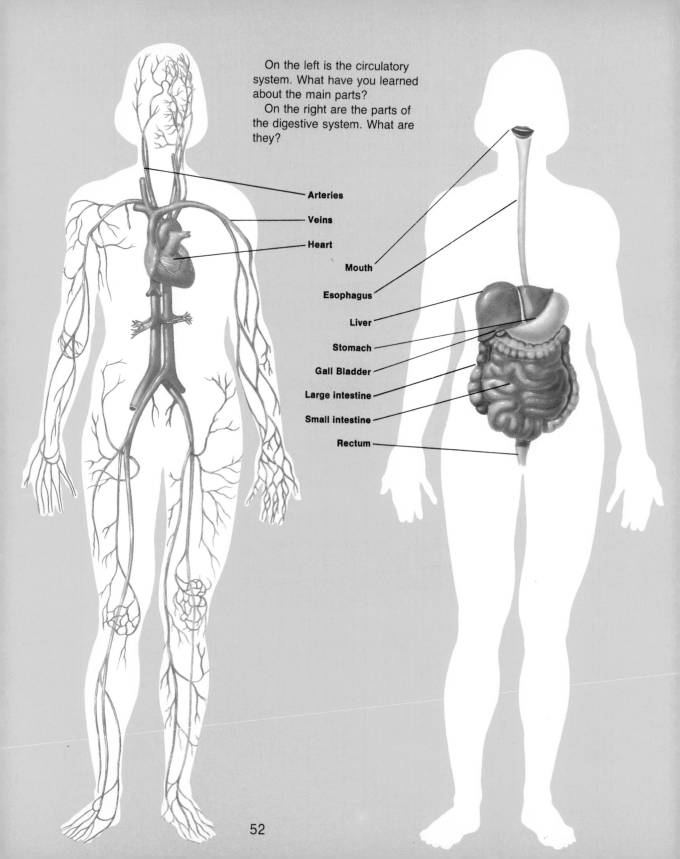

On the left is the circulatory
system. What have you learned
about the main parts?

On the right are the parts of
the digestive system. What are
they?

Arteries

Veins

Heart

Mouth

Esophagus

Liver

Stomach

Gall Bladder

Large intestine

Small intestine

Rectum

The Stomach

The stomach is one of the organs that helps digest food. In digestion, food is changed into a form that the body can use. Digestion starts in the mouth. The teeth break the food into small bits and the saliva softens the food. Then the food moves down the *esophagus,* or food tube, into the stomach. In the stomach, the food is churned with *gastric juices* which help to digest the food.

The partly digested food leaves the stomach a little at a time and goes into the small intestine. When all the food has left the stomach, you begin to feel hungry.

The Liver

The liver makes a digestive juice called *bile,* or *gall.* Bile moves from the liver into the small intestine. There it helps digest the fats in the food you eat.

The Gall Bladder

The *gall bladder* is a tiny organ found near the lower surface of the liver. It stores the bile made in the liver. The gall bladder is not really essential because the liver constantly makes more bile. Thus the gall bladder can be removed if it is infected.

The Pancreas

The pancreas is a digestive organ as well as an endocrine gland. The cells of the pancreas produce several digestive juices which flow into the small intestine. Other cells in the pancreas produce the hormone *insulin.* Insulin controls the use of sugar in the body.

Teacher's Notes
Call attention to the full-page diagram on the preceding page. Ask the students to locate the stomach, the gall bladder, and the liver.
After they have read this page ask:
"What happens to food in the stomach?"
"How does the liver aid in digestion?"
"What does the gall bladder do?"
Glossary words: *digestion, esophagus, small intestine*
See also page T27 for additional teaching suggestions.

Books to Read

Look in the library for books about the human body. Here are some books you may like:

Balestrino, Philip. *The Skeleton Inside You* (Crowell).

Elgin, Kathleen. *The Skin* (Watts).

Kalina, Sigmund. *Your Blood and Its Cargo* (Lothrop).

Ravielli, Anthony. *Wonders of the Human Body* (Viking).

Riedman, Sarah. *How Man Discovered His Body* (Abelard).

Teacher's Notes
Have the students refer to the picture on page 52 again to locate the small intestine, large intestine, and appendix. Then read to find out the functions of these organs. Invite comments on the appendix. After reading this page, you might ask these questions:

"How is food absorbed into the bloodstream?"

"What does the blood do with the digested food?"

Glossary words: *large intestine, villi*

The Small Intestine

The process of digestion is completed in the small intestine. Here the food is mixed with digestive juices from the liver, the pancreas, and the small intestine.

Tiny structures called *villi* line the inside of the small intestine. Food that is completely digested is absorbed into the bloodstream through the walls of the villi.

The blood carries the digested food to all the cells. They use the nutrients from the digested food to produce heat and energy for the body's processes.

The Large Intestine and Appendix

The large intestine, or colon, receives the food that was not completely digested. This food could not be absorbed through the walls of the small intestine. In the colon, water from the undigested food is absorbed into the bloodstream.

The waste matter that the body cannot use collects in the lowest part of the colon. This part is called the *rectum.* The rectum is firmly locked by a ring-shaped muscle. This muscle controls the passing of the wastes from the body in a bowel movement.

A small projection from the large intestine is the *appendix.* Can you find the appendix on page 52? It has no known function in humans. If the appendix is infected, it can be removed.

The Kidneys and Urinary Bladder

There are two kidneys in the body. They filter liquid waste products from the blood. The waste products, known as *urine,* pass from the kidneys to the *urinary bladder.* There the urine is stored until it is ready to be released from the body.

The urinary bladder is a muscular bag. When the bladder is ready to be emptied, a muscle at the lower end relaxes. Then the urine is allowed to leave the body.

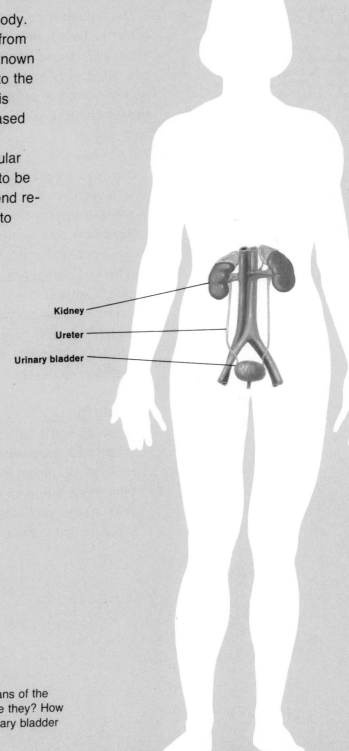

Kidney

Ureter

Urinary bladder

Here you see the organs of the urinary system. What are they? How are the kidneys and urinary bladder connected?

Call attention to the urinary system pictured on the previous page. Ask the pupils what they know about these organs.

(*Note:* Does your school system have an approved course of study in sex education? If so, then this section on the Reproductive System offers a natural opportunity to introduce material on human reproduction. Be sure to check your local school policy about how this material should be handled.)

(*Note:* "Sum It Up" is a feature that occurs at intervals throughout each chapter of this book and of others in the health series. Pupils can use this study aid to review important ideas learned in the preceding pages.)

The Reproductive System

The human body, like all living things, can reproduce. A human being starts life from a *fertilized egg.* The fertilized egg results from the union of a male reproductive cell, the *sperm,* and the female reproductive cell, the *egg.* When these cells unite, they develop into another human being. The new baby has inherited traits from each parent.

The Amazing Body

Now you know some of the functions of your body. You have learned how your organs work together to maintain a healthy body.

Right now your heart is beating. Your blood is circulating. Your stomach is digesting food. Your lungs are breathing. Your glands are secreting hormones. Your eyes are seeing. Your ears are hearing. Your brain is receiving and sending messages, storing impressions, and creating ideas. It is easy then to understand this statement: "Of all the wonders, the human body is one of the most wonderful."

Sum It Up

What are some functions of the skin?
What have you learned about the skeleton?
How do you digest food?
What does the heart do?
What exchange takes place in the lungs?
What do you think is wonderful about the body?

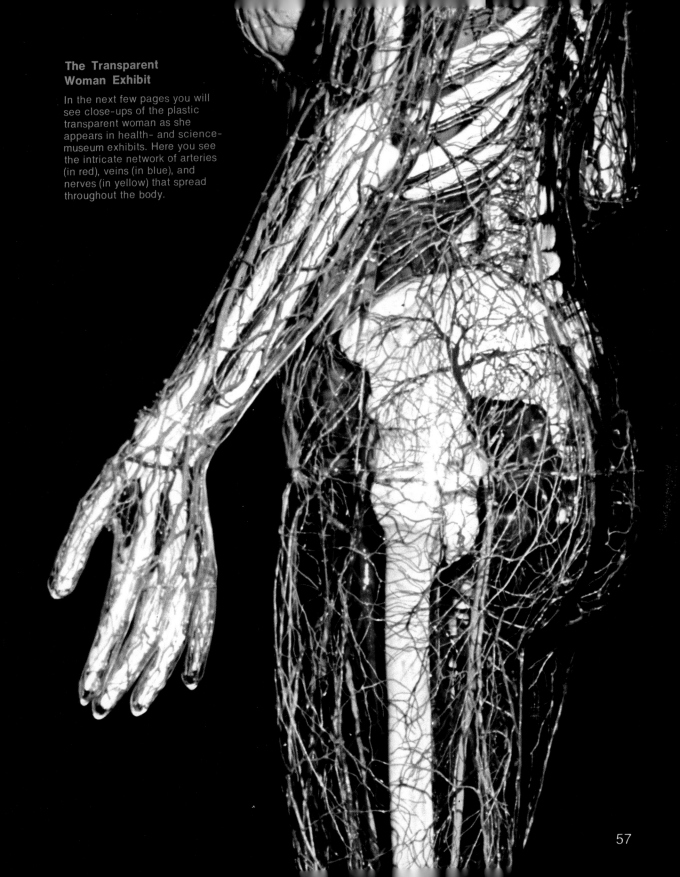

The Transparent Woman Exhibit

In the next few pages you will see close-ups of the plastic transparent woman as she appears in health- and science-museum exhibits. Here you see the intricate network of arteries (in red), veins (in blue), and nerves (in yellow) that spread throughout the body.

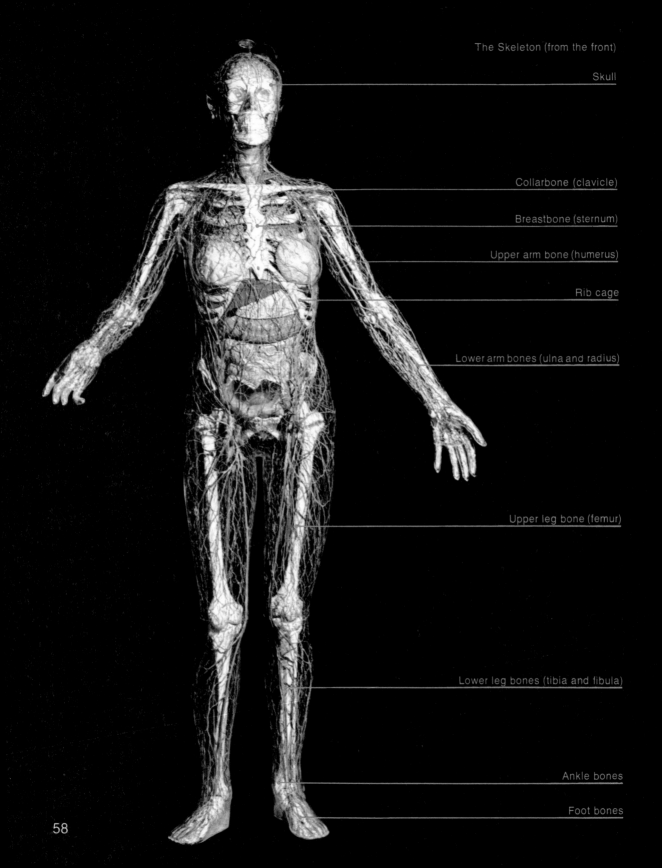

The Skeleton (from the front)

Skull

Collarbone (clavicle)

Breastbone (sternum)

Upper arm bone (humerus)

Rib cage

Lower arm bones (ulna and radius)

Upper leg bone (femur)

Lower leg bones (tibia and fibula)

Ankle bones

Foot bones

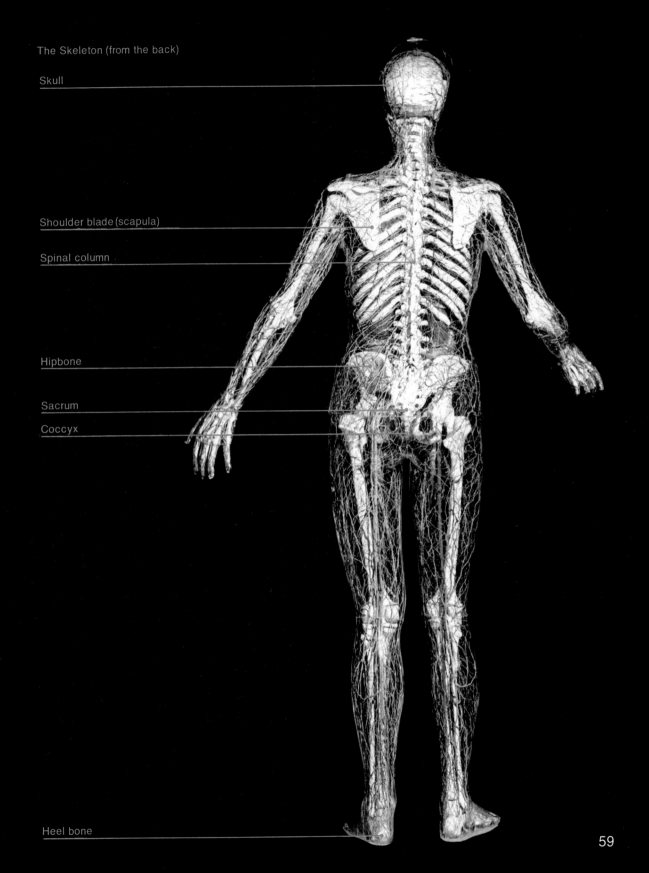

The Skeleton (from the back)

Skull

Shoulder blade (scapula)

Spinal column

Hipbone

Sacrum

Coccyx

Heel bone

Rib cage

Lungs

Heart

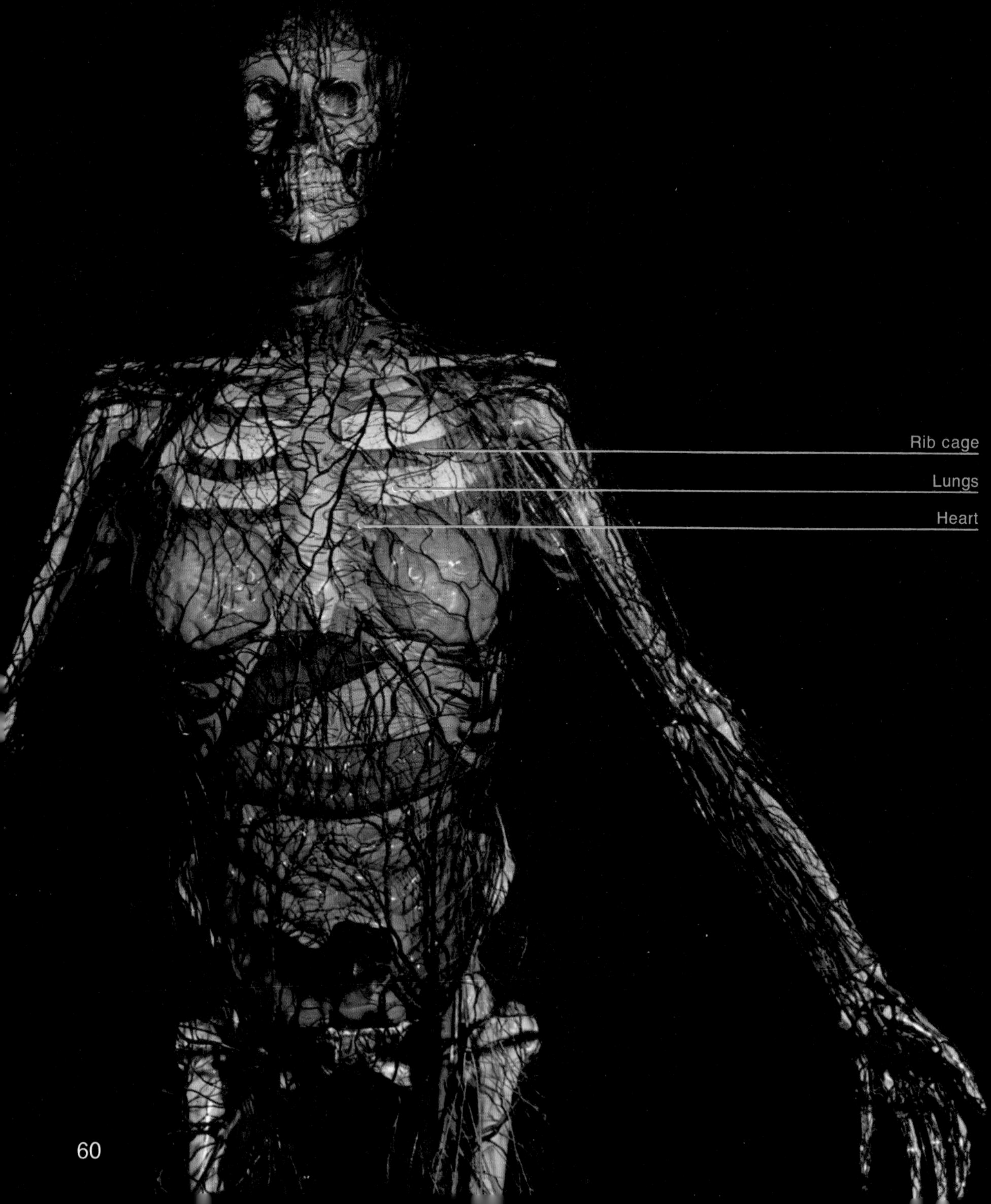

Front View (with lower torso lighted)

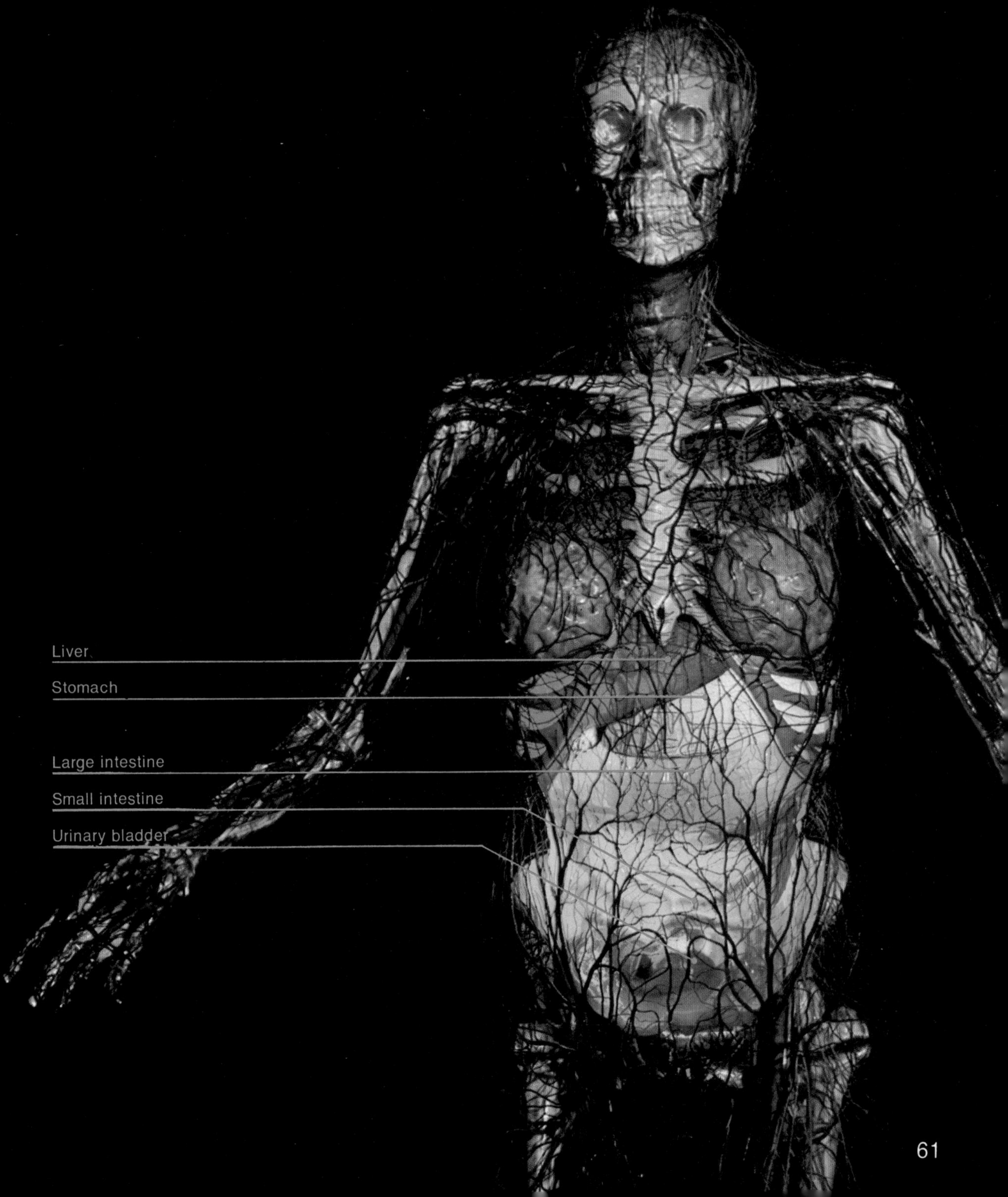

Liver

Stomach

Large intestine

Small intestine

Urinary bladder

HEALTH AROUND US

Teacher's Notes
"Health Around Us" is a recurring feature in this book and in this health series.
Glossary word: *X ray*
See page T27 for additional teaching suggestions.

Fascinating new research tools called *body scanners* are now available to help doctors study the inside of a patient's body.

Until recently doctors used only the usual kinds of X rays. The body scanners, however, use X rays in a new way. These scanners pass a pencil-thin beam of X rays through the patient's body. For example, the X rays may scan a certain organ such as the stomach. Information received is processed by a small computer. The computer then sends a special picture on a screen. This picture looks as if the stomach has been cut in two, from front to back.

The body scanners give the doctor much more information about internal organs of the body than the usual X-ray pictures provide.

A body scanner

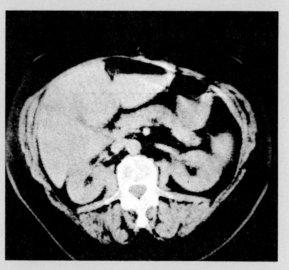

This scan shows the liver, spleen, kidneys, stomach, and pancreas.

Things to Do

Teacher's Notes
"Special Research" offers special challenges to highly motivated or advanced students.
See page T27 for additional teaching suggestions.

1. Write some questions that you want answered about the body. Tell where you may find answers to your questions.

2. Write a paragraph about a time when you were scared or upset. In it, tell about the changes that took place in your body. Did your heart beat faster, for example?

3. Suppose you are a guide in a health museum. You have to explain to a group of younger students the information about the human body on pages 46-56. Choose one of the organs and see if you can re-write the material in a simple way. Write so that a younger child could understand the information.

4. Suppose your class is planning an exhibit on the body and its functions. What special project would you suggest? If possible, make your exhibit. For those who need some helpful hints, the following projects are suggested:

Write a report about the heart (include a display of a plastic model heart).

Write a report about the skeleton. Prepare a display of different animal bones.

Special Research

1. Find out the uses of the instrument called the *electroencephalograph.* It can pick up electrical waves of the brain.

2. Make a report on modern medical research. Look for information about replacing injured tissue, or *transplants.*

Some topics to look up in encyclopedias or reference books are Transplants, Bone Banks, Skin Banks.

3. Find out what you can about the uses of an instrument called an *electrocardiograph.* It can be used to measure the strength of the electrical current in the heart.

4. Make a scrapbook of clippings from the newspaper and magazines about the body and its functions. For example, you may find articles comparing the human brain with man-made computers. Or you may find articles that describe the body's defenses against disease.

5. Investigate some hazards the body can be exposed to during space travel or underwater exploration.

Can You Show What You Know?[1]

Teacher's Notes
Here behavioral objectives in the *cognitive* area are posed in childlike language directly to the students themselves. In turn, boys and girls give evidence by *observable behavior* of what they have learned.
Other hoped-for behavioral objectives lie chiefly in the less easily observed *affective* area—objectives that pertain to feelings, attitudes, and values. Some of them are:

Appreciates the wonders of the human body.

Initiates some independent research about the body and its workings.

Shares interesting information about the body with family members at home.

Page numbers show you where to look back in the chapter for information, if you need it.

1. Describe the major functions of the brain. (46)
2. Tell how messages go to and from the brain. (46)
3. Tell why you don't continue to grow tall all your life. (48)
4. Describe the function of the thyroid gland. (48)
5. Explain where insulin is made and why it is needed. (48)
6. Describe what is under the skin. (49)
7. Describe the important exchange that goes on in the lungs. (50)
8. Tell what happens to food in the mouth. (53)
9. Describe what happens to food in the stomach. (53)
10. Explain what happens to the food in the small intestine. (54)
11. Tell what happens to digested food once it has entered the bloodstream. (54)

[1]Behavioral objectives in the cognitive area are stated here directly to students themselves.

Review It

Teacher's Notes

"Review It" is a feature that occurs at the end of each chapter in this book and in this health series. It gives children a chance to think over what they have learned, to summarize, and to store away important ideas. Page references after each item make this review page a self-help one. However, group discussions can be a valuable aid.

Page numbers show you where to look back in the chapter for information, if you need it.

1. What is one part of the body that protects it from harmful bacteria? (50)

2. What are two hormones produced by the adrenal glands? (48)

3. What are three functions of the skin? (50)

4. What have you learned about the liver? (53)

5. What function does the appendix have in the body? (54)

6. What important work do the kidneys do? (55)

7. What is the function of the urinary bladder? (55)

8. What makes up the circulatory system? (51)

9. What is the difference between the blood that leaves the heart, and the blood that returns to the heart? (51)

10. What speeds up the heart? (51)

Copy each numbered item from List A. After each item, write the letter and words from List B that best describe it. For example: 11. bile b. gall

List A

11. bile

12. capillaries

13. esophagus

14. insulin

15. larynx

16. pituitary

17. veins

List B

a. voice box

b. gall

c. master endocrine gland

d. tiny blood vessels

e. a hormone made in the pancreas

f. blood vessels that carry blood back to the heart

g. the food tube

Health Test for Chapter Two

Teacher's Notes

After students have taken the test and their papers have been scored, the test items can serve as guides for a summary discussion. Volunteers can read aloud their rewording of the false statements and the correct word for the completion statement.

"What Do You Think?" is a special feature that offers pupils a chance to evaluate their newly acquired knowledge.

Part I

On a separate sheet of paper, write the name of the body organ or part responsible for these things:

1. making decisions   brain
2. churning food   stomach
3. forming a protective covering for the body   skin
4. pumping blood to all parts of the body   heart
5. returning to the heart the blood containing waste products   veins

Part II

Write on your paper another name for each term:

6. larynx   voice box
7. food tube   esophagus
8. main artery   aorta
9. storage place for urine   urinary bladder
10. the body's framework   skeleton

Part III

Copy each number on a piece of paper. After each number, write the correct answer, *true* or *false.* Rewrite each false statement to make it true.

F 11. Digestion is completed in the stomach.

T 12. Human beings can reproduce.

T 13. Body cells need digested food and oxygen.

F 14. The liver makes insulin.

T 15. The brain is the center for thinking.

F 16. Urine is stored in the kidneys.

F 17. The brain is part of the skeletal system.

F 18. Motor nerves bring messages to the brain.

T 19. The aorta is the large artery leading away from the heart.

T 20. The lungs contain millions of air sacs.

Number of Answers   20
Number Right   _____
Score (Number Right x 5)   _____

What Do You Think?

What is your opinion of this chapter? Write your answer on a separate sheet of paper.

SCHOOL & HOME

You may want to share with those at home some things you have been learning.

For example, you may want to explain why people do not continue to grow tall all their lives. What will you say?

You may want to make up some riddles for your brothers or sisters to guess. What riddle can you make up about the lungs or the heart or the skin?

Perhaps you want to tell about the amazing things that the brain does. You know that you use the brain to remember. Just for fun, do some remembering with your family. What are happy times that all of you remember? Can you remember things that happened when you were very young? Check with your parents to see if you remember correctly.

Teacher's Notes
Special efforts are made in this book and in this health series to foster school-home communication. This page is an example of how youngsters are urged to share with the family the health ideas they are acquiring at school.

3 Growth

Here is a question that is often asked by young people your age. How does the body grow? How would you answer this question?

Teacher's Notes
"Preview It" is a special feature that
occurs at the beginning of each chapter
in this book and in this health series.
Here students do some *anticipating*.
They skim over the main headings in
the chapter. Most of these headings
are, by design, study questions.
Curiosities are aroused, and pupils are
given a framework for the detailed
information to follow.
Invite conversation about what is
meant by Preview. Ask students how
it might help them get a preview of
what is in a chapter before they start
to read.
See page T29 for additional teaching
suggestions.

Preview It

There is much more to the story of growth than growing in height and becoming heavier. Look through this chapter quickly. Find four main questions that are asked in the titles. What do these questions suggest about what you will learn in this chapter?

Did you notice some interesting pictures as you turned through the chapter? What do the pictures suggest about information that will be discussed in this chapter?

As you read the chapter, look for answers to the four main questions. Also look for answers to such interesting questions as these.

What is a growth spurt?
Why do you stop growing tall?
How do body cells grow?
What is meant by heredity?
What are some traits that you inherit?

Start the chapter now. Read first to find out if you are growing as you should.

Are You Growing As You Should?

A question boys and girls your age often ask is "Am I growing normally?" It is important to know that differences in height and weight among young people your age are common. Each boy or girl is different. Each *has* an individual growth timetable.

There is no one right height or right weight for all girls, or for all boys, of a certain age.

You may find it reassuring to look at the individual growth records below. These have normal weight and height ranges for ages ten to thirteen. Tall boys and girls are usually closer to the heavier weights. Short people are usually closer to the lower weights.

Teacher's Notes
Use the question in the heading to start the preliminary discussion on individual growth differences. The students will want to look up their own height and weight on the metric charts. As a reminder, one inch=2.54 centimeters; one pound=0.5 kilogram.

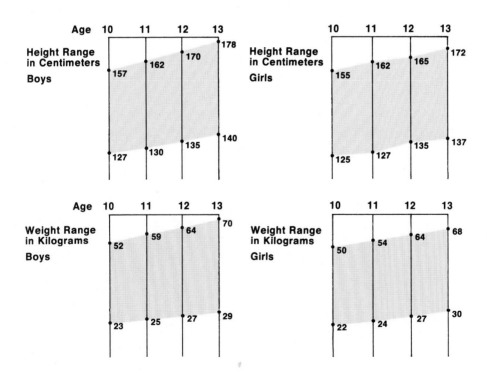

Adapted from "Physical Growth Record for Boys" and "Physical Growth Record for Girls" from PHYSICAL GROWTH RECORD FOR BOYS and PHYSICAL GROWTH RECORD FOR GIRLS by Joint Committee on Health Problems in Education of the NEA and AMA. Reprinted by permission of the American Association for Health, Physical Education, and Recreation.

Growth Patterns

Sometime during the years from nine or ten to fourteen or sixteen, the body has periods of rapid growth. This growth does not occur evenly. Not all parts of the body grow at the same time. And not all parts reach adult size at the same time.

As each part of the body reaches adult size, its growth stops. Meanwhile other parts of the body begin, or continue their growth. This goes on until all parts are fully grown. For example, the feet, hands, and brain are fully grown before the legs, arms, and trunk reach full growth.

For a time, your hands or feet may seem to be out of proportion to the rest of your body. This is because you grow unevenly. At times you may be a little awkward. This is to be expected. You have to get used to a changing size and shape.

This chart shows the height of girls compared with the height of boys at different age levels.

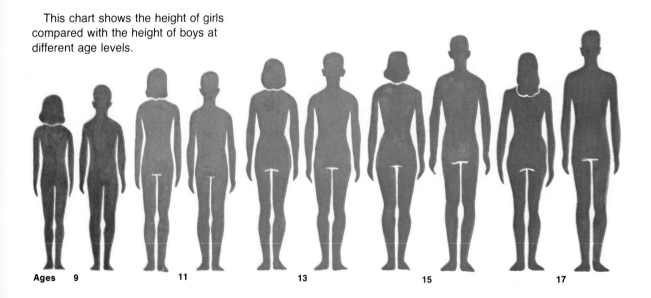

Ages   9   11   13   15   17

In the next few years you may make sudden gains in height and weight. These sudden gains are called *growth spurts.* For example, a girl might gain as much as four to five inches in height in a year. She might gain ten to twenty pounds in that period. Excess fat gained in a growth spurt is not usually kept. The exception is when a pattern of overeating has developed.

Girls generally begin to grow taller and heavier at an earlier age than boys. Most girls begin their rapid growth in height and weight sometime between the ages of nine and thirteen. The greatest gains are usually in the twelfth or thirteenth year.

Most boys begin their growth spurt between ages eleven and fifteen. The greatest gains are often in the fourteenth or fifteenth year.

Remember that every person is different. No two girls or two boys grow in the same way or at the same rate.

Girls usually reach their full growth by age sixteen. Boys usually reach their full growth between the ages of seventeen and the early twenties.

To grow in a way that is right for you, you should follow good health practices. These include getting an adequate daily diet and enough sleep. What is another good health practice?

Sum It Up

How does each boy or girl grow?

What is a growth spurt?

What have you learned about growth that you did not know?

Teacher's Notes

Discuss what is meant by a *growth spurt.* Students will read to find out when these spurts are likely to occur. Mention that growth does depend, in part, upon heredity.

In a follow-up discussion, comment upon the importance of exercise as a good health practice.

See page T29 for additional teaching suggestions.

(*Note:* "Sum It Up" is a feature that occurs at intervals throughout each chapter. Pupils can use this study aid to review important ideas learned in the preceding pages.)

Each Individual Grows In His Or Her Own Way.

All of the boys and girls shown on these two pages are eleven or twelve years old. What does the picture tell you about individual differences in height, weight, and body build?

ENJOY IT

Growing: For Louis

It's tough being short.

Of course your father tells you not to worry,
But everyone else is a giant, and you're just the way
   you were.
And this stupid guy says, "Hey shorty, where'd you
   get the long pants?"
Or some smart beanpole asks how it feels to be so
   close to the ants?
And the school nurse says to tell her again how tall
   you are, when you've already told her.
Oh, my mother says there's really no hurry
And I'll grow soon enough.

But it's tough being short.

(I wonder if Napoleon got the same old stuff?)

How does this young person feel about his height?

If Louis is eleven or twelve, how many years might he have yet
for growing?

Do you think a person's height is the most important thing about
him or her? What else is important?

HEALTH AROUND US

Teacher's Notes
X-ray pictures like the ones shown here are not generally made, but students will be interested in what such pictures can show. See page T29 for additional teaching suggestions.

There are scientific ways to find more about a young person's rate of physical growth. For example, X-ray pictures can be taken of a young person's hand and wrist bones. The X-ray pictures can give a "skeletal age."

Look at the X-ray pictures below. Both show the hands of boys whose actual age is fourteen years and eleven months.

The boy at the left has a skeletal age of thirteen years and six months. There is much cartilage around the ends of the small bones. They have not yet become bony, or *ossified.* This boy is relatively slow-growing. He has several years ahead of him for growth.

The boy at the right has a skeletal age of sixteen years and ten months. This boy is skeletally more mature than his actual age would indicate. His hand bones have matured. He is a fast-grower. He will reach full growth well before the other boy his same age.

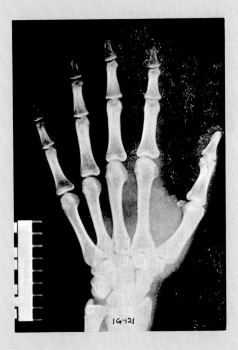

Why Do You Stop Growing Tall?

Perhaps you wonder why you keep growing and adults do not.

To understand this, you need to know about certain glands in your body. These are the *endocrine glands*. They have to do with activities such as regulating when and how you grow.

The endocrine glands make substances called *hormones*. These hormones are sent directly into your bloodstream. Hormones play an important part in growth.

The gland that has the most to do with growth is the *pituitary gland*. This gland is located on the underside of the brain. The pituitary gland produces a number of hormones. One of these is sent into the bloodstream only during the growing years. This hormone keeps your cells growing until you have reached your full size. Then the pituitary gland stops making this special growth hormone. After this you may grow heavier. But you will stop growing taller.

Boys and girls sometimes become a little concerned about how they are growing. They may wonder if a doctor can do something to help speed up or slow down their growth. Rarely would a doctor find that such treatment is needed. A young person may be growing in a way that is different from others the same age. But it is usually the way that is right for him or her.

Books to Read

Here are some books that you may enjoy reading. They can tell you more about how you grow.

Weart, Edith. *The Story of Your Glands* (Coward).

Zappler, Georg. *From One Cell to Many* (Messner).

Which of the endocrine glands is most concerned with your growth?

Are all the endocrine glands the same for boys and girls? Which ones are different? Read on to find out more about the reproductive glands.

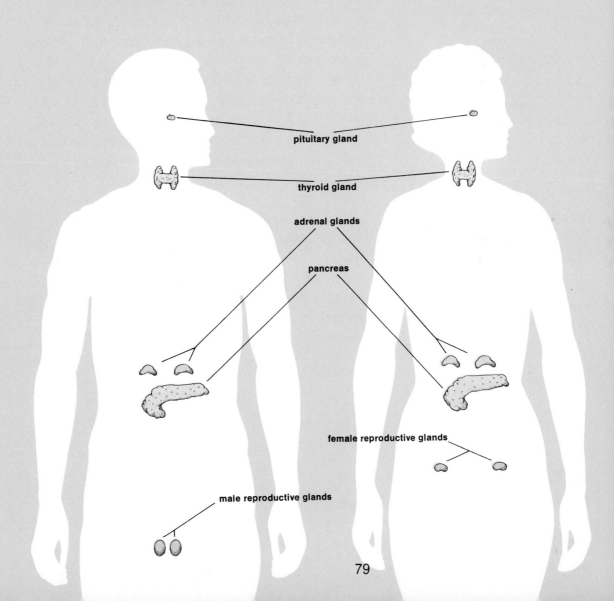

pituitary gland

thyroid gland

adrenal glands

pancreas

female reproductive glands

male reproductive glands

Teacher's Notes
Pupils can read to find out what the reproductive glands do. Also talk over the changes that these glands cause in boys and girls.
You might ask:
"What did you learn about *when* these growth changes take place in girls and in boys?"

The Reproductive Glands

Most of the endocrine glands are the same for boys and girls. However, there are some endocrine glands that are different. These are the *reproductive glands.* They are the *ovaries* in girls and the *testes* in boys. These glands produce hormones whose job it is to develop the sex characteristics.

For example, the male reproductive gland produces a hormone that causes the growth of a beard, a deeper voice, wider shoulders, and the development of *sperm* cells. The female reproductive gland produces hormones that cause the growth of breasts, wider hips, a smooth complexion, and the development of *egg* cells in the ovaries.

Such changes start at different ages in different boys and girls. But generally the changes start in the early teens. The time when these changes occur is called *puberty.* The changes generally start from one and a half to two years earlier in girls than in boys.

Sum It Up

Why don't children go on growing all their lives?

What is the importance of the pituitary gland to your growth?

Why are the endocrine glands important?

What have you learned about the reproductive glands?

What Happens When You Grow?

Suppose you are asked to tell what you are made of. You will probably name such things as skin, muscles, fat, blood, nerves, and bones.

But each of these, in turn, is made up of tiny living parts. Each tiny part is called a *cell.* You cannot see these cells. They are so tiny it takes a powerful microscope to see them.

You are made of billions of these cells. And the cells keep making more of themselves. You grow because the cells in your body keep dividing to make new cells.

Each cell is a "working world" in itself. Each living cell takes in food and oxygen and gives off wastes such as carbon dioxide.

Teacher's Notes

Use the question in the heading to begin preliminary discussion. Emphasize the concept that all living things are made of cells. Mention also that the electron microscope has greatly helped scientists study the cell. Pupils may be interested to know that it takes about 4000 cells, placed side by side, to make a line 2½ centimeters long (one inch).

Glossary words: *oxygen, carbon dioxide*

See T29 for additional teaching suggestions.

Here are some cells of the body, greatly magnified. What kinds do you see here?

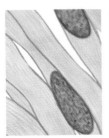 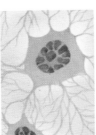 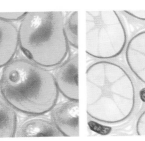 

Muscle cells **Nerve cells** **Fat cells** **Bone cells** **Red blood cells**

Many cells do not look like fat cells. Fat cells do not look like muscle or nerve cells. Muscles, nerves, and fat do not look alike either. So you would not expect them to be made of the same kinds of cells.

Many cells of one kind, which are grouped together and have similar functions, are called *tissue.* For example, many muscle cells grouped together form muscle tissue. Muscles are made of muscle tissue. Many bone cells grouped together form bone tissue. Bones are made of bone tissue.

Cells of a tissue are sometimes compared to bricks joined together to make walls. Unlike brick walls, however, tissues can *grow.* They can grow because each cell of the tissue can divide. It divides to make new cells exactly like itself.

These new cells, in turn, divide to make other new cells. When a cell divides, it always makes more cells of the same kind. When bone cells divide they always make more bone cells.

But not all new cells are used for growing. Some cells in the body are always wearing out. So some new cells take the place of those that wear out. This is why your body does not become worn out in a few years.

However, nerve cells in the brain and spinal cord are not replaced if they are injured.

After a person is fully grown, the cells of the skeletal muscles grow only slightly. This is also true of cells of the heart muscle. Such cells can grow in size. But the number of these cells increases very little in an adult.

Something to Discuss

Why doesn't your body become worn out in a few years, as your clothes do?

How a Cell Divides

All cells are made of a living, jellylike substance called *protoplasm.* Each cell is surrounded by a covering, or *membrane.* This membrane allows materials needed by the cell to enter the cell from the bloodstream. The membrane also allows wastes to move out of the cell into the bloodstream.

Within the cell is a part called the *nucleus.* The nucleus has a membrane of its own around it. The nucleus controls many cell activities such as those of growth and division. Without the nucleus the cell would soon die.

In the process of cell division, the cell first doubles in length. Then changes appear in the nucleus. Next the membrane around the nucleus disappears.

A mass of tiny particles called *chromosomes* becomes visible. The chromosomes contain *genes.* The genes determine which traits are passed on to you by each of your parents. These traits include the color of the hair, skin, and eyes, the body build, and blood type. You will read more about this in the next section.

The chromosomes line up in the center of the cell. They divide before the rest of the cell divides. Half of each chromosome moves to one end of the cell. Half moves to the other. Now the cell is stretched to an elongated shape. Then the cell breaks into two new cells. Each new cell is like the original cell.

Growth of the body during the growing years is made possible by cell division.

Sum It Up

What makes it possible for tissues in your body to grow?

How does a cell divide?

Teacher's Notes

Pupils should study this page to learn the structure of a cell and details of how a cell divides.

Put the words *protoplasm, nucleus, membrane, chromosomes,* and *genes* on the chalkboard. Invite discussion about these terms. Students may be interested to know that the process of cell division is called *mitosis.*

Glossary words: *chromosome, gene, nucleus, protoplasm, membrane*

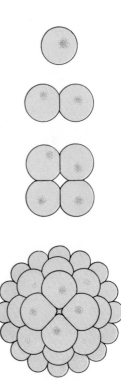

A cell divides to make two cells which are exactly like the original cell. These two cells each divide to form four cells, and so on.

83

Why Do Individuals Differ?

Why *do* individuals differ from one another? Research gives us clues that suggest a very complicated story. It is the story of *heredity.* Heredity involves the passing along of traits from parents to their children.

Your mother and father shared in giving you your inherited traits. These traits were passed on to them from their parents—and so on back through the generations. Heredity is the link that joins the past with the future. Before you read the details of heredity, you might look at the chart on this page. It gives you a brief overview of heredity.

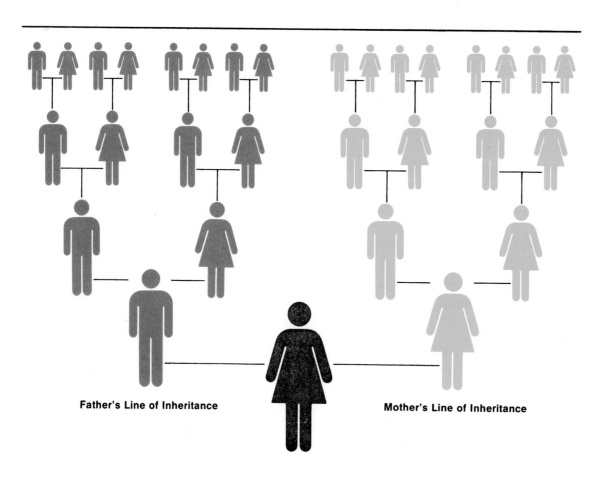

Father's Line of Inheritance   Mother's Line of Inheritance

Chromosomes and Genes

Chromosomes are made of a chemical substance called *DNA*. The DNA records the directions for making you the kind of person you are. Each trait that you inherit, such as eye color, is determined by the chemical structure of DNA. The portion of DNA that is responsible for a specific trait is called a *gene.* There are genes for all your inherited traits. Some traits that you inherit are the color of your eyes and skin, your blood type, the texture and color of your hair, and your sex.

Scientists do not know all the traits that genes pass along. But they do know that you inherit the traits from the twenty-three chromosomes from your mother and the twenty-three from your father. Brothers and sisters get their twenty-three pairs of chromosomes from the same mother and father. Have you ever wondered why brothers and sisters aren't exactly alike?

The reason is this. For every inherited trait, the fertilized egg cell receives one or more genes from the father, and one or more genes from the mother too.

Each parent has at least two genes for a single trait, such as hair color. But both genes are not passed along to each child. Each mature sperm cell and each mature egg cell receives only one of each pair of chromosomes. Thus, each mature cell receives only one of each pair of genes. Which chromosome and gene is just a matter of chance.

It is unlikely that any two egg cells or sperm cells will have the same chromosomes. That is why no two individuals have the very same heredity.

Teacher's Notes

Use the question in the heading on the preceding page to start some discussion. This question usually leads to a comment on identical twins. They look alike because they started from the same fertilized egg. This egg divided and two identical babies were born. *Fraternal twins* are formed from two separate fertilized egg cells. Occasionally three, four, or five babies are born at the same time.

Glossary words: *chromosomes, genes, fertilization, DNA, egg cell, sperm*

Books to Read

Here are some books to look for at the school or public library. They can tell you more about heredity.

Bendick, Jeanne. *How Heredity Works* (Parents' Magazine Press).

Lerner, Marguerite R. *Who Do You Think You Are? The Story of Heredity* (Prentice-Hall).

Randal, Judith. *All About Heredity* (Random House).

Identical twins are the exception. They develop from the *same* fertilized egg. Brothers and sisters who are not identical twins never have the same heredity. They won't receive the same genes from the mother or from the father.

When your father was born, his genes came from both sides of his family. When your mother was born, her genes came from both sides of her family. They pass on still another combination of genes to their children. The thread of life continues in this way from generation to generation.

Human Chromosome (greatly enlarged)

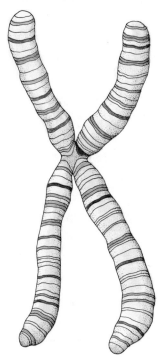

Here you see chromosomes from a bone marrow cell of a male. They are arranged according to their size and shape. The last pair shows an X and Y chromosome, indicating that the cell is from a male. A female cell would carry two X chromosomes.

86

Here you see chromosomes that were stained and scattered before they were photographed. (Picture enlarged about 4800 times.)

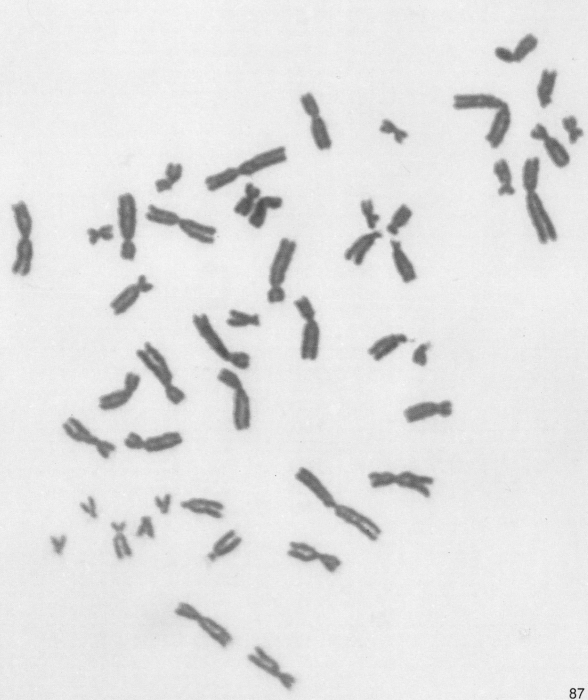

Dominant and Recessive Genes

For every inherited trait, a child gets at least one gene from the mother and one from the father. These genes pair together. One of the pair of genes may be "stronger" than the other. The "stronger" genes are called *dominant.* This means that they are the "most influential." The genes that are not expressed when they are paired with a dominant gene are called *recessive.* Recessive comes from a word which means "held back."

A hereditary trait, such as eye color, is determined by many genes. To simplify how inheritance works, let's assume that only one pair of genes is involved. Suppose a child has a brown-eyed mother and a blue-eyed father. The gene for brown eyes is dominant. The gene for blue eyes is recessive. The child's mother has no gene for blue eyes. Since the gene for brown eyes is dominant, the child will have brown eyes. However, the child will also carry a gene for blue eyes.

A man and woman with such an inheritance may have a blue-eyed child. This can happen even if both parents have brown eyes. The chart on the left shows in a simple way several possibilities of inherited traits.

Some other dominant traits are a straight nose, wide nostrils, dark hair, and full lips. Some recessive traits are a turned-up nose, narrow nostrils, light hair, and thin lips.

For many inherited traits, neither gene in the pair is dominant. Then a child shows a "blend" of both traits.

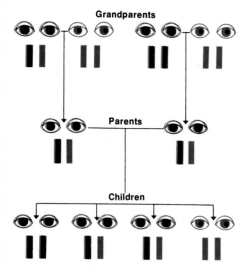

This diagram shows how a child with brown-eyed parents might have a blue-eyed child when both parents carry a recessive gene for blue eyes. The brown block indicates genes for brown eyes; the blue block indicates genes for blue eyes.

How the Sex of a Child Is Determined

When is the sex of a child determined? It is when the egg cell and the sperm cell unite. One of the chromosomes contained in each sperm cell and in each egg cell is the sex chromosome. Men have two kinds of sex chromosomes, X and Y. Each sperm has one or the other. Women have only one kind of sex chromosome, the X chromosome. Every egg cell contains the X chromosome.

If a sperm with a Y chromosome fertilizes the egg cell, the baby will be a boy. If the sperm with the X chromosome fertilizes the egg cell, the baby will be a girl. So you see that it is the father's sperm which determines whether the fertilized egg will develop into a boy or a girl.

Your Heredity and You

What you are and what you become are not due just to your inheritance. The traits you were born with are only the start of your personality development. What you are able and willing to make of your inheritance is just as important as the traits you inherit.

You can think, make decisions, learn, and change all during your life. Whether you make the most of yourself is up to you.

Sum It Up

What is meant by heredity?

What are some traits you inherit?

Why aren't brothers and sisters who are not identical twins exactly alike?

Why do identical twins have the same heredity?

What are dominant genes?

What are recessive genes?

Teacher's Notes

Pupils will read to find out how the sex of a child is determined. Discuss this question:

"Does a person's inheritance completely determine what kind of person he or she will be? What other factors enter in?" (Point out that a person's personality, ability to learn, react, and think are not usually considered to be inherited traits.)

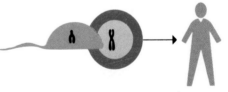

The fertilized egg cell with an XY combination will produce a boy.

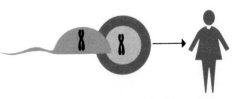

The fertilized egg cell with an XX combination will produce a girl.

Individual Differences That Are Inherited

Individuals differ in such ways as the color and shape of their eyes (top two rows),
and in their fingerprints (bottom two rows).

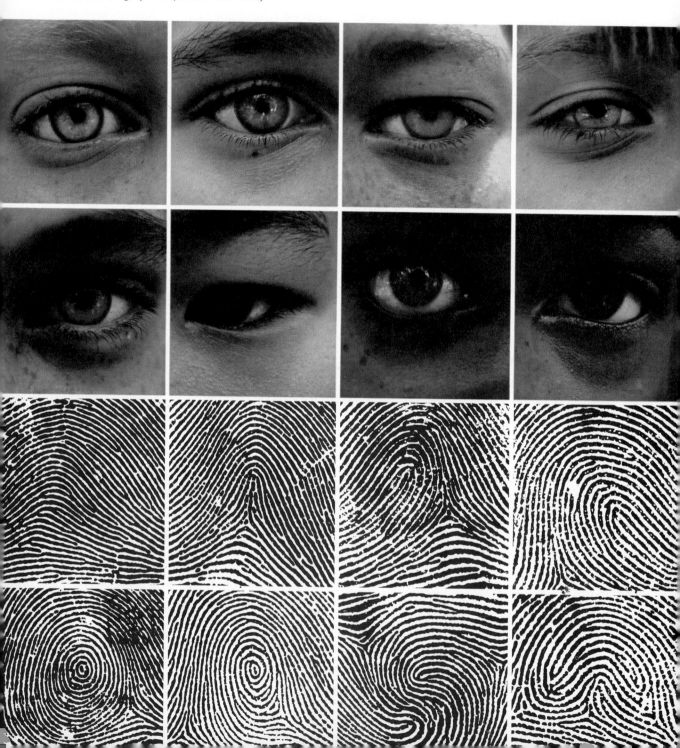

Individuals also differ in skin tones (top two rows), and in hair color (bottom two rows). All these differences are determined by the genes each person inherits. What are some genes that you inherit?

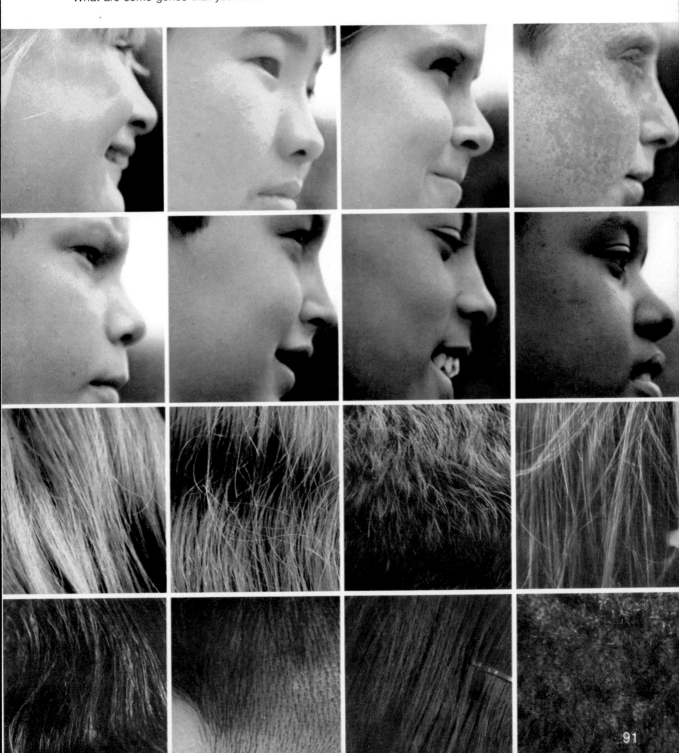

ENJOY IT

Teacher's Notes

A special attempt is made in this health series to enrich children's lives by exposing them to poetry and to art that is related to the lesson topics. This page allows the pupils to look for hereditary traits in a famous painting by Renoir. The students may decide that the child has inherited the mother's nose, mouth, hair color, and skin tones.

See page T29 for additional teaching suggestions.

In this famous picture by the French painter Renoir, you see a pretty mother. You also see an equally pretty child. If you look carefully, you may see some traits the child seems to have inherited from the mother. What are some of them?

On The Terrace by Pierre A. Renoir.
Courtesy of the Art Institute of Chicago.

Things to Do

Teacher's Notes

"Special Research" offers extra research or investigative activities for superior or highly motivated pupils. See page T29 for additional teaching suggestions.

1. You might start to keep your own growth record. At least once a month chart your height and weight. Notice whether or not there are any growth spurts.

	Sept.	Oct.	Nov.	Dec.

Keep a chart each month of your height and weight.

2. Tell which of the following is an inherited trait or something that was learned.

hair color
eye color
liking fried chicken
body build
an enjoyment of reading
blood type

Special Research

Once in a while, in very rare cases, an endocrine gland does not work as it should. Then an unusual thing happens. A person may grow to be very, very tall. Or a person may be a dwarf. Doctors can be of some help with these unusual cases if they can treat the person early in life. You might want to look up in the encyclopedia and find out more about *dwarfs* and *giants*.

Can You Show What You Know?[1]

Teacher's Notes
Here behavioral objectives in the *cognitive* area are posed in childlike language directly to the students themselves. In turn, boys and girls give evidence by *observable behavior* of what they have learned.
Other hoped-for behavioral objectives lie chiefly in the less easily observed *affective* area—objectives that pertain to feelings, attitudes, and values. Some of them are:

Is sensitive to individual differences in growth patterns.

Recognizes that there is no right height or weight for any given individual.

Engages in some individual research to learn more about heredity.

Appreciates the wonders of heredity and how it works.

Page numbers show you where to look back in the chapter for information, if you need it.

1. Tell what is meant by a *growth spurt.* (73)
2. Tell what can help a boy or girl grow in the way that is right for him or her. (73)
3. Name five or six different kinds of body cells. (81)
4. Explain what is meant by body *tissue.* (82)
5. Tell how a cell grows. (83)
6. Explain what keeps your cells growing until you reach full size. (83)
7. Explain what is meant by *heredity.* (84)
8. List some traits that a person inherits. (85)
9. Explain why brothers and sisters are not exactly alike, unless they are identical twins. (85-86)
10. Tell what is meant by dominant genes. (87)
11. Mention some dominant traits. (87)
12. Explain how the sex of a child is determined. (89)

[1]Behavioral objectives in the cognitive area are stated here directly to students themselves.

Review It

Teacher's Notes
"Review It" is a feature that occurs at the end of each chapter in this book and in this health series. It gives children a chance to think over what they have learned, to summarize, and to store away important ideas. Page references after each item make this review page a self-help one. However, group discussion can be a valuable aid.

Page numbers show you where to look back in the chapter for information, if you need it.

1. What have you learned about the growth patterns of girls during the years from nine to sixteen or so? (72-73)

2. What have you learned about the growth patterns of boys during the years from eleven to the early twenties? (72-73)

3. Why might you find some girls in a sixth grade group who are taller than the boys in the group? (73)

4. What are hormones? (78)

5. What are some things that the endocrine glands do? (78)

6. How would you explain the statement "The body grows unevenly"? (72)

7. Why do identical twins have the same heredity? (86)

8. What are recessive genes? (87)

9. What is meant by the statement, "Whether you make the most of your inheritance is up to you"? (89)

Copy each numbered item from List A. After each item, write the letter and words from List B that best describe it. For example:

10. dominant genes   e. strong genes

List A

10. dominant genes
11. endocrine glands
12. gene
13. heredity
14. pituitary
15. protoplasm
16. sperm and egg
17. tissue

List B

a. master gland
b. many cells grouped together
c. reproductive cells
d. jellylike substance in cells
e. strong genes
f. passing along of traits
g. glands that make hormones
h. portion of DNA responsible for a specific trait

Health Test for Chapter Three

Teacher's Notes
After children have taken the test and their papers have been scored, the test items can serve as guides for a summary discussion. Volunteers can read aloud their rewording of the false statements.
"What Do You Think?" is a feature that offers pupils a chance to evaluate some of their newly acquired knowledge.

Copy each number on a piece of paper. After each number write the correct answer, *true* or *false*. Rewrite each false statement to make it true.

T 1. You are made of cells.

F 2. All cells in the human body look just alike.

F 3. When a muscle cell divides, it makes new bone cells.

T 4. Each body cell is surrounded by a covering, or membrane.

T 5. Hormones are sent directly into the bloodstream.

T 6. The reproductive glands help boys and girls grow up to be men and women.

T 7. The feet are fully grown before the legs and arms.

F 8. Boys generally tend to grow taller and heavier at an earlier age than girls.

T 9. A deepening voice is one sign that occurs during puberty in boys.

F10. Girls usually reach their full growth in their early twenties.

T11. The female reproductive cell is the ovum.

T12. Chromosomes are made of a chemical substance called DNA.

T13. A person inherits the color of his or her skin.

T 14. In every human cell except the reproductive cells there are forty-six chromosomes.

T 15. Body build is an inherited trait.

F 16. The gene for blue eyes is a dominant trait.

T 17. Identical twins develop from the same fertilized egg.

T 18. A fertilized cell is one in which the sperm and the egg have joined.

T 19. If the sperm with the X chromosome fertilizes an egg cell, the baby will be a girl.

T 20. What a person becomes is the result of much more than inheritance alone.

Number of Answers   20

Number Right   _____

Score (Number Right x 5)   _____

What Do You Think?

Did this chapter on growth tell you things that you wanted to know? If so, what did you find out? Write your answers on a piece of paper.

SCHOOL & HOME

Family members at home may be interested to hear some things that you have learned about. For example, you might talk about how boys and girls grow and change from the ages of ten to twenty.

Another interesting thing to do is to look at family photographs. Try to find resemblances or traits that have been inherited. Who has Grandpa's red hair? Who inherited Mother's blue eyes?

Teacher's Notes
Special efforts are made in this book and in this health series to foster school-home communication. This page is an example of how youngsters are encouraged to share with the family the health ideas they are acquiring at school.

4 Health Questions Answered

Most newspapers and many magazines have health columns. People write in their health questions, and a doctor suggests some answers. These health columns are very popular. Why do you think this is so?

What are some health questions you would like to have answered?

Preview It

This chapter answers health questions that many boys and girls your age have asked. Look through the chapter quickly. See if you can find eight main questions that are asked. What are these eight questions? Which ones do you most want to have answered?

As you read this chapter, look for answers to the eight main questions. Think of other health questions that you have too. How might you find answers to your own health questions?

As you read the chapter, look for information about other interesting questions such as these.

Do you dream in color?
What is periodontal disease?
How can you lose nutrients in foods by improper methods of cooking?
How does a vaccine help to keep you from getting a disease?

Start the chapter now. Find out what your emotions have to do with how your body works.

Can Emotions Affect How Your Body Works?

Have you ever had a sudden fright? If so, did you notice that your heart began to beat faster? Or perhaps your breathing speeded up. Body changes often occur when you are fearful, angry, worried, or excited. Why is this so?

An important function of your nervous system is to control actions you can direct. These are *voluntary actions* such as talking, running, singing, and so on. But a large part of the nervous system's work is to take care of *involuntary actions.* These are body actions that must go on twenty-four hours a day. These must go on whether you are awake or asleep. There is a close connection between your emotions and the involuntary actions of your body.

What happens when a strong emotion such as fear or anger is aroused? Nerve messages to many organs in your body are changed. They are speeded up or slowed down.

Suppose you are in a class play or a school game. The whole school will see it. You may begin to feel fearful and "jittery" about performing before such a large group. Messages will go from your brain to alert the nervous system about your emotions. Some body changes that can result are shown on the next two pages. What are they?

Such body changes are to be expected now and then. The way your body works depends a great deal on your emotions. However, you want to learn to manage your emotions so that you won't feel fearful, worried, or angry a great deal of the time. Why is this important?

What should you do if you have worried or angry feelings that stay with you for a long time?

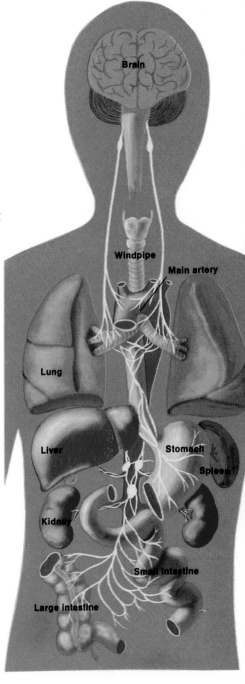

Here you see some of the nerves that carry messages to and from the brain and spinal cord to the body organs.

Messages about the fearful, "jittery" feelings go from the brain to the part of your nervous system that deals with involuntary actions.

Then a whole series of body changes may occur. For example, your heart may beat faster than it usually does.

Your breathing may become more rapid. And your adrenal glands may become more active. They may pour added amounts of the hormone adrenaline into the bloodstream. This hormone stimulates the liver to send sugar into the bloodstream. The sugar burns quickly and produces extra energy.

Sometimes the stomach walls get pale, and the work of the stomach slows down. Sometimes feelings such as fear may cause the stomach walls to get red and the stomach will work too fast.

The stomach may feel "upset" or fluttery too.

Your skeletal muscles may become tense and ready for action. They may twitch, causing trembling.

You may notice that your throat suddenly feels dry. Or there may be an increase in the flow of saliva. You may want to swallow often.

Perspiration may increase on the palms of the hands or under the arms. At times, the kidneys are stimulated, causing frequent urination. Bowel action may be speeded up.

What Is Known About Sleep and Dreams?

Everyone needs sleep. In fact, we spend about one third of our lives asleep. Some people have attempted to go without sleep for long periods of time. They may have been kept awake during emergencies. Or they may have taken part in experiments. These attempts have shown how necessary sleep is.

People who are deprived of sleep become irritable. Their actions slow down. They continually fight the desire to sleep. Finally, they fall into a light sleep for seconds at a time. They may do this while they are standing up or even walking.

Why people sleep and exactly what happens during sleep are scientific puzzles. Sleep researchers are still trying to find answers to many unanswered questions. However, researchers have discovered many things about the nature of sleep.

Body Changes During Sleep

During sleep many changes take place in your body. Some muscles are at rest. They have a chance to recover from the work they have done during the day.

Parts of your brain are less active than usual. But other parts are quite active. Some parts are especially active during dreaming. Other parts must keep active to keep you alive. These parts control breathing and the beating of the heart. But these processes change somewhat during sleep. Both the heartbeat and breathing are slower.

All the senses are dulled during sleep, even the sense of pain.

Why You Need Sleep

Because many of the body's processes slow down during sleep, energy is conserved. Your mind and body have a chance to become refreshed.

Sleep is especially important during growing years. Sleep gives you a chance to save energy for a while. It cuts you off temporarily from the normal, daily stresses.

You need sleep to keep you mentally alert. Suppose you don't get enough sleep night after night. You will soon find that lack of sleep causes your attention to wander. Mistakes and daydreaming increase.

However, missing the needed amount of sleep for just one night is not serious. A person may not be quite as efficient the next day. But there will be no long-range effects.

A person who rests a great deal does not need as much sleep as an active person. But everyone needs some sleep. If people go without sleep over a period of time, their mental processes begin to break down. For example, experiments show that if people are kept awake for four or five days and nights, they lose their judgment and self-control. They may be unable to pass simple tests. They may lose control of their temper. They may begin to see and hear things that don't really exist.

Do you know that an ancient form of torture was to keep a person awake for four or five days and nights?

Teacher's Notes

After students have read this page, you might ask:

"What does sleep do for you?"

"What is the connection between schoolwork and getting adequate sleep?"

"How might you find out if you are getting enough sleep for *you?*"

Something to Try

Generally young people your age need nine or ten hours of sleep at night. But sleep needs differ in individuals.

Try this activity to find out your sleep needs. Keep a sleep diary for several days. Note how much sleep you have each night. Note also how you felt an hour or so after waking up each morning. Did you feel rested and in good humor? If so, you are probably getting the sleep you need.

Teacher's Notes

Discuss what students have learned about dreams that they did not know before. Sleep researchers know how people behave when they are kept from dreaming because of experiments in sleep laboratories. People have been wakened at the start of REM periods. When people are prevented from dreaming, they try to make up the lost dreaming time. Then the REM period occurs more frequently than usual.

Glossary word: *electroencephalograph*

Dreams

There are two kinds of sleep. One kind is with dreams. One is without dreams.

During dream sleep your eyeballs move around underneath your eyelids. This eyeball movement is called the REM period. REM stands for rapid eye movement.

Scientists have learned a lot about dreaming. They have done this by watching people while they sleep. Volunteers, who are willing to be watched, go into sleep laboratories. There, scientists use a special machine called an *electroencephalograph*. It records the tiny electrical waves that the brain produces. These are *brain waves*.

The volunteers sleep all night in the sleep laboratory. Before they go to sleep, little pieces of metal are taped to their head. Wires from these metal pieces are connected to the electroencephalograph. This does not hurt the volunteers. But it does record each volunteer's brain waves.

When a volunteer starts to dream, the electroencephalograph shows an increase in activity. When the activity decreases, the dream is over. A bell is rung to awaken the volunteer. The volunteer then tells his dream into a tape recorder. Then the volunteer goes back to sleep.

It has been found that everyone dreams. But some people don't remember dreaming. Most people dream four or five times a night. Dreams may last just a few minutes or an hour.

On the top you see large, slow brain waves. At this point, the volunteer is asleep without dreams.

The bottom brain wave shows an increase in activity. At this point, dreaming is taking place.

You usually dream about yourself and people and events in your life. Sometimes you imagine people and events in your dreams. Sometimes dreams are filled with fear, anger, or worry. There are scientists who think such dreams are useful in helping us get rid of these troublesome feelings.

You may think that you dream in black and white. But scientists have learned that most dreams have color in them. Scientists believe that people need to dream. Or at least people need the sleep periods in which dreams occur.

Sum It Up

What are some ways in which emotions can affect the way the body works?

What are some changes in your body during sleep?

How does sleep help you? How can lack of sleep affect you?

What have you learned about dreams?

Here you see a volunteer in a sleep laboratory. A research worker is watching the volunteer's brain waves and eye movements from another room.

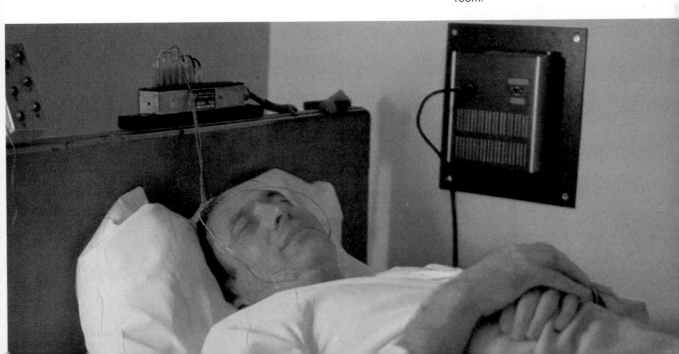

Use the question in the heading to begin preliminary discussions. After the pupils have read the page, ask them what is meant by physical fitness. Also discuss the advantages of being physically fit.
Mention that the exercises shown on the next page are designed to strengthen muscles in different parts of the body. Ask if they know which muscles are being strengthened in each exercise.
See page T31 for additional teaching suggestions.

How Can You Be Physically Fit?

To be physically fit means that you are in the best possible physical condition for you. It means that you get the exercise you need every day. All your muscles, including the heart muscle, are strong and firm.

If you are physically fit, you can take part in games without getting overtired too soon. You can do a good day's work at school without ending up worn out.

You feel better, sleep better, and eat better when you are physically fit. Your posture is usually good too. When you do become tired, your body usually makes a quick comeback.

How can you become physically fit and stay physically fit? You should exercise each day. You should exercise enough to make you pleasantly tired. But you do not want to feel exhausted.

Whatever kind of exercise you choose, it should be fun for you. If physical activity seems hard and boring, you will soon give it up. Some games and sports and other kinds of physical activities are shown on pages 110 and 111. What other ways do you like to get your exercise?

Young people are often advised to engage in some kind of physical activity that can be done all their lives. Why is that a good plan? Which activities shown on pages 110 and 111 can be enjoyed throughout a lifetime? What are some other activities of this kind?

If you aren't able to keep physically fit through sports alone, try doing some exercises regularly. Some exercises you might do are shown on the next page. Be ready to demonstrate each one. What other exercises do you know?

Something to Do

You might draw a picture of you in an activity or sport that you enjoy. Or make a clay model of yourself playing a game. Or you might write about your favorite sport and tell why you like it.

Run in Place   50 slow

Twister   5 each way

Robot   20 times

Propeller   10 each way

Windmill   10 times

Run in Place.   25 slow, 50 fast, 25 slow

"The Basic Workout" from *Vim: A Complete Exercise Plan for Girls 12 to 18* and *Vigor: A Complete Exercise Plan for Boys 12 to 18*. Published 1964 by President's Council on Physical Fitness.

Enjoying Sports

Which of these sports do you enjoy? Which ones can you do by yourself? Which ones are good year-round sports? Which sports could you do all your life?

ENJOY IT

When you watch an acrobat, the arms, legs, and body may seem unusually long. That is how the artist drew them in this picture called *The Acrobat*. The artist is Marc Chagall, a Frenchman.

Your eyes may become "acrobats" as you move them about in studying this picture. They may move in circles to follow the action of the hands, the hoop, and the patterns in the costume. What else in the picture shows movement?

Teacher's Notes

A special attempt is made in this health series to enrich children's lives by exposing them to poetry and to art that is related to the lesson topics. Here students see Chagall's portrayal of an "acrobat."

Invite comments about the picture. Volunteers might look through art books to find other examples that show physical activity. The book *Famous Paintings* by A. Elizabeth Chase (Platt and Munk) has "Children's Games" by Pieter Bruegel the Elder and "The Dancer" by Degas.

See page T31 for additional teaching suggestions.

The Acrobat by Marc Chagall. From the Albright-Knox Art Gallery, Buffalo, New York, Room of Contemporary Art Fund.

ENJOY IT

The Runner

On a flat road runs the well-trained runner,
He is lean and sinewy with muscular legs,
He is thinly clothed, he leans forward as he runs,
With lightly closed fists and arms partially raised.

What do you think makes a runner "well trained"?
What advantages do well-trained runners have in a race?

"The Runner"
by Walt Whitman.

113

Teacher's Notes
Use the question in the heading to start the initial conversation. After studying the page, put these key words on the chalkboard and see what ideas the words suggest about the care of the teeth: *dental caries, plaque, calculus, dental floss, toothbrush, dental hygienist.*
Students may ask about orthodontists. They are special dentists who use bands, wires, and tiny springs to straighten teeth. After the students have read the following page, invite volunteers to demonstrate how to brush the teeth. Also discuss the purpose of disclosing wafers.
Glossary words: *dental caries, calculus, plaque*
See page T31 for additional teaching suggestions.

How Should You Take Care of Your Teeth?

Tooth decay is the most widespread disease in this country. This will give you an idea of the problem. Suppose that all the dentists in this country were put to work doing nothing but repairing dental cavities, or *dental caries.* By the time the dentists finished, they would have to start over again.

However, some progress is being made in reducing the number of cavities. People are learning better ways to remove *plaque* from the teeth. Plaque is a sticky, colorless film of harmful bacteria. Plaque forms constantly on everybody's teeth. It forms near the gumline and in between the teeth. It sticks in grooves too. If plaque is not removed, it hardens. It is then called *calculus,* or *tarter.* Calculus can be removed only by a dentist or a dental hygienist. Calculus will not form if plaque is removed daily.

In the presence of sugar, bacteria in plaque form acids. The acids make holes in the enamel covering of the teeth. Then cavities form. The body cannot repair these cavities. The dentist has to remove the decay and put in fillings.

How to Remove Plaque

How can you remove plaque each day? Use dental floss to remove plaque between your teeth. Ask your dentist to show you how to do it. Then use a toothbrush to clean the teeth and gums. The pictures on the next page show how to do this. What procedures should you follow?

If you can, floss and brush your teeth after eating. Otherwise floss and brush them thoroughly at least once a day.

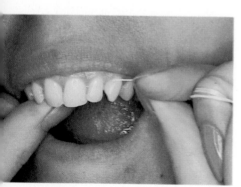

What is being done here to remove plaque?

114

Place the head of your toothbrush alongside your teeth. Angle the bristle tips against the gumline.

Move the brush back and forth. Use short, gentle strokes. Do this to the outside of all your teeth. Keep the bristles angled against the gumline.

Brush the insides of your teeth and gums. Move the brush back and forth. Brush back and forth along the tops of the teeth.

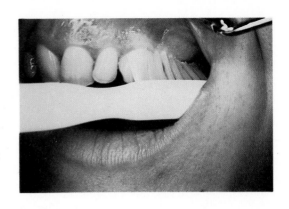

Brush the inside surfaces of your front teeth and the nearby gums.

Use the "toe" of your toothbrush. Brush up and down.

There is something you might do now and then. It helps you see how well you are removing plaque.

Ask at home if some disclosing wafers can be bought at the drugstore. These wafers stain the teeth with a harmless dye. These stained areas show plaque that needs to be removed.

You brush your teeth as you usually do. Then you look for stain on them. If all stain is not removed, you must floss and brush some more. Keep brushing until all the stain (and plaque) are removed.

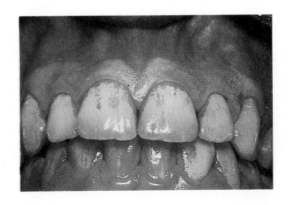

The Best Kind of Toothbrush and Toothpaste

The best kind of toothbrush is one that has a flat brushing surface and soft bristles. It should be small enough to reach all areas of the mouth.

Research has shown that a toothpaste with accepted fluoride in it helps prevent tooth decay. See if your toothpaste has fluoride in it. You can tell because there will be a statement from the American Dental Association on the package.

Periodontal Disease

Besides tooth decay, another dental problem is *periodontal disease.* Periodontal disease is a group of diseases. These diseases affect the tissues around the teeth. The tissues fasten the teeth to the jawbones. If early stages of the disease are neglected, the gums become soft and bleed easily. The teeth may become loose. In an advanced stage of one type of periodontal disease, pus forms around the teeth. The gums shrink. And perfectly good teeth may loosen and fall out.

Periodontal disease occurs most frequently at middle age or older. But young people may also suffer from this disease. Calculus has something to do with starting this disease. Calculus will not form if you floss and brush your teeth daily. If it does form, who will remove it? Other causes of periodontal disease are poor teeth-cleaning habits and irregular teeth.

Sum It Up

What can help you become physically fit?

What is plaque? How can it be removed?

What is the correct way to brush your teeth?

What kind of toothbrush and toothpaste should you use?

TELL IT

These students have been reading about teeth. They have learned some interesting things about the care of teeth. They have found out about some advances in dental health. What can you learn from their reports?

Each time sweet foods are eaten bacteria in plaque on the teeth form acids. The acids start to attack the teeth. This causes cavities.

To help prevent cavities, cut down on sweet foods. It is better to eat sweets after meals than to snack on them all day long. That is because each time you eat sweet foods there is an acid attack on the teeth.

Andrew

Before long there may be foods with harmless chemicals in them. The chemicals will help keep acids from forming cavities in the teeth.

Judy

New plastic coverings, or sealants, are being made and tried out. These sealants will cover the chewing surfaces of the teeth and help prevent cavities. A dentist has to put on the sealant. Just how long the sealants will last is not known for certain.

Yolanda

Teacher's Notes
Use the question in the heading to start some preliminary conversation. What do the students know about nutrients? After studying this page and the next, discuss the body's need for nutrients. You might ask these questions:

"What information was known about nutrients by the early 1900's?"

"What is the disease called scurvy?"

"How was a cure for it found?"

"What still remained a mystery about scurvy?"

Glossary words: *nutrient, protein, fats, carbohydrate, mineral*

See page T31 for additional teaching suggestions.

What Are Nutrients?

Nutrients are nourishing substances in foods. Nutrients supply the materials your body needs for growth, repair, and upkeep. Nutrients also help regulate your body processes and provide heat and energy.

By the early 1900's nutrition scientists had identified four main classes of nutrients in foods. These were *proteins, fats, carbohydrates,* and *minerals.* There was another important class of nutrients that had not yet been discovered. But there had been mysterious hints about it for hundreds of years.

A Mysterious Substance in Lemons

One hint appeared and reappeared over the years. In the early days of exploration, the life of a sailor carried great health risks. Fresh foods were hard to get. And sailors' diets consisted chiefly of hard biscuits and salt pork. It was common for many sailors to suffer and frequently die from *scurvy.* This disease caused bleeding gums, loss of teeth, and internal bleeding. On Vasco da Gama's first voyage around the Cape of Good Hope in 1497, 100 of the 160 crew members died from scurvy.

For the next hundred years or so, a high death rate from scurvy continued among sailors. Then in the early 1660's, some British sailors were given the juice of lemons (called limes). It prevented scurvy. But no one paid much attention.

What Do You Think?

Lemons were part of a nutrition puzzle. Their juice prevented scurvy. But why lemons prevented scurvy remained a mystery for many years. Do you know why?

In 1746, a Scottish naval physician, James Lind, studied scurvy. He proved that lemon juice in the diet could prevent or cure the disease. British sailors were then given lemon juice on all voyages. Soon other navies began this practice. By the early 1800's scurvy stopped being a major health problem. But not for another hundred years did people know why a special nutrient in lemons prevented scurvy.

A Mysterious Substance in Milk, Vegetables, Fish, and Meat

Another disease that once caused much sickness is *beriberi*. This is a disease of the nerves. It eventually paralyzes the body. Beriberi was especially common in Far Eastern countries. Here the diet was mainly polished rice.

In 1882, a Japanese medical officer named Kanehiro Takati had a theory. He thought that a poor diet caused the Japanese sailors' illness. He tested his theory. One ship of Japanese sailors took a nine-month cruise. These sailors had the usual diet, chiefly rice. Another ship took the same route. These sailors had increased amounts of meat, fish, and vegetables. Condensed milk was added to the diet. And less rice was served. There were 160 cases of beriberi on the first ship and 25 deaths. There were 10 cases on the second ship among men who had not eaten all parts of the new diet. Soon the Japanese navy adopted the new diet.

Later other doctors proved that whole grains, lean meats, dried peas and beans, yeast, and milk contained something that would prevent or cure beriberi. But not until 1926 did people know about the helpful nutrient in these foods.

Teacher's Notes
Continue the discussion by asking:
"What do you know about beriberi?"
"How was a cure for it found?"
"What was still a mystery about the disease?"
See page T31 for additional teaching suggestions.

Do You Know?

These foods were part of a nutrition puzzle too. Sailors who ate them did not get beriberi. Those who ate chiefly polished rice were likely to get the disease. Do you know the answer to the puzzle?

119

Teacher's Notes
Explain that scurvy and beriberi are known as "food deficiency diseases." They occur because of a lack of a certain nutrient in the diet. Suggest that students read on to learn about two other food deficiency diseases, rickets and pellagra. Mention that all of these diseases still exist in the world today.

However, today we know exactly what causes these diseases.

You might ask these questions:

"What have you learned about rickets?"

"How was a cure for rickets found?"

"What is pellagra?"

"How was a cure for pellagra found?"

A Mysterious Substance in Codfish Liver and Codfish Oils

Rickets is a disease of the bones. It occurs mainly in babies and young children. Rickets causes crooked bones or crippling. In past years it was a common disease in certain areas of this country as well as other countries. In fact, it still occurs in people who do not have an adequate diet.

Doctors looking for a cure made some discoveries. They found that rickets did not occur in some parts of the world. In these areas, people ate codfish livers. Or they had codliver oil in their diets. Eskimos, for example, never had rickets.

Doctors also discovered that light from the sun or sun lamps helped undernourished children who had rickets.

But what was it in codfish livers, in codliver oil, and in sunlight that prevented rickets? It was not until 1919 that the nutrient was discovered.

Pellagra—and Another Mystery

Another puzzling disease of the early 1900's and for years before was *pellagra.* Pellagra was found in this country and others. It was found among people whose diet was chiefly corn meal, molasses, and pork fat. Symptoms included soreness of the mouth, skin rashes, and loss of memory. For years no one knew what caused pellagra or how to treat it.

In 1914, Dr. Joseph Goldberger, a doctor in the United States Public Health Service, made a discovery. He found that children who ate fresh meat and drank milk did not get pellagra. Later he learned that yeast would cure the disease. But what was it in milk and fresh meat that prevented pellagra? What was it in yeast that cured it? It was not until the late 1930's that the mystery was solved. Then the special nutrient was identified.

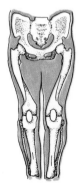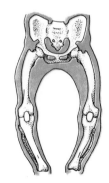

On the left are normal leg bones.
On the right are bowed leg bones,
resulting from rickets.

Vitamins

What were the mysterious substances in certain foods that could prevent or cure scurvy, beriberi, rickets, and pellagra? To find the answer, scientists worked in laboratories. Gradually they learned that foods supply not only proteins, carbohydrates, minerals, and fats, but also other essential substances. These must be in the diet for a person to stay well. These substances were named *vitamins.* The name comes from the word "vita" which means "life."

At first the exact chemical nature of vitamins was not known. So they were named by the letters A, B, C, and D. Now chemists know the exact nature of the most common vitamins. Scientists can manufacture many of these vitamins in the laboratory. And now the chemical names are used for some of these vitamins. For example, ascorbic acid is the chemical name for vitamin C.

With knowledge of vitamins, the mystery of the cures for scurvy, beriberi, rickets, and pellagra was solved.

Teacher's Notes

Students can read this page to find out what the mysterious substances were in foods that could cure scurvy, beriberi, rickets, and pellagra.

You might ask:

"What was the mysterious substance?"

"What is the meaning of the word *vitamins?*"

"What other way can we obtain vitamins besides from foods?" (Chemists manufacture synthetic vitamins in laboratories. Students have seen these vitamins on shelves in the drugstores.)

"What is ascorbic acid?"

Glossary words: *vitamin, ascorbic acid*

Today nutrients such as vitamins can be made in the laboratory, or *synthesized.*

121

Students can now read to find the
exact cause of scurvy, beriberi,
pellagra, and rickets.
Use the "Sum It Up" questions to
guide a summary of pages 118–122.
Also explain that water is grouped
with the main classes of nutrients
because water is needed to carry
nutrients to the cells. It also carries
the wastes away, helps to regulate
body temperature, helps digest food,
replaces daily water loss, and helps to
sustain the health of all the body cells.
Glossary word: *niacin*

A lack of vitamin C, found in citrus fruits such as lemons, causes scurvy. Lack of vitamin B_2 causes beriberi. A lack of vitamin D causes rickets. And a lack of the vitamin *niacin* causes pellagra.

At the present time nutrition scientists have discovered at least thirteen vitamins that are needed for good nutrition. Others may still be found.

The Six Main Classes of Nutrients

With the discovery of vitamins, the study of nutrition entered a new era. Further advances have been made in recent years. Nutrition scientists have found many more nutrients in foods. It is believed that others may be discovered.

These nutrients are grouped into six main classes. They are *vitamins, minerals, proteins, carbohydrates, fats,* and *water.* Each nutrient performs a special job in your body.

You need all of these nutrients in your diet to keep you healthy. You get most nutrients from many different foods. Vitamin D, however, can also be made by the body. It is made when your skin is exposed to certain invisible rays in the sunlight.

No one food such as milk, meat, bread, fruit, or vegetables alone contains all the nutrients your body needs. What does that suggest about the need for a varied diet?

Sum It Up

What helps prevent scurvy? beriberi? rickets? pellagra?
What are nutrients? What do they do for your body?
What are the six main classes of nutrients?

How Can You Get All the Nutrients You Need?

How can you be sure to get all the nutrients you need in your diet? How can you be sure to get all the right amounts of them?

A daily food guide is the best answer to this important food problem. You can see a suggested food guide on pages 124 and 125. Try to include in your daily diet the different groups of foods in the amounts suggested. The guide will help you get enough of all the nutrients you need daily.

A Food Diary

A good way to see if you are eating enough of the right kinds of foods is to keep a food diary. In your diary list all the foods you eat or drink during the day. Put in the number of servings too. Be sure to include snacks.

It is a good idea to keep your food diary for several days. Over a period of days you can get an idea if you are omitting foods from any of the food groups. You may want to talk over your food diary with your family.

An example you can follow is shown below.

Teacher's Notes
Use the question in the heading to start some preliminary discussion. Remind the students that there are many different nutrients in foods and that all are needed in the daily diet. Have the students study the Food Guide on pages 124–125 to see if they are getting the right foods. They might copy the food groups and servings to take home for reference.
Encourage the students to keep a food diary for a few days. These diaries should be kept private.
See pages T31 for additional teaching suggestions.

A Food Diary

	MILK (SERVINGS)	MEAT (servings)	VEGETABLE-FRUIT (servings)	BREAD-CEREAL (servings)
Breakfast	1 glass		orange juice (1 glass)	cereal (1 bowl)
Lunch				
Supper				
Snacks				
Total Servings				

Each day your food should supply you with many different nutrients. Using the Daily Food Guide below can help you choose food wisely. With it, you can plan to get needed nutrients from a variety of foods.

Vegetable-Fruit Group: **Four or more servings, including a citrus fruit or other fruit or vegetable for vitamin C. A dark-green or deep-yellow vegetable for vitamin A—at least every other day. Other vegetables and fruits.**

Meat Group: **Two or more servings of beef, veal, pork, lamb, poultry, fish, eggs.
As alternates—dry beans, dry peas, nuts, peanut butter.**

Some other foods not specified here but which almost everyone eats regularly are butter, margarine, and other fats including vegetable oils, such as olive oil; sugars; and unenriched grain products.

Milk Group: Some milk for everyone
Children under 9: 2 to 3 cups
Children 9-12: 3 or more cups
Teen-agers: 4 cups
Adults: 2 cups

Bread-Cereal Group: Four or more servings
Whole-grain, enriched, or restored

125

Teacher's Notes
Use the question in the heading to
encourage some discussion about the
importance of having breakfast. After
reading the page, ask these questions:
"Why is breakfast an important meal?"
"What is known about the breakfast
habits of many people?"
"What is known about the importance
of breakfast to workers and students?"
"What is known about the value of
breakfast to those who want to lose
weight?"

Does It Matter If You Skip Breakfast?

Breakfast is the most important meal of the day. It is the meal that "breaks the fast" since supper the night before. Skipping breakfast may mean going without food for about eighteen hours. Important nutrients missed at breakfast may not be made up in remaining meals.

Some years ago nationwide surveys showed that many people in this country have poor breakfast habits. This is still true. Since these surveys, research has been done on the need for breakfast. Some of the most famous studies have been the Iowa Breakfast Studies.

In one of the Iowa Studies seventy people were tested. The people were both male and female. They ranged in age from twelve to eighty-three years. While they were being tested, they ate a variety of experimental breakfasts. Sometimes they ate no breakfast.

Specially designed equipment tested how well the people's bodies were working. Blood tests and exercise tests gave information too. Look at the exercise test shown at the left.

What were the results? Results showed that an adequate breakfast can help a person do more work than a person with a poor breakfast. This was especially true of mental activities such as schoolwork. Usually the person who had the adequate breakfast was quicker in actions and did not tire so easily.

Many people skip breakfast because they think this will help them lose weight. The Iowa Studies showed that the opposite is true. Breakfast skippers usually become so hungry that they eat large amounts of food later in the day. And sometimes they may gain weight.

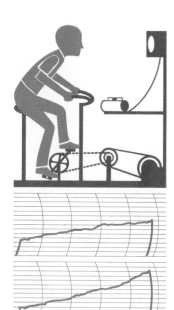

Here is a test used in the Iowa Breakfast Studies. In this test a person's maximum work output was measured on days when he or she ate breakfast and on days when he or she did not. The person rode a stationary bicycle for one minute at maximum effort. The results were recorded. The tests showed that a person can do more and better work with breakfast than without breakfast.

What is an adequate breakfast? Fruit or fruit juice (preferably citrus fruit), cereal and/or bread, and milk make up one pattern for a breakfast. Eggs, cheese, sausage, peanut butter, and other foods can be substituted or added to give variety.

If a person tires of the usual breakfast menu, an equally nutritious but different one can be tried. Many people enjoy such foods as a grilled cheese sandwich, fish cakes, fried potatoes, spaghetti, or pizza. Other people like refried beans, cornbread, grits, soup, rice, or fried chicken.

There are variations in food patterns. All of them are fine if somewhere in the day's diet enough foods from the food guide are included.

What is a food you like for breakfast? What is your family's most preferred food for breakfast? Would you expect your family to serve exactly the same foods for breakfast as other families? Why or why not?

At the right is a recipe for oatmeal that is enjoyed by a nutrition scientist and his family. You might want to copy it. Take it home and see if you can try it some day soon.

Sum It Up

How can you be sure you are getting enough of the essential nutrients daily?

Why is it important to have an adequate breakfast?

Teacher's Notes
Discuss one breakfast and ask how this breakfast can be varied.
Have the students read the recipe for oatmeal and raisins. Ask them what has been done to add extra nutrients to the usual oatmeal recipe. (The nonfat dry milk and raisins are rich with calcium and iron.)
Students might copy this recipe and try it at home. If so, give them time later to talk over their response to it. See page T31 for additional teaching suggestions.

Something to Do

You might try this recipe at home.

Oatmeal with Raisins
4 cups water
1 teaspoon salt
2 cups quick-cooking oatmeal
1 1/3 cups nonfat dry milk powder
raisins
brown sugar for sprinkling
cinnamon (optional) for sprinkling

Bring water to a boil. Add salt. Mix oatmeal and nonfat dry milk. Stir mixture gradually into boiling water. Continue stirring over medium heat for one to two minutes. Turn off heat; let stand a few minutes. Add raisins, brown sugar, and, if you wish, cinnamon. Serves six.

From ''What Nutrition Experts Feed Their Own Families'' by Martin Cohen, *Today's Health* (September 1973). Published by the American Medical Association. Reprinted by permission.

HEALTH AROUND US

The next time you go shopping, look carefully at the labels on foods. The labels on many containers give valuable information about nutrition.

Look at the two nutrition labels below. These come from boxes of breakfast cereals. What information is given on the labels?

If you wanted the cereal which supplies the most nutrients, which one would you buy? Why?

Teacher's Notes

"Health Around Us" is a recurring feature in this book and in this health series. This page draws attention to the labels on packages. The labels contain information about the calories per serving, the amounts of proteins, carbohydrates, fats, vitamins, and minerals. This is all in terms of the new U.S. Recommended Daily Allowances.

(*Note:* A *calorie* is the unit used to measure the amount of energy produced by the food you eat.)

See page T31 for additional teaching suggestions.

Cereal A

NUTRITION INFORMATION PER SERVING

Serving Size 1 ounce (1 cup)
Servings per Container 9

	1 ounce	+ ½ cup Milk
Calories	110	190
Protein, gm	2	6
Carbohydrate, gm	24	30
Fat, gm	1	5

PERCENTAGE OF U.S. RECOMMENDED DAILY ALLOWANCES (U.S. RDA)

Protein	2%	10%
Vitamin A	45%	50%
Vitamin C	45%	45%
Thiamin	45%	50%
Riboflavin	45%	60%
Niacin	45%	45%
Calcium	2%	15%
Iron	45%	45%
Vitamin B₆	45%	50%
Vitamin B₁₂	45%	50%

Cereal B

NUTRITION INFORMATION PER SERVING

SERVING SIZE: ONE OUNCE (1 CUP)
SERVINGS PER CONTAINER: 12

	1 OZ.	WITH ½ CUP WHOLE MILK
CALORIES	110	190
PROTEIN	3 g	7 g
CARBOHYDRATES	23 g	29 g
FAT	0 g	5 g

PERCENTAGE OF U.S. RECOMMENDED DAILY ALLOWANCE (U.S. RDA)

	1 OZ.	WITH ½ CUP WHOLE MILK
PROTEIN	4	15
VITAMIN A	100	100
VITAMIN C	100	100
THIAMIN	100	100
RIBOFLAVIN	100	110
NIACIN	100	100
CALCIUM	*	15
IRON	100	100
VITAMIN D	100	110
VITAMIN E	100	100
VITAMIN B₆	100	100
FOLIC ACID	100	100
VITAMIN B₁₂	100	100
PHOSPHORUS	2	10
MAGNESIUM	2	6

WRITE IT

Can you destroy nutrients in foods by the way you prepare them? Some boys and girls your age looked into this matter. You can see their reports below. What information do they give you?

Teacher's Notes

After reading the cooking tips that the pupils have written, see if the students have any other suggestions. (Serve raw foods immediately after cutting, slicing, shredding, or chopping, because foods lose much of their vitamin content when exposed to air. Also do not let vegetables or fruit soak in water before cooking them, because minerals and vitamins dissolve in water.)

See page T31 for additional teaching suggestions.

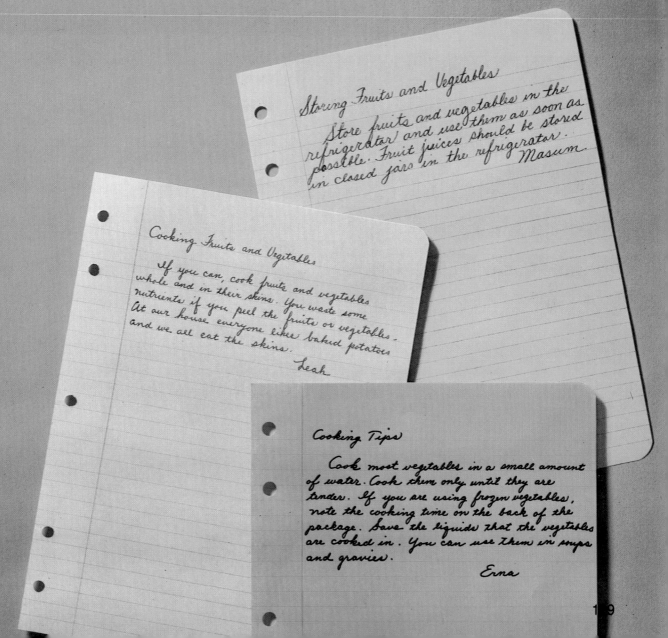

Storing Fruits and Vegetables

Store fruits and vegetables in the refrigerator and use them as soon as possible. Fruit juices should be stored in closed jars in the refrigerator.

Masum

Cooking Fruits and Vegetables

If you can, cook fruits and vegetables whole and in their skins. You waste some nutrients if you peel the fruits or vegetables. At our house everyone likes baked potatoes and we all eat the skins.

Leah

Cooking Tips

Cook most vegetables in a small amount of water. Cook them only until they are tender. If you are using frozen vegetables, note the cooking time on the back of the package. Save the liquids that the vegetables are cooked in. You can use them in soups and gravies.

Erna

What Happens in a Health Checkup?

Doctors believe it is a good idea to have regular health checkups. For boys and girls your age, a checkup is recommended every two or three years. However, in some cases more frequent checkups may be advised.

When the doctor sees you regularly, he or she can check your continued growth and development. Booster shots can be given if they are needed. The doctor keeps a record of you when you are in good health. Then the doctor is better able to help you if you get sick. If the doctor discovers any minor problems in a checkup, they can be corrected. It is better to find and correct any problems before they get worse.

At a checkup you get to know your doctor better too. You have a chance to ask him or her any questions you may have about your health.

Your Temperature

The doctor or a nurse will take your temperature during a checkup. This is one way to tell how well you are at this time. Also the doctor may be planning to give you a booster shot. You would not get a shot if you had a fever. A fever is a temperature which is higher than normal.

There are differences among individuals. But normal body temperature is about 37° Celsius. If it goes up a degree or two, you may have an infection. The body's reaction to harmful germs is usually a fever.

Your Height, Weight, and Posture

The doctor or a nurse will weigh and measure you. Your height and weight can then be compared with measurements made at your last visit.

The doctor may ask you to sit, stand, and walk. This is to check your posture. Some boys and girls have flat feet. Some walk with toes pointed in or out. The doctor may suggest the need for special shoes. Or the doctor might give suggestions about your posture.

The doctor may tell you to sit way back in a chair with your feet on the floor. Then you will "feel" the correct sitting posture.

To get the "feel" of good standing posture, put your back against a wall. The back of your head and your shoulders should touch the wall. Keep your chin level and your abdomen flat. Keep your knees relaxed. If your posture is correct, your ear, shoulder, and hip will be in a straight line. Both shoulders should be level. If you practice this posture, it can become natural for you. What are the advantages of good posture? What do you think adequate food, rest, and sleep have to do with your posture?

Teacher's Notes

After study of this page, ask these questions:

"What is normal body temperature?"

"What might an above-normal temperature indicate?"

"What are some other things the doctor or nurse does during a checkup?"

Mention that good posture usually goes along with good health. Invite students to demonstrate poor and good sitting and walking postures.

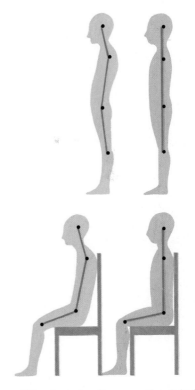

Why does the figure on the right in both pictures show good posture?

With good posture you can sit and stand and move about for long periods of time without getting tired.

131

Teacher's Notes

Invite comments on these questions:

"What is the ophthalmoscope? Why is it an important tool?"

"What can the doctor find out when using the otoscope?"

"What is the doctor looking for when he or she looks into your nose and throat?"

Glossary words: *ophthalmoscope, otoscope, larynx*

Checking Your Eyes, Ears, Nose, and Throat

The doctor has instruments to help see inside your eyes, ears, nose, and throat.

An *ophthalmoscope* is used to see through the pupil of the eye to the *retina.* The retina is the thin film of nerve cells lining the inside back of your eyeball. On the retina nerves and blood vessels can be seen clearly. They are not covered with skin or muscles. Early signs of some diseases may show in the blood vessels and nerves of the retina. Some of these are kidney disease, diabetes, and high blood pressure. See the picture on page 133.

The doctor or nurse may ask you to cover one eye at a time and read aloud lines of letters on an eye chart. Each line of letters is smaller than the one above. How well you can read the chart at a distance can help the doctor know how well you can see.

The doctor uses an *otoscope* to check inside each ear. An otoscope is like a flashlight with a magnifying glass. With it the doctor checks your eardrum. He or she can look for signs of disease or for too much wax inside the ear. Too much wax in the ear can keep you from hearing properly. The doctor can easily remove the wax.

To examine your nose, the doctor uses another electrically lighted instrument. This helps in viewing the cavities of the nose. The doctor looks for signs of infection or swelling.

The doctor looks down your throat with the aid of a tongue depressor. You may be asked to say "Ah-h-h-h." The doctor looks for signs of disease in the tonsils and other areas of the throat.

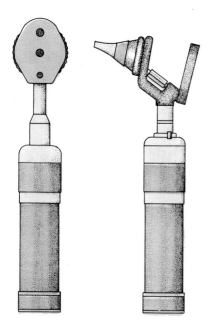

Ophthalmoscope   **Otoscope**

This is how a healthy normal retina looks through an ophthalmoscope.

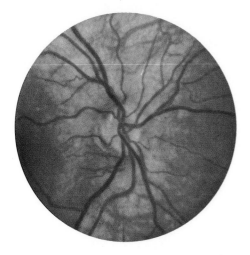

Here you can see an eye that has been injured. Note the dark scar at the left of the eyeball.

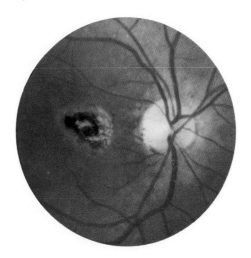

The condition of blood vessels in this eye indicates the early stages of diabetes.

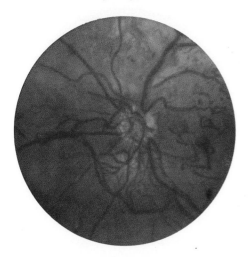

This shows how the retina looks in an advanced stage of diabetes.

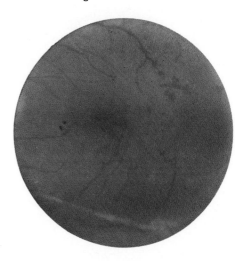

With the otoscope, the doctor can see conditions inside the ear. This shows how a normal, healthy ear looks through an otoscope.

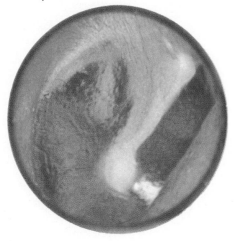

Inflamed tissue and clouding of details in this ear indicates that it is infected.

This picture shows that an eardrum has been pierced.

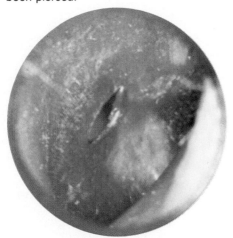

A small stone has lodged in this ear.

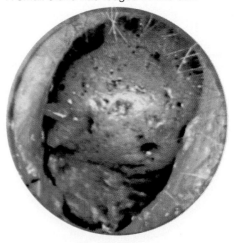

Using a tongue depressor, the doctor checks the patient's throat. This is how a normal throat looks.

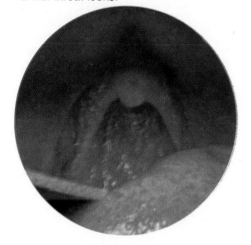

This is a normal larynx.

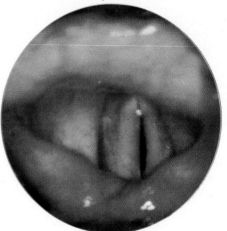

In this picture the tonsils are enlarged and inflamed.

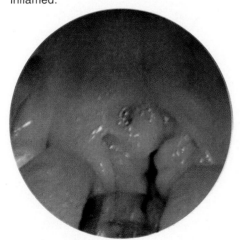

Here you see a sore throat.

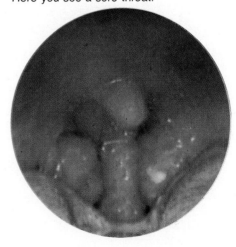

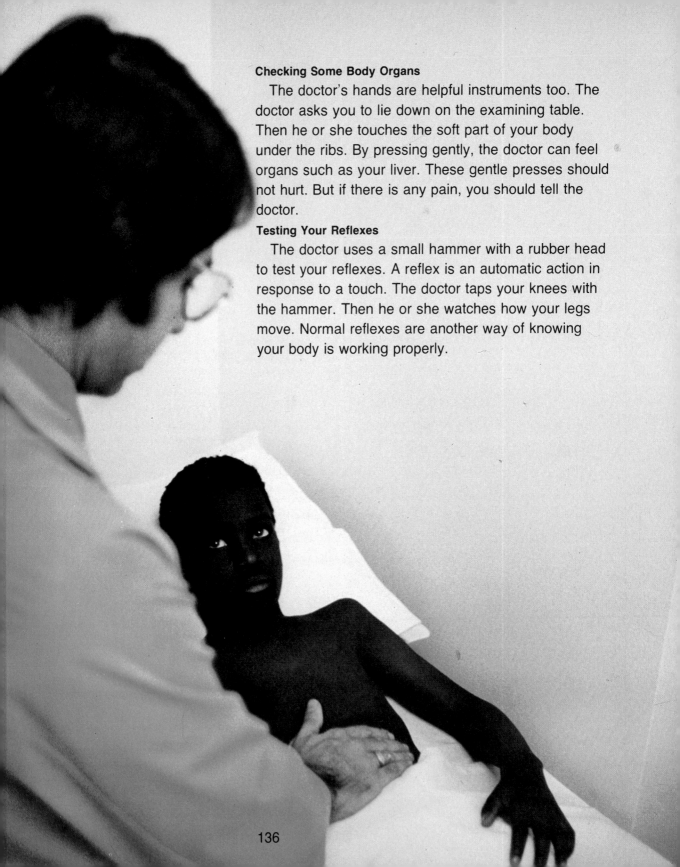

Checking Some Body Organs

The doctor's hands are helpful instruments too. The doctor asks you to lie down on the examining table. Then he or she touches the soft part of your body under the ribs. By pressing gently, the doctor can feel organs such as your liver. These gentle presses should not hurt. But if there is any pain, you should tell the doctor.

Testing Your Reflexes

The doctor uses a small hammer with a rubber head to test your reflexes. A reflex is an automatic action in response to a touch. The doctor taps your knees with the hammer. Then he or she watches how your legs move. Normal reflexes are another way of knowing your body is working properly.

Studying Your Heart and Lungs

There are a variety of methods to study your heart and lungs.

The doctor taps the chest and listens to the chest sounds. A drumlike sound tells that the tapping is over air. A dull, flat sound gives a clue that there may be something wrong in one or both lungs.

The doctor may feel your pulse at your wrist. This tells how fast your heart is beating. The doctor also uses the *stethoscope*. It is used to study the heartbeat and the passage of air into the lungs.

A heartbeat sounds something like "lub dub, lub dub." If one of the heart valves does not close tightly, there may be a rushing or blowing sound. This is called a *murmur*. There are other causes of heart murmurs too. Some murmurs are important. Others are not. The doctor will decide by studying the heart.

The doctor puts the stethoscope on your back to listen to the sound of air going in and out of your lungs. The doctor may say, "Take some deep breaths." If your lungs are in good shape, the doctor will hear a "swish, swish" sound. If you have a cough, the doctor may hear a rattling sound.

Teacher's Notes

Invite discussion on these questions:
"When using the stethoscope, what does the doctor hear?"
"Why does the doctor tap the chest?"
"What is a heart valve?" (It is the part found between the upper and lower chambers on each side of the heart. The valves allow the blood to pass through one way only.)
"What is a heart murmur?"
"What is the purpose of taking the pulse?" (To check the heartbeat. The normal heartbeat of a twelve-year-old is about 90 times a minute. It is about 70–80 times a minute in adults. This count will vary in different conditions and different individuals.)
Glossary word: *stethoscope*

Teacher's Notes

Discuss the purpose of taking a blood count in a health checkup. Ask:

"What may an increased number of white cells tell the doctor?"

"What might a low red-cell count indicate?"

(*Note:* Blood for a blood test may come from the finger or from a vein.)

Glossary word: *anemia*

Testing a Sample of Your Blood

Tests can be made on just a few drops of your blood. The tests indicate some important things about your health. Some blood tests can be done right in your doctor's office. Others are sent to laboratories where the blood is tested on complicated instruments.

One test the doctor can do in the office is a *blood count.* This test tells the number of red blood cells and white blood cells you have.

For a red-blood-cell count, a small, measured amount of blood is mixed with another liquid. One drop of this mixture is spread over a counting chamber. See the picture below. The surface of the chamber is marked off into little squares. The chamber is put under a microscope. Then the red blood cells in several squares are counted. A low number of red blood cells may indicate some form of *anemia.* If this is the case, the doctor may prescribe medicine, or a better diet.

For a white-blood-cell count, another portion of the blood sample is mixed with an acid liquid. The acid dissolves the red blood cells. Then a white-blood-cell count can be made. White blood cells fight off disease germs that enter the body. A high white-blood-cell count may mean that your body is fighting an infection.

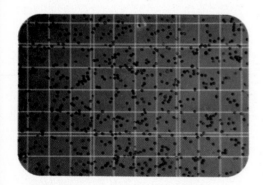

Here you see a blood counting chamber. This is how the red blood cells look in a normal red-cell count. What might a low red-cell count indicate?

Testing a Sample of Urine

Urine tests give valuable clues about health. That is why they are a part of most health checkups.

Urine tests can tell if there is an infection in the kidneys, urinary bladder, liver, pancreas, heart, and stomach. For example, the amount of sugar in the urine can tell how well the cells of the pancreas are working. Too much sugar in the urine is a clue that a person may have *diabetes*.

Here you can see how some very simple urine tests are made. Colored squares on a plastic strip are used. The strip at the left shows how a completely normal sample looks. The five strips at the right show changes that may occur in the color squares when the urine is tested. The strip is dipped into a urine sample. It is then quickly removed. Each square is compared with the normal square. Color changes indicate conditions in the body that may need more study.

Teacher's Notes
The urine test shown on this page can be done in the doctor's office. A complete study of the urine, or a *urinalysis*, is usually done in a laboratory.
Glossary word: *urinary bladder*

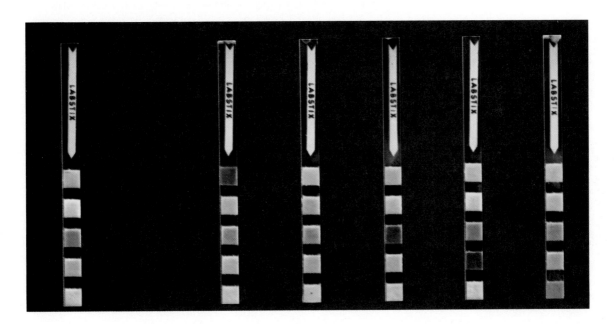

Teacher's Notes

Discuss what is meant by *immunity*. Have students look it up in the Glossary. Also talk about ways to get immunity. Ask:

"What is a vaccine? What is its effect on the body?"

Encourage students to check on their present immunity record. Each student could make a record of communicable diseases he or she has had and the dates. Notice if immunization was given for diphtheria, tetanus, whooping cough, polio, and German measles.

Glossary words: *immunity, vaccine*

Checking Your Immunization Record

As part of the health checkup, the doctor looks at your immunization record. Any needed vaccines can be injected in your body in a shot. Or polio vaccines can be given in a syrup or sugar cube.

The purpose of vaccines is to cause your body to build *antibodies.* Antibodies are substances in the blood that help your body fight off diseases.

Suppose you have not had a measles shot. The doctor can give it to you now. The doctor uses a needle to inject the vaccine. This vaccine contains weakened measles germs. You are not harmed by these germs. But your body starts to make antibodies that fight measles germs. These antibodies remain in your body for a while. Then you have an immunity to measles. That means that you are protected against the disease.

Some vaccines such as whooping cough vaccine contain killed germs. Your body reacts as if the killed whooping cough germs were live ones. It builds antibodies to fight whooping cough germs and gives you immunity to whooping cough.

The protection given by some vaccines may not last too long. To maintain immunity against some diseases, you may have to get booster shots from time to time.

Against what diseases have you been immunized? How can you find out?

Sum It Up

Why does a doctor use the stethoscope?

What do blood counts and urine tests tell the doctor about your health?

What is the purpose of vaccines? How do they work in the body?

Books to Read

Look for books about doctors at the school or public library. Here are some that may interest you.

Barr, George. *Young Scientist and the Doctor* (McGraw-Hill).

Berry, James. *Why You Feel Hot, Why You Feel Cold: Your Body's Temperature* (Little, Brown).

Cobb, Vicki. *How the Doctor Knows You're Fine* (Lippincott).

TELL IT

A doctor who has training in a given field of medicine and who specializes in treating problems in that area is a *specialist.* There are many kinds of specialists. The students you see here have learned the names of some specialists. What are they? What do they do?

What can you find out about these specialists?

urologist　　　　*orthopedist*　　　　*otologist*

Teacher's Notes
Here are some specialists your students may learn about:
urologist—specialist in problems of urinary organs.
orthopedist—specialist in defects and injuries of the bones, muscles, and joints.
otologist—specialist in problems of the ear.

A *psychiatrist* specializes in preventing, diagnosing, and treating emotional problems.

A *pediatrician* specializes in the treatment of children and teen-agers.

An *ophthalmologist* specializes in treating all defects, injuries, and diseases of the eyes.

A *dermatologist* specializes in treating skin problems.

Beth

Eric

Maria

John

Things to Do

Teacher's Notes

Ask students to keep a Health Question Box. Have volunteers find the answers to questions that they do not know.
See page T31 for additional teaching suggestions.

1. You may want to try feeling your *pulse*. Touch your left wrist below the thumb. Use two fingers from your right hand to do this. Press down gently. See if you can feel a push, push, push. You are feeling a movement in a blood vessel called an artery. This movement in the artery is the pulse. Your pulse tells you how fast your heart is beating.

In boys and girls your age, the pulse beats about ninety times a minute. If you have a watch with a second hand, count your pulse.

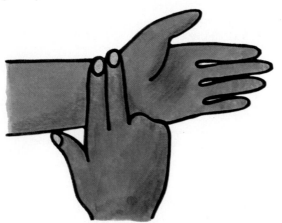

2. Here is something else to try. Hop up and down on one foot twenty times. Now sit down and count your pulse. Is it beating faster or slower than it was when you first felt it? What does this tell you?

3. You might want to look in the school or public library for books about doctors. Here are some that you might enjoy:

Anckarsvard, Karin. *Doctor's Boy* (Harcourt).

Baker, Rachel. *The First Woman Doctor: The Story of Elizabeth Blackwell, M.D.* (Messner).

Goodsell, Jane. *The Mayo Brothers* (Crowell).

Grant, Madeleine P. *Alice Hamilton: Pioneer in Industrial Medicine* (Abelard-Schuman).

4. Bring to class labels from food cans and packages. Make a bulletin-board display of them.

Study the labels to see what nutrition information is given. Also notice whether any recipes are given on the labels.

Look at the parts of labels at the right.

What can you learn from studying them?

Special Research

Many people believe things about foods that aren't true. These things they believe are called *food fallacies.* Here is a fallacy.

Fallacy: You have to eat special foods if you want to lose weight.
Fact: Successful weight control depends on careful control of food intake. It also involves having an adequate diet and getting plenty of exercise.

See if you can find some other food fallacies. Be ready to give the correct facts about them as well.

Net Wt....16 oz. (1 lb.) or 454 grams Cups....Approx. 2

INGREDIENTS: PEAS, WATER, CARROTS, SUGAR, SALT.

NUTRITION INFORMATION—PER ONE CUP SERVING
SERVINGS PER CONTAINER APPROX. 2

| CALORIES | 100 | CARBOHYDRATE | 19gm |
| PROTEIN | 5gm | FAT | 0gm |

PERCENTAGE OF U.S. RECOMMENDED DAILY
ALLOWANCES (U.S. RDA) PER ONE CUP SERVING

PROTEIN	6	NIACIN	8
VITAMIN A	420	CALCIUM	4
VITAMIN C	25	IRON	8
THIAMIN (B_1)	8	PHOSPHORUS	10
RIBOFLAVIN (B_2)	8	MAGNESIUM	8

DISTRIBUTED BY DEL MONTE CORPORATION
SAN FRANCISCO, CA 94105, U.S.A.— PACKED IN U.S.A.

0   24000 01319

For good nutrition eat a variety of foods.

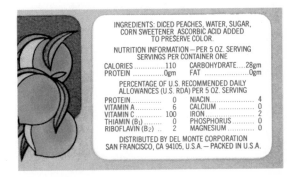

INGREDIENTS: DICED PEACHES, WATER, SUGAR, CORN SWEETENER ASCORBIC ACID ADDED TO PRESERVE COLOR.

NUTRITION INFORMATION—PER 5 OZ. SERVING
SERVINGS PER CONTAINER ONE

| CALORIES | 110 | CARBOHYDRATE | 28gm |
| PROTEIN | 0gm | FAT | 0gm |

PERCENTAGE OF U.S. RECOMMENDED DAILY
ALLOWANCES (U.S. RDA) PER 5 OZ. SERVING

PROTEIN	0	NIACIN	4
VITAMIN A	6	CALCIUM	0
VITAMIN C	100	IRON	2
THIAMIN (B_1)	0	PHOSPHORUS	0
RIBOFLAVIN (B_2)	2	MAGNESIUM	0

DISTRIBUTED BY DEL MONTE CORPORATION
SAN FRANCISCO, CA 94105, U.S.A.— PACKED IN U.S.A.

Can You Show What you Know?[1]

Teacher's Notes

Here behavioral objectives in the *cognitive* area are posed in childlike language directly to the students themselves. In turn, boys and girls give evidence by *observable behavior* of what they have learned.

Other hoped-for behavioral objectives lie chiefly in the less easily observed *affective* area— objectives that pertain to feelings, attitudes, and values. Some of them are:

Realizes the close connection between emotions and body functions.

Appreciates the need for sleep.

Engages in activities that contribute to physical fitness.

Enjoys a health-related painting or poem.

Assumes responsibility for proper care of teeth.

Is alert to the need for getting an adequate diet.

Is aware of the need for periodic checkups.

Page numbers show you where to look back in the chapter for information, if you need it.

1. Mention some body changes that may occur when you are worried and fearful. (102, 103)
2. List three body changes that take place during sleep. (104)
3. Tell one reason why you need sleep. (105)
4. Mention two things that you have learned about dreams. (106)
5. Describe what is meant by physical fitness. (108)
6. Demonstrate one exercise that can help you keep physically fit. (109)
7. Explain what is meant by plaque. (114)
8. Tell how to remove plaque. (114)
9. Demonstrate how to brush your teeth. (115)
10. Tell what nutrients are and how they help your body. (118)
11. List four food groups in a suggested Food Guide and the servings needed daily from each group. (124, 125)
12. List the six main classes of nutrients. (122)
13. Explain the importance of breakfast. (126, 127)
14. Tell five things a doctor may do in a health checkup. (130-137)

[1]Behavioral objectives in the cognitive area are stated here directly to students themselves.

Review It

Teacher's Notes

"Review It" is a feature that occurs at the end of each chapter in this book and in the series. It gives the children a chance to think over what they have learned, to summarize, and to store away important ideas. Page references after each item make this review page a self-help one. However, group discussion can be a valuable addition.

Page numbers show you where to look back in the chapter for information, if you need it.

1. How do emotions affect how your body works? (102)

2. How do people act who have been deprived of sleep? (104)

3. What is the REM period? (106)

4. How do you know what kinds of dreams people have? (106)

5. What are the advantages in being physically fit? (108)

6. What are some sports that are likely to be carried into adult life? (109)

7. How are cavities formed in the teeth? (114)

8. What are the best kinds of toothbrush and toothpaste? (116)

9. What is the advantage in having a good posture? (131)

10. Why is it wise to have regular health checkups? (130)

Copy each numbered item from List A. After each item, write the letter and words from List B that best describe it. For example:

11. anemia h. disease in which there is a low red-blood-cell count

List A

11. anemia
12. calculus
13. dental caries
14. ophthalmoscope
15. nutrients
16. periodontal disease
17. REM
18. rickets
19. scurvy
20. vaccine

List B

a. nourishing substances in foods

b. tooth decay

c. a shot that builds antibodies

d. rapid eye movement

e. plaque that has hardened on teeth

f. disease due to vitamin C deficiency

g. disease due to vitamin D deficiency

h. disease in which there is a low red-blood-cell count

Health Test for Chapter Four

Teacher's Notes

After students have taken the test and their papers have been scored, the test items can serve as guides for a summary discussion. Volunteers can read aloud their rewording of the false statements and wording of the completion statements.

"What Do You Think?" is a special feature that offers pupils a chance to evaluate some of their newly acquired knowledge.

Copy each number on a piece of paper. After each number write the correct answer, *true* or *false.* Rewrite each false statement to make it true.

T 1. The way your body works depends partially on your emotions.

F 2. During sleep the heartbeat speeds up.

F 3. Lack of sleep makes you mentally alert.

T 4. The brain waves can be recorded on an electroencephalograph.

F 5. Only a few people dream at night.

T 6. Getting the exercise you need helps you become physically fit.

T 7. Dental floss helps remove plaque from between your teeth.

T 8. The best kind of toothbrush is one with soft bristles.

T 9. In periodontal disease the teeth can become loose.

F 10. Skipping breakfast is a good way to help a person lose weight.

Copy each sentence and fill in the missing word or words.

11. The six main classes of nutrients are minerals, proteins, water, carbohydrates, fats, and vitamins .

12. Four food groups in a suggested Food Guide are fruits and vegetables, bread and cereal, meat group, and the milk group.

13. The purpose of vaccines is to cause the body to make antibodies to protect it against diseases.

14. The sticky, colorless film that forms on teeth is plaque .

15. Look for a toothpaste with an accepted fluoride in it.

16. Actions that you can control are called voluntary actions.

17. Most dreams have you in them.

18. You can find nutrition information on a food label .

19. Early signs of some diseases may show in the retina of the eye.

20. A reflex is an automatic action in response to touch.

Number of Items	20
Number Right	_____
Score (Number Right x 5)	_____

What Do You Think?

What information from this chapter do you plan to use in your daily life?

SCHOOL & HOME

You have learned many things in this chapter that you can share at home.

What can you tell your family about sleep and dreams?

What can you tell about physical fitness? What can you and your family do to help keep physically fit?

What can you and your family do to be sure that you are removing all the plaque from your teeth?

What kind of toothbrush and toothpaste can you recommend to the family?

How can you and other family members try to get enough of the necessary nutrients each day?

Suppose you are asked to buy some cereal at the store for your family. What can help you choose one that is rich in nutrients?

5 First Aid and Safety

Why do you think everyone needs to know about first aid?

What are some first-aid procedures that you want to learn?

What do you think boys and girls your age need to know about safety?

Preview It

First aid is the first care given to an ill or injured person. In the case of serious accidents, proper first aid may help save a life. In such cases, the person giving first aid should continue until a doctor takes over.

When injuries are minor, first aid may be the only care needed.

Look quickly through the first part of the chapter on pages 152-157. What are six emergency situations mentioned in the titles? As you read, find out the correct first aid for these emergencies.

Now look at the last part of the chapter on pages 159-162. What questions on safety do you find? As you read, look for the answers to these questions. Also be ready to suggest other safety questions you want answered.

Begin the chapter now. Start by finding out what you know about first aid.

How Much Do You Know About Emergency Situations?

Teacher's Notes
Students might jot down their ideas of what to do in each of the emergencies listed. Discuss each emergency. Then have the students turn to check their ideas with those on the designated pages.
See page T33 for additional teaching suggestions.

An emergency is an unforeseen happening that calls for immediate action. Even though we try to avoid accidents involving emergencies, they do occur now and then. We need to know how to give prompt and correct first aid.

Here are some general guides to keep in mind in case of emergencies:

1. Try to keep calm.

2. Ask an adult for help if it is possible.

3. Send someone to call a doctor at once.

4. Keep the injured person comfortable and as calm as possible.

5. Reassure the injured person that help is coming.

Now check what you know about first aid. Read each emergency listed below. Think about what should be done. Then turn to the pages listed. Check to see if you knew exactly what to do.

What should you do if a person is choking? (152)

What should you do if someone's breathing has stopped? (153)

What should you do in case of fainting? (154)

What should you do in case of severe bleeding? (155)

What should you do if a child has swallowed or inhaled something poisonous? (156)

What should you do in case of a broken bone? (157)

151

What Should You Do If a Person Is Choking?

Choking occurs when some food or other object gets stuck in the throat. This usually happens in the voice box, or *larynx,* which is at the entrance to the windpipe.

Ordinarily the choking person coughs up the object. If the person gasps for breath, suggest deep, slow breathing.

If the object is not coughed up *at once,* try the following procedure:

1. Stand behind the choking person.
2. Grasp both arms around the victim's waist. One hand should grip the other wrist. Place the thumb side of your wrist against the victim's stomach. It should be below the ribs but above the navel.
3. Press upward, forcefully and quickly.
4. If the object is not expelled, try again and again quickly. If the object remains stuck in the victim, rush the victim to the nearest hospital emergency room.

This procedure is called the *Heimlich Maneuver.* It is named after Dr. Henry Heimlich. If done correctly, the procedure compresses the lungs and expels the object that caused the choking.

What Should You Do
If Someone's Breathing Has Stopped?

Teacher's Notes
You might have the students turn to page 164. This tells them how to make a Mouth-to-Mouth Rescue Breathing Mannequin. Volunteers might make a Breathing Mannequin to demonstrate Rescue Breathing.

There is only one way to save the life of a person whose breathing has stopped. It is to get air in and out of the victim's lungs. This can be done by using the *Mouth-to-Mouth Rescue Breathing procedures.* Study the four steps shown below carefully. What are they?

1. Use fingers to clear victim's mouth of foreign matter, if any.

2. Lift neck. Put folded coat or blanket under shoulders. Tilt head back as far as possible. Pull or push jaw into jutting-out position to keep air passage open.

3. Pinch nostrils shut. Take a deep breath and seal your mouth over victim's. Blow until you see the victim's chest rise. (For infant, blow in both nose and mouth.)

4. Remove your mouth and listen for outflow of air. For an adult, repeat steps three and four about twelve times a minute. For a child, twenty times. Continue until trained medical help arrives.

Teacher's Notes
Invite discussion on the causes of
fainting. Remind the students that
medical aid should be sought
immediately if the first-aid procedures
mentioned do not work for the victim.
It is also a good idea to suggest to the
victim to see a doctor after he or she
has recovered from fainting.

What Should You Do In Case of Fainting?

A person faints when the blood supply to the brain
is suddenly reduced. Some people feel faint in crowds
or in stuffy places. Some people faint upon hearing bad
news. Other people faint if they are very frightened.

If a person feels faint. . . .

Lower the head between the knees, if the person is
sitting. The blood will rush to the brain. How will that
help?

If the person is lying flat, put a coat or some other
object under the person's legs and feet. This will put
the head lower than the rest of the body. Then gravity
will pull the blood flow down to the brain. How will that
help?

*If the person has fainted and has temporarily lost con-
sciousness. . . .*

Keep the person lying flat on the back. Make certain
the head is lower than the feet.

Loosen any clothing that might prevent the person
from breathing easily. This could be a tight collar, a tie,
or a tight belt.

If the person does not regain consciousness within a
few minutes, a doctor should be called.

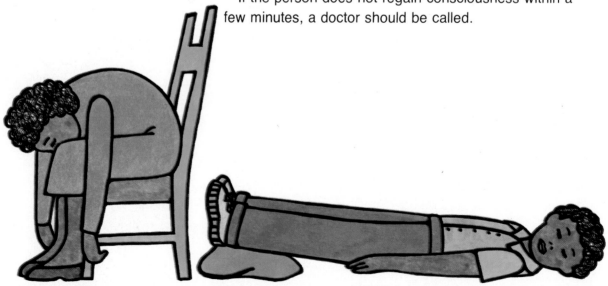

What Should You Do
In Case of Severe Bleeding?

Severe bleeding occurs when large blood vessels have been injured. The blood flows out of the vessels too quickly for the blood to thicken or *clot.*

To stop the bleeding, place a clean cloth or pad of material over the wound and press down. The pressure squeezes the blood vessels against the tissue, muscle, or bone. This decreases the amount of blood that can flow through the vessels.

If an arm or leg is bleeding, raise it slightly. Place it on a pillow or a piece of clothing. Raising the bleeding part allows gravity to help slow the bleeding. This is because the blood has to flow uphill.

Keep the pressure on the wound until the bleeding stops. Then wind strips of cloth tightly around the pad to hold it in place.

If you are alone with the victim, try to stop the bleeding at once. Do this before you call a doctor. Remember, time is very important!

If others are around, they can get a doctor while you apply pressure to the wound. Or they can help rush the person to a doctor or an emergency room of a hospital. Keep the pressure on the wound even as the person is rushed to the doctor or hospital.

Teacher's Notes

After the students have read this page, ask these questions:

"What causes severe bleeding?"

"Why does pressing down on the wound help to stop the bleeding?"

"What is a *sterile* bandage?" (Pupils may check *sterile* in the Glossary.)

"What is the purpose of raising an arm or leg that is bleeding freely?"

Glossary word: *sterile*

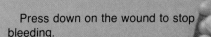

Press down on the wound to stop bleeding.

155

What Should You Do If a Child Has Swallowed or Inhaled Something Poisonous?

How can you tell if a child has swallowed or inhaled something that is poisonous? You cannot always know for sure.

Some household chemicals and drugs contain poisons that could harm a child, if they are swallowed or inhaled. Most household cleaners and pesticides have labels which indicate that they are poisonous.

Therefore, perhaps this is the best rule to follow: Regard all household products such as cleaning fluids, bleaches, and detergents as poisonous. Also remember that medicines can be poisonous if an overdose is swallowed.

If you suspect that a child has swallowed something that may be poisonous, get medical help immediately. Here is what to do:

1. Call your doctor, a hospital emergency room, or a poison-emergency center if there is one in your town. If you cannot find the telephone number quickly, call the operator and ask her to put the call through for you.

2. When the call goes through, tell exactly what the child has swallowed or inhaled, if you know.

3. Follow exactly the instructions that the doctor will give to you.

Some Things to Do

1. Check to see if there is a poison-emergency center in your city.

2. Work with a group to plan skits. Show what to do in case of fainting or taking something poisonous.

3. Look at various containers at home to see what warnings they have on them.

What Should You Do In Case of a Broken Bone?

Teacher's Notes
Invite discussion of how to prevent broken bones. For example, students can be aware of situations that cause falls—objects on stairs, failure to use the handrail, icy walks, stunts on bikes, and so on.

It may be clear to the victim that he or she has broken a bone. The victim may have heard the bone snap. The broken part may be out of shape. Or the victim may be unable to move the injured part.

Sometimes though, the injured person may be able to move the broken bone. This can be dangerous, because movement may make the damage worse.

If the bone has broken into two or more pieces, the jagged edges of the break may rub together. Or they may cut into the surrounding tissue.

If you suspect that a bone has been broken, *do not* try to move the victim. Keep him or her quiet. Put a coat or sweater around the person for warmth. Call a doctor. Or have someone else call the doctor. Then follow the doctor's instructions.

Usually this is all you should do. But if the break is an open fracture, the bone may have torn the skin. This kind of break may cause bleeding. Then you must stop the bleeding by applying pressure directly to the wound.

Sum It Up

How can you help a person who is choking?

What first aid would you give someone who feels faint?

What first aid would you give to a person who has stopped breathing?

How can you stop severe bleeding?

What first aid would you give to a child who has swallowed something poisonous?

What is correct first aid for a broken bone?

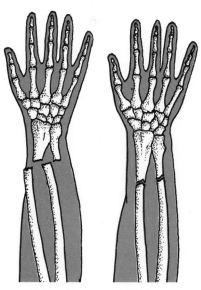

Open fracture   **Closed fracture**

157

TELL IT

These boys and girls have found the first-aid procedures for some minor injuries. What first-aid tips do they give you? You might look up the first-aid procedures for these minor injuries: *bruise* and *frostbite.*

Teacher's Notes
Small everyday bruises need no first-aid treatments.
For frostbite, press against the part with a warm hand. As soon as possible, put the frostbitten part in lukewarm water or a warm blanket.

Wash a *small cut or scratch* with soap and water. Wash away from the cut so you won't push germs into it. Then there will be less chance to get an infection. Cover the cut with a sterile bandage. The bandage will help keep out germs.

If you have a *nosebleed,* sit with your head straight. If you tip your head back, the blood will go into your throat. Pinch the ends of your nostrils together. This will squeeze the blood vessels, and give the blood a chance to clot. If the bleeding doesn't stop, get help from an adult.

Suppose you have a *blister* that has not broken. Cover it with a sterile bandage. The fluid in the blister will be reabsorbed into the body. If the blister breaks, treat it as a cut. This will avoid an infection.

If you have a *small burn* with no blisters, soak it in water. Add ice to the water. Soak the burn until there is no pain when you take it out of the water.

Lolita

Diana

Steve

William

How Can You Play Softball Safely?

Many accidents occur while playing softball. What are some safety guides that might prevent some of these accidents?

Compare your ideas with those on the next page.

Safety in Softball

As you read the following safety guides, consider the reasons for them. Also see if you can think of other safety guides to add.

Batters: Drop the bat or put it down. Do not throw it. Use a bat with tape on the handle. Be ready to move out of the way of a bad pitch.

Basemen: The baseline is for runners. Therefore, the basemen should play at or near their bases, *not* in the baselines.

Base runners: Base runners should run along the baseline. Unless you have been taught how to slide correctly, do not slide into a base.

Catchers: Be alert to all pitches and to the batter's swing. Wear proper protective equipment.

Outfielders: Call fly balls that are between fields. The first one to call "I have it" should take the ball. Keep your eyes on the ball. Be in position to catch it.

Question: What are six parts of the body that may be injured in softball?
Answer: Unscramble the words: hdea, ecnk, ram, egl, ooft, ngfeirs.

How Can You Keep Safe When You Swim?

Swimming is a popular sport. But it is also an activity in which accidents often occur among young people.

What can help keep swimmers safe?

Check your ideas with those on the next page.

Teacher's Notes

Discuss the safety guides for the various sports that the students enjoy. Volunteers might make safety posters. Students might also consider what their school does to help prevent accidents in the gym or on the playground.

See page T33 for additional teaching suggestions.

Safety When Swimming

Be ready to suggest a reason for each of the following safety guides. What other safety guides for swimming can you add?

Never swim alone. Have a buddy swimming with you. You watch your buddy. And your buddy watches you.

Swim only in protected areas. Obey the rules set by the lifeguard.

Do you swim in water which is too deep for your ability.

If you are swimming in a pool, know where the shallow water ends and the deep water begins.

Avoid swimming when you are tired, chilled, or overheated.

Avoid pushing, shoving, or other kinds of horseplay in the water. Never call for help as a joke.

Remember that it is never safe to hold a person's head under the water.

Dive only in deep water and in places intended for diving. It is unsafe to dive in shallow water. Other unsafe places are those where there may be rocks and where the depth of the water is unknown. Be sure a lifeguard is present.

Avoid using floating devices. They may cause you to float too far from shore. Or you may slip off the floating device into deep water.

Never run along the deck or edge of a pool. It is wet and slippery.

Sum It Up

How can you help prevent accidents when you play softball?

How can you help prevent accidents when you are swimming?

Books to Read

Look for some books in the school or public library about safety. Here are two that may interest you.

Frey, Shaney. *The Complete Beginner's Guide to Swimming* (Doubleday).

Gore, Harriet M., and Lindroth, D. *What to Do When There's No One But You* (Prentice-Hall).

162

SAFETY AROUND US

Your radio and television warn you of emergency weather conditions. For example, you may hear of a *tornado watch.* This means that a tornado may strike your area within several hours.

Or you may hear of a *tornado warning,* or *severe weather warning.* This means that a tornado is likely to strike your area immediately or within the hour.

In the event of a tornado warning, go to a safe place. If possible, get next to a strong wall or stay in the inner part of a hallway. Find a place where flying glass or other objects can't hit you. Try a closet, the basement, or a room without windows.

If you are outside and can't get indoors, seek shelter. Find a low place such as a ditch. Lie down. Cover your face with some sort of clothing. This will protect your nose and eyes from dust and dirt. Why is this important?

Teacher's Notes

This page helps alert the students to the important warnings and instructions that may be given on the radio or TV. "Safety Around Us" is a recurring feature in this health series. It focuses on one of the safety problems presented in each of the safety chapters.

See page T33 for additional teaching suggestions.

Things to Do

1. Falls are a leading cause of accidents. Look at the posters below. What do they suggest about some causes of falls?

Write three safety guides to help prevent falls.

Also make your own safety poster. What will your message be?

2. Write a paragraph about a sports accident you have seen or heard about. Tell how the accident may have been prevented.

3. You might make a Mouth-to-Mouth Rescue Breathing Dummy. Follow these steps:

Step 1. Take an empty, thoroughly washed, plastic, water bottle. Sketch in the face on the bottle and cut out a hole for the mouth.

Step 2. Use rubber bands to attach a small, lightweight, plastic bag to the neck of the bottle.

Step 3. Tape a paperback book to the top of the bag. When the bag fills with air, the book will press down on it and force the air out. Thus the action of the lungs is imitated.

Use this dummy to practice Mouth-to-Mouth Breathing as shown on page 153.

4. Make a safety word puzzle similar to the one Cindy made. Use the letters of your first name as starters. Pick a topic such as a sport, a safety procedure, or a fall.

Traffic Safety

C	Cross streets at the corner.
I	If it's night, wear something light.
N	Never cross streets from between parked cars.
D	Do use a crosswalk if there is one.
Y	You should look both ways and around the corner before crossing a street.

5. Look at the posters below. What do they suggest about causes for some pedestrian accidents?

Write three useful pedestrian safety guides.

Special Research

Investigate and make a report on the *Emergency Broadcasting System.* This is a warning system that Civil Defense authorities have set up in case a nuclear attack should occur.

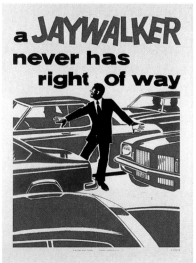

Can You Show What You Know?[1]

Teacher's Notes
Here behavioral objectives in the *cognitive* area are posed in childlike language directly to the students themselves. In turn, boys and girls give evidence by *observable behavior* of what they have learned.
Other hoped-for objectives lie chiefly in the less easily observed *affective* area—objectives that pertain to feelings, attitudes, and values. Some of them are:
Initiates discussions at home about what to do in emergencies.
Is aware of some of the causes of accidents that require first aid.
Observes safety precautions in sports.

Page numbers show you where to look back in the chapter for information, if you need it.

1. Explain what is meant by *first aid*. (150)
2. Demonstrate the Heimlich Maneuver. (152)
3. Describe four main steps to follow in Mouth-to-Mouth Rescue Breathing. (153)
4. Describe the first aid to give to a person who has fainted. (154)
5. Tell how to help someone who feels faint. (154)
6. Demonstrate how to apply first aid for severe bleeding. (155)
7. Explain what to do if a child has swallowed poison. (156)
8. Tell how to give first aid to a person who may have broken a bone. (157)
9. Tell what first aid to give for a small cut or scratch. (158)
10. Demonstrate the correct first aid for a nosebleed. (158)
11. List four safety guides for softball players. (160)
12. List four safety guides for swimmers. (162)
13. Tell what to do in case of a tornado warning. (163)

[1]Behavioral objectives in the cognitive area are stated here directly to students themselves.

Review It

Teacher's Notes
"Review It" is a feature that occurs at the end of each chapter in this book and in the series. It gives children a chance to think over what they have learned, to summarize, and to store away important ideas. Page references after each item make this review page a self-help one. However, group discussion can be a valuable addition.

Page numbers show you where to look back in the chapter for information, if you need it.

1. What may cause a person to feel faint? (154)

2. How does it help a person who feels faint to put the head between the knees? (154)

3. What is the first thing to do in case a child has swallowed something poisonous? (156)

4. What causes choking? (152)

5. What causes severe bleeding from a wound? (155)

6. Why should you press down on a wound that is severely bleeding? (155)

7. Why do you press forcefully into the victim's stomach in the Heimlich Maneuver? (152)

8. What are some signs of a broken bone? (157)

9. Why should a person with a broken bone be kept quiet? (157)

10. How would you describe an open fracture? (157)

11. What is the purpose of Mouth-to-Mouth Rescue Breathing? (153)

12. How do you know if the Mouth-to-Mouth Rescue Breathing is getting air into the victim's lungs? (153)

13. What first aid should you give for a blister that has not broken? (158)

14. What first aid should you give for a blister that breaks? (158)

15. What first aid should you give for a mild burn with no blisters? (158)

16. What are some safety guides for a batter in softball? (160)

17. What is one important safety guide for outfielders in softball? (160)

18. What are some safe places for diving? (162)

19. What is the difference between a tornado watch and a tornado warning? (163)

20. What is one thing you can do to prevent falls? (164)

21. What are some things you can do to be a safe pedestrian? (165)

Safety Test for Chapter Five

Teacher's Notes
After students have taken the test and their papers have been scored, the test items can serve as guides for a summary discussion. Volunteers can read aloud their wording of the completion statements.
"What Do You Think?" is a special feature that offers pupils a chance to evaluate some of their newly acquired knowledge.

Copy each sentence and fill in the missing word or words.

1. If the blood supply to the brain is suddenly reduced, a person feels _faint_.

2. A person who has fainted should be kept _lying_ down with the head _lowered_.

3. If a child has swallowed something poisonous, get _help_ immediately.

4. To stop severe bleeding, _press down_ on the wound.

5. If an arm or leg is bleeding severely, _raise_ it slightly.

6. If someone's breathing has stopped, use _Mouth_-to-_Mouth_ Rescue Breathing.

7. For a small cut, use _soap_ and _water_ to clean it.

8. In case of a small burn with no blister, _soak_ the injured part in _cold water_.

9. For a nosebleed, _pinch_ the _nostrils_ together.

10. A softball batter shouldn't _throw_ the bat.

11. Always swim with a _buddy_.

12. Swim where there is a _lifeguard_.

13. Dive only in _deep_ water.

14. An outfielder in softball should yell _I have it_ when catching fly balls.

15. Never hold a person's _head_ under water when you go swimming.

16. The radio and TV will give a tornado _warning_ if a tornado is likely to strike at once or within an hour.

17. When you get a tornado warning, look for a _safe_ place.

18. If you are in the open and a tornado approaches, _lie_ down.

19. Avoid _running_ along the edge of a swimming pool.

20. If you suspect a person has broken a bone, do not try to _move_ the person.

Number of Answers	20
Number Right	_____
Score (Number Right x 5)	_____

What Do You Think?

What did you learn in this chapter that you think you will use in your daily life? Write your ideas on a piece of paper.

SCHOOL & HOME

There is plenty of information in this chapter that may help you at home. What did you learn that can help you in emergencies?

Suppose someone at home needs first aid. What kinds of first aid do you now know how to give?

You might also work with family members to "fall proof" your home. Look around for hazards that might cause falls. Here are some suggestions.

Are objects kept off the stairs?

Are scatter rugs firmly fastened down?

Are spilled liquids promptly wiped up?

Is soap picked up if it falls on the bathroom floor, bathtub, or shower?

Are electric cords placed where people will not trip over them? What else might you look for?

Teacher's Notes
Special efforts are made in this book and in this series to foster school-home communication. This page is an example of how students are encouraged to share with the family the safety ideas they are acquiring at school.

6 Drugs and You

What do you think is meant by the term *drugs?*
What are some things you think you and others
ought to know about drugs?

Warning: The Surgeon General Has Determined
That Cigarette Smoking Is Dangerous to Your Health.

Preview It

Before you start this chapter, you should have in mind what is meant by the term *drug.* A drug is any prepared substance that if taken into the body causes changes. The changes may affect the way the brain works. Or they may affect the way other parts of the body work. The changes may also affect a person's emotions.

As you know, medicines are one kind of drug. Medicines can help treat an illness. They can prevent an illness as is the case with vaccines. Medicines can also help relieve pain. But medicines can be misused too. You will learn how in this chapter.

Alcohol, tobacco, and marijuana are among the substances people may use to change how they feel. In each of these substances there is a drug.

You may be surprised to know that things like solvents and various sprays are sometimes considered along with drugs. They are not intended to be breathed. But when they are inhaled, they may cause changes in the body.

Now look through the chapter quickly. What are the four questions asked in the main titles? Look for information in the chapter that will help you answer these questions.

What Should You Know About Drug Safety?

One Saturday Marta was looking at television. In the middle of the program, there was a commercial.

A woman told about some cold tablets. She said, "Stop those cold miseries. Don't suffer with a sore throat and stopped-up nose. Try Bell's Cold Tablets."

"I'm going to ask Mother to get some of those when she goes shopping today," thought Marta. "I think I'm getting a cold. My throat's a little sore."

What do you think of Marta's plan to try the tablets? What are some things about drugs and drug safety that she might consider first?

Teacher's Notes
Suggest that students read this page and the next one for basic information about drugs and drug safety. Then ask: "What are medicines?"
"Why is it a good idea not to take medicine for every minor ache and pain?"
"What is meant by the 'risk factor' in taking any drug?"
"What are side effects of a drug?"
Students should be aware that drugs can be dangerous even under a doctor's supervision. Many people are in hospitals because of unexpected reactions to drugs.

Marta has been persuaded by a TV commercial to try medicine she may not really need. This often happens.

However, as people learn more about drugs, they are less likely to take a pill for every minor ailment.

Drugs can change the way the body works. And medicines are a kind of drug that can help prevent or treat an illness or deaden pain. Anything powerful enough to cause changes in the body should be used cautiously. In fact, it is a good idea not to take any medicine for minor aches and pains. Everyone can learn to take a little discomfort. The body soon heals itself. And no chances are taken with safety.

Individual Differences in Reactions to Drugs

There is something about drugs that everyone should know. Each person reacts differently to them. So nobody knows for sure how a drug will affect him or her. Even doctors cannot be sure how a drug may affect a person. There is a risk in taking any drug. Every drug has the potential to cause some unwanted effects in some people. These unwanted effects are *side effects.*

Side Effects

Side effects from a drug can be mild. They may include a mild headache, a slight rash, some drowsiness, or slight nausea.

Or the side effects may be more severe. They may last longer too. They may include prolonged vomiting, bleeding, blurred vision, impaired hearing, a feeling of weakness, or even death.

Dangerous side effects may occur if two different medicines are mixed. Never take two or more kinds of medicine unless your doctor has been consulted.

Books to Read

Look for books on drugs at the school and public libraries. Here are two books you might find:

Christian, Samuel, and Gorodetzky, Charles. *What You Should Know About Drugs* (Harcourt).

Madison, Arnold. *Drugs and You* (Messner).

Teacher's Notes
Ask:
"What is an OTC drug? Why do people take OTC drugs?"
"Why is it important to read the labels on drug containers?"
Students can read pages 176–177 for more information about labels on medicines. See page T35 for additional teaching information.

Over-the-Counter Drugs

Over-the-counter drugs, or OTC drugs, can be bought without a doctor's prescription. OTC drugs are sold at drugstores, in food stores, and in other places. Some people take OTC drugs for such problems as minor headaches, indigestion, small aches, and pains.

Prescription Drugs

Prescription drugs, or Rx drugs, can be prescribed only by a doctor. They can be sold only by a registered pharmacist. These drugs are generally more powerful than OTC drugs. They are also more likely to cause side effects.

The Importance of Labels

It is most important to read carefully the labels on both Rx and OTC drugs. Read the information given on the next two pages. What important information is given on an over-the-counter drug? What important information is given on a prescription drug?

What have you learned about OTC drugs?

175

Drug Labels and You[1]   Labels on medicines tell you how to use them correctly. Labels on OTC drugs are especially important. The labels are your main source of information about correct use.

Labels On Over-the-Counter Medicines

Information on OTC drug labels includes
Name of the product
Net quantity of contents
Active ingredients
Name and place of business of the manufacturer, distributor, or packer.

Directions for use of the product
1) An indication of the symptoms to be treated
2) Individual dose
3) How frequently medicine can be taken
4) Total dose that can be taken in a day
5) Limit on length of treatment (or number of days the medicine can be taken).

Warnings
Many OTC medicines should not be taken by people with certain health problems. Here is an example: "CAUTION—Should not be taken by persons with high blood pressure, heart disease, diabetes, or thyroid disease unless directed by a doctor."

Always read a warning carefully. A drug that is safe for many others may be dangerous for you.

Side effects
Labels on OTC medicines tell you about some side effects that may occur.

If an OTC drug has ill side effects, stop taking it at once.

If an OTC medicine does not relieve symptoms promptly, stop taking it. You may have an illness that should be treated by a doctor. Make an appointment with a doctor.

From "We Want You to Know About Labels on Medicines," Public Health Service, Food and Drug Administration DHEW Publication No. (FDA) 73-3028.

The law requires that important information be given on labels.
But the information offers no help unless you read and use it.
Always read the labels. And always follow the directions exactly.

Labels On Prescription Drugs

Prescription drugs also have labels. The labels are written on the containers by the pharmacist. The pharmacist writes the instructions as directed by your doctor.

Information on prescription drug labels includes

Doctor's name
Pharmacy name
Patient's name
Directions for use.

Directions for use of the product

Instructions on the label tell you how much medicine to take and how often.

Unlike an OTC label, the label on a prescription drug does not usually tell you what the drug will do for you. The label does not tell about side effects. It does not warn about special precautions to take. This information must come from your doctor. It is important that you understand the doctor's instructions. It is important that you follow them exactly.

Some things to remember about prescription drugs

Every time you take the medicine, read the label. Be sure you are taking the medicine correctly.

Never take a medicine that was prescribed for someone else. And never let someone else take a medicine that was prescribed just for you.

Remember, prescription drugs are powerful. They can be dangerous if not used properly.

If a prescription drug causes side effects, call your doctor.

Teacher's Notes
Use the question in the heading to start preliminary discussion. Then ask:
"If someone has had no ill effects from a drug, should someone else assume the drug to be safe for him or her?"
"What have you learned about the hazards of mixing drugs?"
(*Note:* In the marginal activity the directions on the container have been carelessly obscured. This is a prescription drug. So a pharmacist can be called to check the correct directions.)
See page T35 for additional teaching suggestions.

What Are Some Drugs That May Be Misused?

Any drug can be misused. It is misused if it is taken when no drug is really needed. It is misused if it is not taken exactly according to directions.

But when you hear about drugs being misused, people often mean certain kinds of drugs. And they mean that these drugs are being used in disapproved, unsupervised ways.

Why do people sometimes use certain drugs in disapproved, unsupervised ways? The reasons are many. Some people may experiment with drugs because their friends are doing it. Some people misuse drugs because they say the drugs give them pleasure. Some misuse drugs as a way of escaping problems.

You now know enough about drugs to understand possible dangers in drug misuse. Some people can experiment with a drug and have no bad effects. But others may get dangerous side effects from the same drug. There is a risk in taking any drug. No one knows for sure how it will affect him or her.

Also, people who do not know much about drugs may mix the drugs they take. Mixing of some drugs can be dangerous. For example, people have died after mixing alcohol with sleeping pills.

The following pages describe some of the drugs that are sometimes misused. These drugs may be used in ways they were not meant to be used. Sometimes these drugs may be bought or sold illegally.

What Is Wrong Here?

What has happened to this prescription drug? What do you think should be done about it?

Stimulants

Stimulants are drugs that increase the activity of the brain or other parts of the nervous system. Some stimulants are very weak. For example, coffee has the drug *caffeine* in it. There are small amounts of caffeine in tea, cocoa, and some colas. Caffeine is a very mild stimulant. So for most people there is little harm in moderate amounts of these drinks.

Some stimulant drugs, though, can be very harmful if misused. These are the *amphetamines*. Amphetamines should be taken only under a doctor's supervision. Doctors may use these drugs to treat some disorders of the nervous system. They may prescribe them to help some people lose weight. But the doctors watch their patients closely.

Improper use of amphetamines may cause nervousness, sleeplessness, and stomach upset. In large doses, amphetamines may make a person confused and anxious. These drugs may affect vision too. Truck drivers who use amphetamines to stay awake on long trips may have accidents. Why might this be so?

People who misuse amphetamines by taking large doses for a long period of time may become mentally unbalanced.

Depressants or Sedatives

Depressants or *sedatives* are drugs that can be useful in calming the nerves. In certain doses they can encourage sleep. Some common depressants are the *barbiturate* drugs. Any depressant should be prescribed by a doctor.

Teacher's Notes

After studying this page, ask these questions:

"What are stimulant drugs? Why may doctors prescribe them?"

"Which stimulant drugs can be very harmful if misused? Why?"

"What are some slang terms for amphetamines?"

"How do you think people get amphetamines without a doctor's prescription?" (Sometimes they get them from acquaintances. They may or may not be "pushers" or sellers of drugs. These drugs may be obtained in illegal ways and people who sell them are subject to legal penalties if they are caught.)

Glossary words: *amphetamine, barbiturate, depressant, stimulant*

Do You Know?

Some common amphetamines are Benzedrine and Dexedrine. These are some slang terms for stimulant drugs:

Uppers
Pep pills
Bennies (short for Benzedrine)

179

Doctors may use barbiturates to encourage sleep. But the drugs should be used only for a few days. Misusers of barbiturates tend to take them more often or in much higher doses than a doctor would prescribe. With some people this can result in a craving for the drugs. Then people may need them in higher doses for the effects to be felt. If such people are withdrawn suddenly from the drugs, they become violently ill. These people should be withdrawn from the barbiturates in a hospital.

Minor Tranquilizers

Minor tranquilizers are a mild form of depressants. Minor tranquilizers may be prescribed by doctors to relieve nervousness or to help people who often feel under stress. These drugs should be used exactly as the doctor directs.

Hallucinogens

Hallucinogens are drugs that produce changes in the way people sense things. Thus a whisper may sound like a shout. A table may feel as if it had a coat of fur. Colors may seem more vivid. The sense of time may be lost.

LSD is a strong hallucinogen. Experimenting with LSD can be dangerous. A user may get feelings of great panic. This is known as "a bad trip." A person never knows when a bad trip will result from taking LSD. Different people react differently to the drug. A person who uses it with no ill effects one time may have a bad trip another time.

In some cases LSD users become mentally ill. Treatment in a mental hospital is sometimes necessary.

LSD can be used legally only by research scientists. Any other use is against the law.

Do You Know?

Most barbiturates are in the form of colored pills or capsules. Here are some slang names for them:

Downers
Reds
Yellow jackets
Goofballs

180

Marijuana, often called *pot,* is a mild hallucinogen. It is usually smoked in marijuana cigarettes. These are sometimes called "joints" or "reefers."

The drug marijuana causes changes in the body. These changes differ from person to person. Some users feel relaxed, calm, and happy. Others may feel worried or confused. Some may become loud or talkative. Some laugh and giggle a lot. Vision may be affected, making it difficult to judge distances accurately.

Much more research is needed and is being done on the long-time physical effects of marijuana. Meanwhile remember that the use of marijuana is still illegal in many states.

Narcotics

Narcotics is a legal term that covers a variety of drugs that lawmakers think are especially dangerous. Some narcotics have medical use. They are given as pain killers and are prescribed and supervised by doctors. The risk comes when narcotics are taken without medical supervision. All narcotics must be used with great care.

Morphine and *codeine* are narcotics prescribed by doctors to produce sleep and relieve pain after operations and in serious illnesses. *Heroin* is not used medically in this country. All these drugs are made from *opium,* a substance made by a certain kind of poppy.

A danger in narcotics use is that a person can become "hooked" on them. This means he or she must have increasing amounts to feel well. When the person cannot get enough of the drug, *violent* illness may occur.

Teacher's Notes
You might mention that there is still controversy and scientific uncertainty about the effects of marijuana. Marijuana comes from the hemp plant. It is usually smoked in cigarettes. Some nicknames for marijuana are grass, pot, joints, and Maryjane. (*Note:* A person who is "hooked" on a narcotic is said to be dependent on the drug.)
Glossary words: *marijuana, narcotic*

Something to Do

Try to find out what the marijuana laws are in your state. Look for this information in the library or call a law office.

Teacher's Notes

It is safe to use products such as solvents and sprays if they are used as directed in the instructions. Usually solvents and sprays should be used in well-ventilated places. In such places, not enough vapors will be breathed to be dangerous.

(*Note:* "Sum It Up" is a feature that occurs at intervals throughout each chapter of this book and others in the health series. Pupils can use this study aid to review important ideas learned in the preceding pages.)

Glossary word: *solvent*

Solvents and Various Sprays

Solvents include such things as lighter fluid, cleaning fluid, gasoline, paint thinner, and airplane glue. *Sprays* include such things as hair sprays, pesticides, deodorants, and oven cleaners.

Solvents and most sprays are not intended to be breathed deeply into the body. But people who misuse these substances do this. Then changes occur in the body just as they do when drugs are taken.

Deliberate inhaling of vapors from solvents and sprays may have an intoxicating effect. This "lift" does not last long. Soon other effects may occur. A person may feel giddy or dizzy. He or she may have trouble speaking clearly. Vomiting may start. A person may become drowsy. He or she could "pass out."

Harmful effects from inhaling solvents or sprays include damage to the nose, throat, and lungs. Constant sniffing can damage the brain or other organs.

Sum It Up

What are drugs? Why is there a risk in taking them?

What is the difference between OTC drugs and Rx drugs?

How can labels on drugs help protect a user?

How can drugs be misused? Why may people misuse drugs?

What have you learned about stimulants? Depressants? LSD? Marijuana? Narcotics?

How may solvents and various sprays be misused?

What can be the harm in such misuse?

What Should You Know About Alcohol?

Stan is going to give a report on alcohol. But first he has made a quiz about it. He wants to see how much his classmates already know.

You can see Stan's quiz in the picture here.

How would you answer each of the questions?

Now turn to pages 184 and 185. Compare your answers with the information there.

HOW MUCH DO YOU KNOW ABOUT ALCOHOL?

1. Is alcohol a stimulant or depressant drug?

2. What is an example of an alcohol problem?

3. What is an alcoholic?

4. What are the dangers of experimenting with alcohol?

? ? ? ? ? ? ? ? ? ? ? ? ? ? ? ? ?

Alcohol Is a Depressant

Alcohol is a depressant or sedative drug. It is the drug in such drinks as whiskey, gin, rum, and vodka. Beer and wine have alcohol in them too. But there is less of it.

Alcohol causes changes in people who drink it. Alcohol affects the way people's minds and bodies work. It affects emotions as well.

One thing alcohol does is to slow down the activity of the brain. This slows other parts of the body also.

Alcohol can cause a person to think less clearly than usual. It may make a person less skillful in use of the muscles. The more alcohol a person drinks, the more noticeable these effects will be.

Individual Differences

Different people react differently to alcohol. And alcohol may affect the same person in different ways at different times.

After drinking too much alcohol, some people may become loud. Some may become quarrelsome.

Some people take alcoholic drinks only now and then. They may drink wine on ceremonial occasions, for example. Or they may use alcoholic drinks for refreshments once in a while.

Other people may use alcohol more often or more heavily. They may or may not be able to control their use of it. Some of these people may have "alcohol problems." They may drink too much and get sick. They may get into fights or get involved in accidents. Sometimes they get very sleepy, or even "pass out." They may even become violent or harm others.

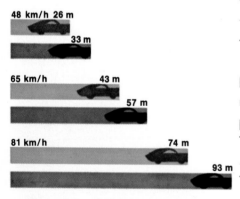

48 km/h 26 m

33 m

65 km/h 43 m

57 m

81 km/h 74 m

93 m

Green bars show normal stopping distances for passenger cars when the driver has had no alcohol. Purple bars show some likely stopping distances for a driver who has had a small amount of alcohol. What has happened to this driver's reaction time? How might this slowing of reaction time cause an accident?

Alcoholics

Still other people go beyond alcohol problems. These people are intoxicated often enough to prevent them from leading normal lives. Family problems may result. Jobs may be lost.

Heavy drinkers who cannot control their use of alcohol are *alcoholics*. Alcoholics are troubled people who need help. The help can be given by a doctor. Or it can be given by others who understand the problem.

An organization known as Alcoholics Anonymous, or A.A., has helped many alcoholics stop drinking. In A.A., those who have overcome alcoholism work with people trying to control this illness. A.A. members encourage the strugglers to live useful, satisfying lives *without any use of alcohol.*

There are special branches of A.A. to help family members of an alcoholic. The branch for wives, relatives, and friends is called Al-Anon. The one for sons and daughters, ages twelve to eighteen, is Alateen. The one for sons and daughters who are under twelve is Alatots.

Alcohol and Young People

Young people who experiment with alcohol may become intoxicated. This can happen after drinking very little. Alcohol acts in relation to weight of the user. And most boys and girls are lighter than adults.

There is a very special danger for young people in experimenting with alcohol. They may foolishly have drinking contests. They may not know that too much alcohol at one time can be a poison. Death can result.

Teacher's Notes

Remind the students that an alcoholic is dependent on increasing amounts of alcohol. If an alcoholic should stop drinking suddenly, he or she will suffer from withdrawal symptoms.
Why do people become alcoholics? There is no single answer for all people. Most alcoholics have trouble solving problems. They can escape reality through alcohol. Alcoholics need the skilled help of doctors and other groups who understand that alcoholism is a serious problem.

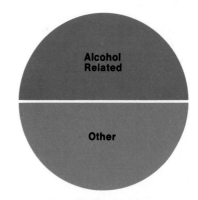

Fatal Traffic Accidents

Something to Discuss

About half of all the people killed in traffic accidents each year die because they or others were driving when drunk.

What do you think about this safety guide: "Never drive an automobile after drinking alcohol"?

185

Teacher's Notes
After study of this page, ask:
"What is the drug in tobacco and tobacco smoke?"
"How does nicotine affect the body?"
"What have you learned about carbon monoxide and its effects on the body?"
"What are tars? Why can they be harmful?"
Glossary words: *nicotine, carbon monoxide*
See page T35 for additional teaching suggestions.

What Is Harmful About Smoking?

What evidences are there in the world around you that smoking can be harmful?

You might compare your ideas with the ones shown on the next few pages. Then read on to find out more about *why* smoking is harmful.

When a Cigarette Is Puffed

When a cigarette is puffed, smoke is formed. In this smoke is a mixture of gases, vapors, and chemicals.

As the tobacco in the cigarette and the paper around it burn, *carbon monoxide* is formed. Carbon monoxide is a harmful gas. It is the same harmful gas found in car fumes. Car fumes can suffocate people in poorly ventilated places.

In the smoker's body, the carbon monoxide replaces some of the oxygen in the blood. This reduces a person's oxygen supply. The tired feeling some smokers have can be traced to this carbon monoxide.

Also in the cigarette smoke is the drug *nicotine.* It speeds up the heartbeat. Some smokers feel more alert for a while after smoking. Some say they feel relaxed. The nicotine leads many smokers to form the habit of smoking. The habit may become so strong that it is very difficult to break. Perhaps you know someone who is trying to stop smoking. Sometimes people go to Stop Smoking clinics.

Tars are also in the cigarette smoke. Tar is a yellow or brown substance containing hundreds of chemicals. Some of them can cause cancer.

When a smoker inhales, some smoke, with all the harmful things in it, goes into the lungs.

Do You Know?

Some people smoke because they say it gives them a "lift." They think it is pleasurable. But many other people do not start to smoke. And many have given up cigarette smoking. They have decided that some pleasures such as smoking cost too much in the long run. For cigarette smoking can cause lung cancer and other serious health problems.

Lung Cancer

A great danger in cigarette smoking is that it can cause lung cancer. The smoke from cigarettes may injure or destroy lung cells. If the damage continues over a period of time, the cells may become cancerous. Cancer cells multiply in an uncontrolled way. Eventually they prevent the lungs from working properly. By the time symptoms are noticed, it may be too late to save a person's life.

Pipe and cigar smoking do not contribute greatly to lung cancer. But they do increase the risk of cancer of the lip, tongue, and larynx.

Emphysema

Cigarette smoking can be a factor in causing *emphysema.* In emphysema the air sacs in the lungs are destroyed. They may even break. Stale air is trapped in the lungs. Proper amounts of fresh air, with oxygen, cannot get in. Breathing becomes very difficult. The heart must work harder to pump the blood through damaged lungs.

Heart Disease

Cigarette smoking overworks the heart by making it beat too rapidly. Smoking makes the arteries contract, or become narrower. Then the heart has to work harder to push blood through them. Cigarette smokers are more apt to have heart problems than nonsmokers.

Sum It Up

What changes in the body does alcohol produce?

In what ways can drinking too much alcohol affect various people?

How may alcoholics be helped if they want help?

What is harmful in cigarette smoke?

Why is cigarette smoking dangerous to health?

Teacher's Notes

Remind the students that the sale of cigarettes and alcohol to minors is illegal.

Also explain to students that the nicotine in cigarettes is a drug. Cigarette smokers become dependent on this drug. They need more and more cigarettes to get the same effect. People can suffer great discomfort if they stop smoking suddenly.

NO SMOKING

FAVOR DE NO FUMAR

DEFENSE DE FUMER

Something to Discuss

Do you know that smoking can be unpleasant for people nearby? Smoking can also harm the health of nearby nonsmokers. Smoke can cause people to cough or sneeze. It can irritate the eyes. It can cause difficulty in breathing for some people with allergies. Smoke pollutes the air too. What is being done to curb smoking in public places?

TELL IT

You can find evidence that smoking is harmful on every pack of cigarettes. By law, a special notice has to be on every pack. It says *Warning: The Surgeon General Has Determined That Cigarette Smoking Is Dangerous to Your Health.*

Cigarette makers are not allowed to advertise cigarettes on television or radio. There used to be cigarette commericals on TV and radio. But now there are none.

Rachel

I read a pamphlet called *Second-Hand Smoke.* It said that at least 34 million people in this country are sensitive to cigarette smoke. It also said people should not have to breathe in second-hand smoke.

Lynn

Smoke from other people's cigarettes makes the heart beat faster. It raises the blood pressure. And it increases the carbon monoxide in the blood. This cuts down on the usual supply of oxygen in the blood.

Lewis

HEALTH AROUND US

Perhaps you wonder how scientists study the effects of harmful substances in cigarette smoke. Sometimes they use the "smoking machine." You can see a picture of a smoking machine below.

The smoking machine puffs away on cigarettes just as people may do. But the machine also traps the tars from the cigarette smoke. The tars are used in research work. At times the tars have been painted on the backs of mice in laboratories. The tars have been shown to produce cancers in the mice.

Teacher's Notes
"Health Around Us" is a recurring feature in this book and in this health series. As an adjunct to the smoking-machine demonstration, you or some other adults might do the "handkerchief demonstration." An adult inhales several puffs from a lighted cigarette. Then the adult exhales through a clean handkerchief which is held close to the mouth. There will be a little stain on the handkerchief. All the tars stayed behind in the lungs. Then the adult puffs on a cigarette, but tries to keep the smoke in the mouth. Exhale into the handkerchief and you will see a much darker stain.
Glossary words: *emphysema, cancer*

A Smoking Demonstration

The American Cancer Society lends a set of "smoking lungs" for a demonstration. The small air spaces in these plastic lungs resemble small air sacs in the human lungs. Study the picture below and the one on the next page. What does the demonstration show?

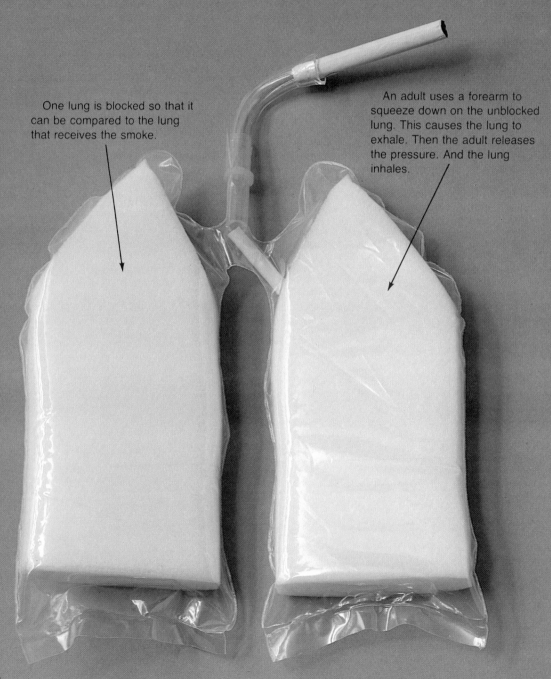

One lung is blocked so that it can be compared to the lung that receives the smoke.

An adult uses a forearm to squeeze down on the unblocked lung. This causes the lung to exhale. Then the adult releases the pressure. And the lung inhales.

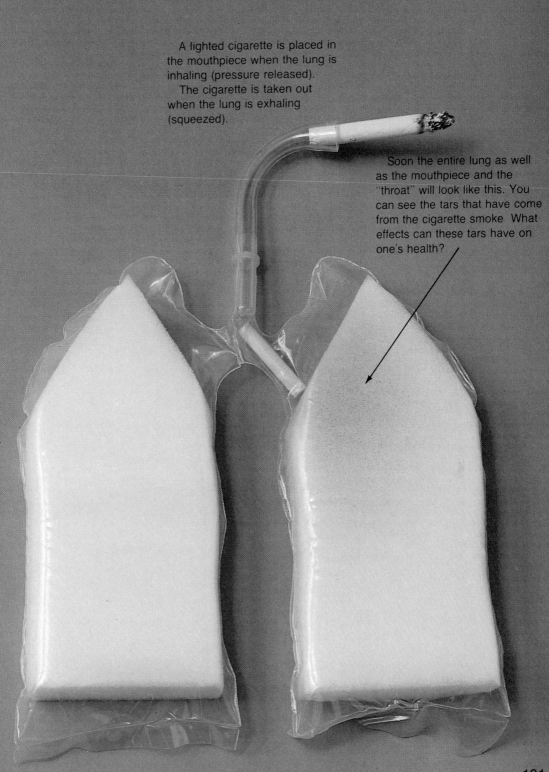

A lighted cigarette is placed in the mouthpiece when the lung is inhaling (pressure released).
The cigarette is taken out when the lung is exhaling (squeezed).

Soon the entire lung as well as the mouthpiece and the "throat" will look like this. You can see the tars that have come from the cigarette smoke What effects can these tars have on one's health?

Things to Do

Teacher's Notes
Students may ask if filter-tip cigarettes prevent tars and nicotine from reaching the smokers' lungs. Filters trap some tars and nicotine, but not all.
See page T35 for additional teaching suggestions.

1. Cigarette makers can no longer advertise on radio or TV. But they still can advertise in newspapers and magazines. Look for some of these advertisements. See what reasons are suggested for smoking a certain brand of cigarettes. Notice also what important health information is not mentioned in the ads. Keep in mind, too, that cigarette filters cannot trap *all* the tars and nicotine.

Look at the cigarette ad at the right. What means are used to persuade people to use that brand?

2. Make a bulletin-board display of cigarette ads from newspapers and magazines. Take time now and then to talk over the sales points given. What do you think of them? What warning must appear with every ad?

LOOK for Long Bills

Good taste...

More puffs...

Low tar...

More puff...

Low nicotine...

More puffs...

Love from the first puff

LONG BILLS

LONG BILLS MENTHOL

Warning: The Surgeon General Has Determined That Cigarette Smoking Is Dangerous to Your Health

3. Now look for some advertisements about alcohol in newspapers and magazines. Bring the ads to class.

Study each ad carefully. Be ready to tell how readers are being persuaded to buy a given brand of whiskey or gin or some other kind of alcohol. What information about alcohol is not given?

4. Discuss this statement with your classmates: "Many young people just don't know what they are getting into when they experiment with drugs."

5. Bring in clippings from the newspaper about accidents. Make a special note of the accidents that are the result of the use of alcohol by car drivers or pedestrians.

6. Have one member of your group write to the American Cancer Society (219 East 42nd Street, New York, New York 10017) to ask for free materials about the effects of smoking on health. Later post the material on your bulletin board. Or put it on the library table.

7. Investigate the cost of smoking cigarettes. Find out what one pack of a given brand costs. Suppose a person smokes a pack a day. How much money will he or she spend in a week? Year?

Special Research

1. Investigate the drug *cocaine.* This is a stimulant drug that is sometimes misused. You might look for information in the book *Drugs and You* by Arnold Madison (Messner).

2. Investigate and make a report on the topic "How Did Smoking Start?" A book that can help you is *Smoking and You* by Arnold Madison (Messner).

Can You Show What You Know?[1]

Teacher's Notes
Here behavioral objectives in the *cognitive* area are posed in childlike language directly to the students themselves. In turn, boys and girls give evidence by *observable behavior* of what they have learned.
Other hoped-for behavioral objectives lie chiefly in the less easily observed *affective* area— objectives that pertain to feelings, attitudes, and values. Some of them are:
Is alert to the health hazards of cigarette smoking.
Is aware of the potential for unwanted effects that any drug may have.
Appreciates that drugs may have different effects on different people.
Recognizes the problems that misuse of alcohol may cause.
Is aware of possible legal penalties for the use of marijuana.
Is alert to the dangers of mixing medicines.

Page numbers show you where to look back in the chapter for information, if you need it.

1. Tell what a drug is. (172)
2. Explain what is meant by the side effects of a drug. (175)
3. Discuss one serious danger of mixing two or more drugs. (174, 175, 178)
4. Tell the difference between an over-the-counter drug and a prescription drug. (175)
5. Explain why it is most important to read the information on medicine labels. (176-177)
6. Tell what stimulant drugs are and why they can be harmful if misused. (179)
7. Mention a hazard in the misuse of barbiturate drugs. (180)
8. Explain what is meant by drugs that are hallucinogens. (180)
9. Discuss why all narcotic drugs must be used with the greatest care. (181)
10. List three harmful effects of inhaling solvents or certain sprays. (182)
11. Explain under what conditions alcohol can be a poison. (185)
12. List three reasons why cigarette smoking is dangerous to people's health. (186-187)

---

[1]Behavioral objectives in the cognitive area are posed here directly to the students themselves.

Review It

Teacher's Notes
"Review It" is a feature that occurs at the end of each chapter in this book and in this series. It gives children a chance to think over what they have learned, to summarize, and to store away important ideas. Page references after each item make this review page a self-help one.

Page numbers show you where to look back in the chapter for information, if you need it.

1. Why is there a risk in taking any drug? (174)

2. What information is given on the label of an over-the-counter drug? (176)

3. What information appears on the label of a prescription drug? (177)

4. What should you do if you get some annoying side effects from an over-the-counter drug? (176)

5. What should you do if you get side effects from a prescription drug? (177)

6. Why may people sometimes use drugs in unsupervised, disapproved ways? (178)

7. What effects do stimulant drugs have on the body? (179)

8. What is the drug in coffee, tea, cocoa, and some colas and what have you learned about it? (179)

9. What can be some effects of improper use of amphetamines? (179)

Copy each numbered item from List A. After each item, write the letter and words from List B that best describe it. For example:

10. amphetamines   d. stimulant drugs

List A

10. amphetamines
11. barbiturates
12. caffeine
13. carbon monoxide
14. LSD
15. marijuana
16. morphine
17. nicotine

List B

a. drug in coffee and tea
b. drug in cigarette smoke
c. a narcotic drug
d. stimulant drugs
e. depressant drugs
f. harmful gas in cigarette smoke
g. a strong hallucinogen
h. a mild hallucinogen

Health Test for Chapter Six

Teacher's Notes
After students have taken the test and their papers have been scored, the test items can serve as guides for a summary discussion. Volunteers can read aloud their rewording of the false statements. "What Do You Think?" is a special feature that offers pupils a chance to evaluate some of their newly acquired knowledge.

Copy each number on a piece of paper. After each number write the correct answer, *true* or *false.* Rewrite each false statement to make it true.

F 1. Alcohol is a stimulant.

T 2. It is very difficult for some people to break the habit of smoking.

F 3. Everyone who takes an alcoholic drink is an alcoholic.

T 4. Alcohol can be a poison if too much is taken into the body at one time.

F 5. Smoking slows the heartbeat.

T 6. Alcoholics cannot control their heavy use of alcoholic drinks.

F 7. A prescription drug is known as an over-the-counter drug.

T 8. A danger in narcotic drugs like morphine is that a person may become "hooked" on them.

F 9. People do things more safely after a few alcoholic drinks.

T 10. A great danger in cigarette smoking is that it can cause lung cancer.

F 11. You can use all the amphetamine you wish with no harmful effects.

T 12. Stop taking an over-the-counter drug if you have bad side effects.

T 13. Some people may unwisely experiment with drugs because their friends are doing it.

F 14. Scientists know all there is to know about the effects of marijuana.

F 15. Carbon monoxide is a harmless gas found in cigarette smoke.

F 16. It is a good idea to take a drug the minute you feel an ache or pain.

T 17. You should always read and follow the directions on drug labels.

T 18. The use of marijuana is illegal in many states.

T 19. LSD is a strong hallucinogen that can have very dangerous effects.

F 20. Cigarette smoking is not dangerous to people's health.

Number of Answers   20

Number Right   _____

Score (Number Right x 5)   _____

What Do You Think?

What did you learn in this chapter that you think is important to know? Write your answer on a piece of paper.

SCHOOL & HOME

One slogan about smoking is "The best tip is not to start." You might talk about this at home. What are some reasons for not starting to smoke?

If someone at home smokes, you might discuss what happens when a person quits. The body starts repairing itself quickly. For most people who quit, the risk of developing lung cancer decreases. The risk of smoking-related heart disease goes down.

You might also join some family members at home in a drug safety check. Here are some things to look for and correct if necessary:

Is old medicine thrown away? If not, it should be. Old medicine can lose strength or get stronger. In either case, it should be thrown away.

Is medicine kept where small children can't get it? Does it have "child-proof" containers?

Do family members avoid calling medicine like aspirin "candy"? Young children may look for the "candy" and may take overdoses.

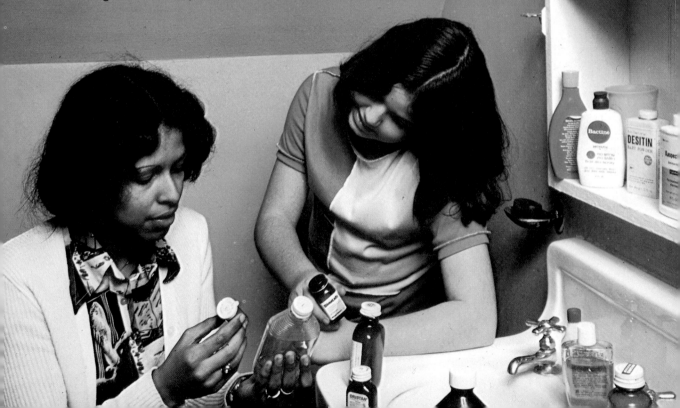

7 The Long Struggle Against Communicable Diseases

Long ago people did not know how to stop the spread of communicable diseases. What do you think health conditions were like then?

How do you suppose people learned to fight communicable diseases?

What pioneers in health do you know?

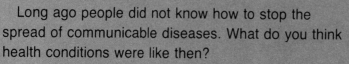

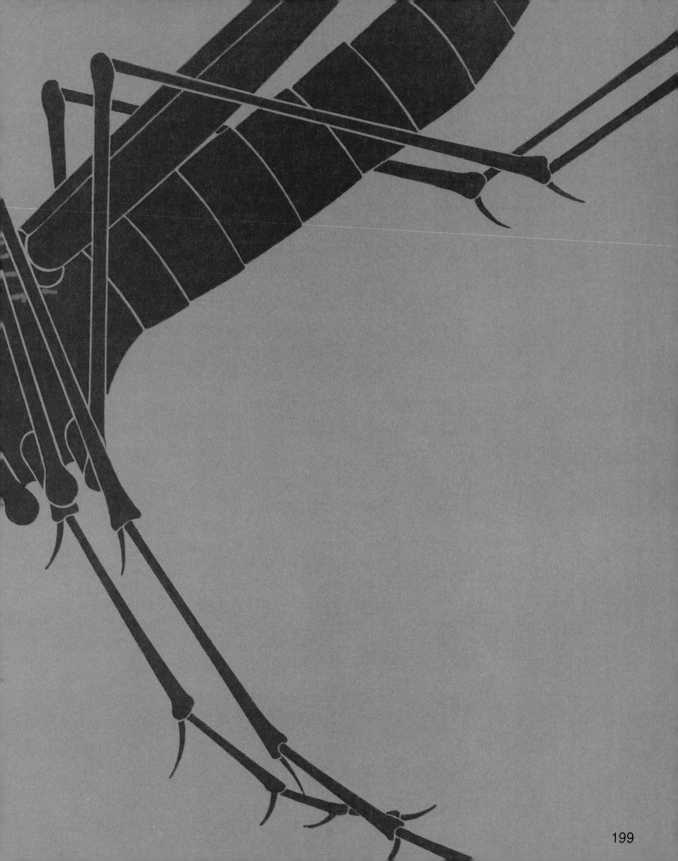

Teacher's Notes

"Preview It" is a special feature that occurs at the beginning of each chapter in this book and in this health series. Here students do some *anticipating.* They skim over the main headings in the chapter. Most of these headings are, by design, study questions. Curiosities are aroused, and pupils are given a framework for the detailed information to follow.

See page T36 for additional teaching suggestions.

Preview It

Before you begin this chapter, you might think about *communicable diseases.* They are the diseases that can be spread from one person to another. Among such diseases are smallpox, plague, yellow fever, malaria, polio, and measles.

People today know what causes communicable diseases. They are caused by tiny living plants and animals called *microbes,* or *microorganisms.* The kinds that cause diseases are known as *disease germs.*

Long ago, people knew nothing of this world of tiny living things. A microscope is needed to see microbes. And the microscope was just starting to be developed around the year 1600. Even when microbes were first seen under a microscope, people didn't know what they were. More than two hundred years passed before the role of microbes in diseases was understood.

In this chapter you will learn what happened in the years from the 1600's to the present time. You will become acquainted with various health pioneers. These pioneers helped in the long struggle against communicable diseases.

Look through the chapter quickly. What eight main questions are asked in the titles? Look for answers to the questions as you read the chapter.

Begin the chapter now. Read first to get an idea of the health conditions in communities of long ago.

What Were Health Conditions in Early Days?

What are the strange costumes that you see below? They are plague costumes. The ones shown here were worn by some people in the 1600's. They thought the costumes would keep them from getting bubonic plague. People didn't know how to stop this terrible disease from spreading. But they tried everything that they could think of.

Bubonic plague, or Black Death, caused thousands of deaths over the centuries. History records many epidemics. One such *epidemic,* or rapid spread of the disease, took place in London in 1665.

Teacher's Notes

Invite comments on the costumes shown on this page. Call attention to the extra features on the costume at the right.

After the pupils have read the page, ask these questions:

"What was the bubonic plague?"

"Why did people think that wearing strange costumes would combat the plague?"

See page T36 for additional teaching suggestions.

These costumes were worn in an attempt to ward off the plague. Note the windmill on the hat, the bags of aromatic herbs on the skirt, and the oversized shoes, on the costume on the right. All were worn to prevent infection.

Teacher's Notes
Ask:
"What was alarming about the Great London Plague Epidemic of 1665?"
"What means were used to stop the plague?"
"Why couldn't the epidemic be fought successfully?"
"What makes you think there were other plague epidemics in Europe around this time?" (There were plague epidemics from early history.)

Throughout 1665, the death rate in London mounted. Everyone was terrified. In May of that year, 43 died. In June, 590 died and 6137 people died in July. In August, 17,036 people died. In September, the death toll was 31,159. In all, over 70,000 people died before the end of the year.

Two thirds of London's inhabitants fled from the city. Those who remained tried all kinds of things to stop the spread of the disease. Other methods besides wearing plague costumes were used. For example, people who had been in contact with the sick had to carry crosses or white sticks. Crosses were painted on the doors of the sick. Belongings of the dead were burned. Infected people were locked in their houses for a two-week period. Fires were built to "purify" the air. But all these methods failed.

The plague continued until it had run its course. The disease could not be fought effectively because no one knew what caused it. That discovery was to come after many years, as you will learn in this chapter.

Nine years before the Great Plague in London, there was one in Rome. Here you see belongings of the Rome plague victims being burned. What else do you notice in the picture?

202

Health Conditions in the Colony of Jamestown

In 1607, the settlers in Jamestown in North America had serious health problems. Jamestown was on the bank of the James River in what is now called Virginia.

Hot, humid weather occurred in the summer of 1607. Food spoiled. Water became contaminated. It had a bad taste. And it was full of deadly germs. But the colonists knew nothing about germs. Sickness spread rapidly. By the end of the summer, only about 50 of the original 104 colonists were alive.

The City of New York in 1865

Even as late as 1865, health and sanitary conditions in cities like New York were terrible.

Garbage and filth of every kind were tossed into the streets. Human wastes filled the gutters and caused very unpleasant odors.

A survey was taken in New York in 1865. It showed that 1200 cases of smallpox and 2000 cases of typhus occurred in a two-week period. The cause of the diseases was unknown.

The Missing Knowledge

People who lived long ago failed in their fight against communicable diseases. They did not know what caused such diseases and how they spread. They had no scientific knowledge about how to control communicable diseases.

The story of how people learned to fight communicable diseases is a fascinating one. It involves gradual knowledge about *microbes,* or *microorganisms,* especially harmful microbes or *disease germs.* The story also involves scientific "detective work" that took place over several hundred years.

Teacher's Notes
Mention that bubonic plague, malaria, yellow fever, measles, scarlet fever, and smallpox were among the diseases that afflicted the early colonists. It is estimated that half the children died in infancy.

In colonial North America, some colonists believed "evil spirits" caused communicable diseases. These people often fastened a fish to one leg to frighten away the "evil spirits." Do you think the method worked?

What Did Leeuwenhoek Discover?

No one knows who made the first microscope. Some say it was made by an Italian scientist, Galileo. Others say it was made in 1590 by a Dutchman who made eyeglasses. He lived at the time of Galileo.

There is no doubt, however, about who first saw microbes under a microscope. It was another Dutch investigator named Anton van Leeuwenhoek, who is shown at the left. Leeuwenhoek also made drawings of what he saw.

Leeuwenhoek was born in Holland in 1632. In his youth he worked for a cloth merchant. Here he learned to look at different textiles under a fine, hand lens.

In later years, Leeuwenhoek learned to grind lenses and to mount them. He put many things under the lenses to study. He looked at a sheep's hair, a bit of dust, a moth's wing. He also began to write letters to the Royal Society of London. In the letters he described the things he saw under his lenses.

In 1676 he wrote of seeing tiny living things in a drop of water. He called these things "tiny animals." We now know that some were the little plants that we call *bacteria*. Some were the one-celled animals that we call *protozoans*.

Later Leeuwenhoek studied scrapings from his teeth under his lenses. He studied drops of his own saliva. And he saw many more "tiny animals." He also made drawings of them. These were the first sketches ever made of microbes.

Neither Leeuwenhoek nor the Royal Society realized that the "tiny animals" had any connection with communicable diseases. Two hundred years passed before Leeuwenhoek's discoveries were used in medicine.

Teacher's Notes

One reason Leeuwenhoek was successful in seeing microbes was that he had developed over 200 accurate lenses. Some were powerful enough to magnify an object more than 250 times. They were powerful enough to see bacteria but not viruses. It was not until the electron microscope was developed that viruses were seen.
You might ask:
"What were the 'tiny animals' that Leeuwenhoek saw?"
"How did the world learn about them?"

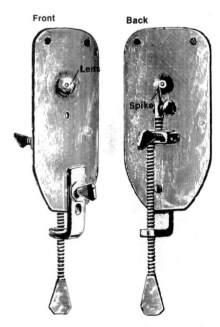

Front   Back

Here is one of Leeuwenhoek's microscopes. It contained a single lens held in a peephole on a flat wooden plate. The object to be viewed was placed under the lens. Solid objects could be held on a spike on the backside of the plate.

After the students have read this page, ask:

"How *do* microbes reproduce?"

"Why are microbes 'here, there, and everywhere'?"

You may want to have the students look at the activity of growing microbes which is suggested on page 226 of the pupils' text.

See page T37 for additional teaching suggestions.

What Did Spallanzani Learn About Microbes?

In the years after Leeuwenhoek's discovery, scientists asked many questions about the "tiny animals." They wanted to know from where the "tiny animals" came. They also asked, "How do these 'tiny animals' multiply so fast?"

The "tiny animals" were now starting to be called microbes. Some scientists thought they came into being "out of nothing." Others thought the microbes laid eggs. A Swiss scientist suggested that a microbe reproduced itself by dividing into two parts. He said each part became a new microbe.

In Italy, a scientist named Lazzaro Spallanzani felt the Swiss scientist was right. In the late 1700's, Spallanzani invented a way to trap a single microbe. He watched the microbe under his microscope. Soon an amazing thing happened. The rod-shaped microbe began to get thinner in the middle. Meanwhile the two thick ends began to wiggle and tug. Suddenly the two halves pulled apart with a violent jerk.

Where there had been one microbe, now there were two. In about twenty minutes these two microbes divided to make four.

Each time Spallanzani performed this experiment, he saw the same thing. He did some fast figuring. If one microbe divided in two every twenty or thirty minutes, that could produce a billion microbes in about fifteen hours! It was easy now to explain why microbes were here, there, and everywhere.

Spallanzani had added a basic link to the growing chain of knowledge about microbes.

20 minutes

40 minutes

60 minutes

Here is a diagram of Spallanzani's discovery. How many microbes grow from one microbe within an hour?

206

What Did Jenner Contribute to Disease Prevention?

Teacher's Notes

As background information on Edward Jenner, you might mention that he discovered how to make a vaccine that would *prevent* smallpox. This is one of the great discoveries in the history of medicine. Students might study this page to learn about the disease, and to find out what led Jenner to think he could prevent people from getting smallpox.

Then ask:

"What made Jenner think cowpox might have some connection with preventing smallpox?"

"How did Jenner build on earlier knowledge about inoculations?"

Glossary word: *inoculate*

See page T37 for additional teaching suggestions.

For thousands of years smallpox was a greatly feared disease. This disease causes little sores to form on the face and body. Then crusts, or scabs, fall off the sores. When the scabs fall off, scars are left. Many people who got this disease died. Sometimes entire families died during epidemics of the disease.

The Investigations of Edward Jenner

Around 1790, an English scientist Edward Jenner began some studies that led to the conquest of smallpox. Jenner began to investigate a statement often made by dairymaids. This was the statement. "If you have cowpox, you'll never get smallpox."

Jenner, who is shown on the next page, studied many people who had cowpox. Finally he decided that cowpox and smallpox were similar. Cowpox was a mild form and smallpox a deadly form of the same disease. Jenner also observed that people who got cowpox never did get smallpox. So he decided that if cowpox prevented smallpox, people should be inoculated with cowpox. Then they would never get smallpox.

What Was Known About Smallpox Inoculations

Actually inoculation for smallpox was not unknown. It had been used in ancient China. People were inoculated by having pieces of a scab from a smallpox victim put in their nose. People treated in this way sometimes developed a light case of smallpox. But some people died after getting the disease in this way.

In England, this method had also been used. But many times the inoculated people died of smallpox.

What Jenner proposed to do was to inoculate with material from a person with the milder cowpox.

Something to Do

1. Look in the school or public library for the book *Edward Jenner and Smallpox Vaccination* by Irmengarde Eberle (Watts).

2. A member of your group might write to the Metropolitan Life Insurance Company, 1 Madison Avenue, New York, N. Y. 10010 for a free set of the *Health Heroes* pamphlets for your classroom library.

A Historic Inoculation

In 1796, Jenner performed the first planned experiment to prove the effectiveness of protection against smallpox. This was done with material taken from a cowpox sore. This procedure is now called a *vaccination*. The word comes from the Latin word *vacca* which means cow.

Jenner inoculated an eight-year-old boy named James Phipps. Jenner used matter taken from a sore on the hand of a milkmaid who was sick with cowpox. The boy got a sore arm. But he had no other ill effects.

After six weeks Jenner inoculated the boy twice with material taken from a smallpox sore. The boy did not get smallpox. Jenner's earlier inoculation of cowpox material had made the boy immune to smallpox. Jenner repeated this experiment with three other people. Not one got smallpox. Then Jenner sent an account to the Royal Society in London.

Before long, Jenner's method of vaccination against smallpox was used all over Europe. But no one understood *why* inoculating people with cowpox made them immune to smallpox. The explanation was to come later from the work of Louis Pasteur and others.

Sum It Up

What were health conditions like in communities of long ago?

Why weren't people able to fight communicable diseases effectively?

What was Leeuwenhoek's great contribution?

What knowledge about microbes did Spallanzani contribute?

For what will Jenner always be remembered?

Teacher's Notes

Students can read this page to learn about the inoculation that made medical history. Then ask:

"How did Jenner inoculate James Phipps?" (With material from a milkmaid's cowpox sore. He made two small incisions in the arm where he put the cowpox material.)

"Why did Jenner inoculate James Phipps again with material from a smallpox sore?" (This was the only way to prove that the earlier inoculation had made the boy immune.)

Glossary words: *vaccination, immunity*

(*Note:* "Sum It Up" is a feature that occurs at intervals throughout each chapter of this book and others in the health series. Pupils can use this study aid to review important ideas learned in the preceding pages.)

How Did Pasteur Help in the War Against Disease?

Louis Pasteur, shown on the left, was born in France in 1822. This was twenty-three years after Spallanzani died.

As a young man, Pasteur trained in the field of chemistry. Later he became a professor of science. One of his special interests was studying microbes which he called "wee germs."

Microbes in Food

The first work that brought Pasteur fame had to do with the fermentation of foods. *Fermentation* causes milk to sour and various foods to spoil.

Pasteur's studies led him to conclude that microbes from the air get into foods. Then these microbes multiply quickly. The microbes cause fermentation, a chemical change in foods. Pasteur learned that some microbes are helpful. Such microbes help in making bread, cheese, and pickles. Other microbes cause foods to spoil.

By experimenting, Pasteur found a temperature at which harmful microbes could be killed in wine without harming its flavor. This process is now known as *pasteurization*. It involves heating liquids long enough and to a temperature high enough to kill harmful germs. It is a process that has saved the lives of countless people. This process is still used to make milk safe by killing the harmful bacteria in it.

As Pasteur studied the changes that microbes can make in foods, an exciting idea came to him. Could microbes be the cause of many diseases in humans?

Teacher's Notes

After study of this page, ask:
"What was Pasteur's background for scientific work?"
"In what country and in what century did he live?"
"What information did Pasteur discover about food spoilage?"
"What theory was beginning to form in Pasteur's mind about the cause of diseases?"
Glossary word: *pasteurization*
See page T37 for additional teaching suggestions.

Books to Read

Look in the school or public library for these books:
Dietz, David. *All About Great Medical Discoveries* (Random).
Villiard, Paul. *The Hidden World: The Story of Microscopic Life* (Four Winds).

Teacher's Notes
Students can read this page and the
next to find out how Pasteur saved the
silkworm and French livestock
industry.
Glossary words: *vaccine, antibody*
See page T37 for additional teaching
suggestions.

Microbes and Silkworms

In 1864, the French silkworm industry was being ruined. A disease was killing off the silkworms. The government asked Pasteur to help with the problem. Pasteur found that two kinds of microbes were killing the silkworms. He then worked out ways to stamp out the disease.

By this time Pasteur was becoming very sure of something. *He believed that harmful microbes could cause diseases not only in silkworms but in people too.*

Vaccination for Anthrax

In the early 1880's, the French livestock industry was in trouble. There was a fast-spreading disease called *anthrax*. It was killing cattle, sheep, and horses. Once again the French government asked Pasteur for help.

First Pasteur repeated and confirmed the earlier experiments of the scientist Robert Koch. Koch had proved that certain rod-shaped bacteria cause *anthrax*.

Through experiments, Pasteur found that he could protect healthy sheep from getting anthrax. He did it by using heat to weaken anthrax germs. Then he injected the weakened germs into the healthy sheep. This was the process of vaccination that Jenner had discovered. But Pasteur was to provide the explanation of *why* it worked.

Many people did not believe in Pasteur's anthrax vaccination. So Pasteur agreed to a public demonstration of the vaccine.

Pasteur picked twenty-five sheep from a group of fifty. He inoculated them with anthrax vaccine. These twenty-five sheep were marked. The remaining unmarked sheep were given no vaccine.

Here is the silkworm, or caterpillar, that spins silk to form a cocoon. What part did the silkworms play in the development of Pasteur's "germ theory" of diseases?

212

Twelve days later, the marked sheep were given a second vaccination. After several weeks came the big test. All fifty sheep were injected with deadly anthrax bacteria. This was not the weakened form of bacteria used in the vaccine.

Within a few days, every one of the unvaccinated sheep got anthrax and died. The vaccinated sheep all remained alive and well.

Pasteur had proved that for certain diseases vaccination provides immunity. This was his explanation. "When weakened germs of a given disease are injected into the body, the body is later able to fight off invading germs of that same disease."

Scientists who lived after Pasteur's time were able to explain this more fully. When weakened germs of a given disease are injected into the body, it produces *antibodies.* These antibodies can kill the invading germs.

Pasteur's sheep experiment

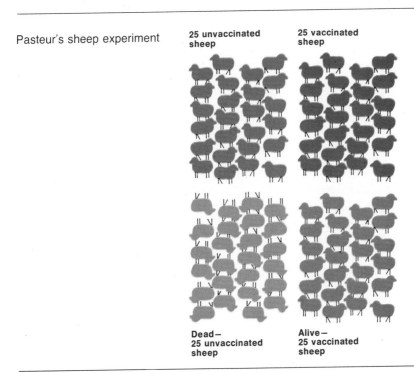

25 unvaccinated sheep

25 vaccinated sheep

**Dead—
25 unvaccinated sheep**

**Alive—
25 vaccinated sheep**

Should germs of this same disease later enter the body and start to multiply, the antibodies remaining in the bloodstream fight them off. The antibodies help keep a person from getting ill with the disease. Each kind of disease germ stimulates the production of an antibody that works against that disease germ alone.

Immunization Against Rabies

Pasteur also discovered how to prevent the disease called *rabies.* Rabies is a disease that still terrifies people. It is a disease caused by a bite from a dog or other animal infected with rabies. Until Pasteur's discovery, to be bitten by a rabid animal meant death.

Pasteur was sure that rabies was caused by a disease germ. So he tried to find the rabies germ in the saliva of rabid dogs. But he never could see the germs when he put their saliva under a microscope. No microscope of that time was powerful enough to make the tiny germ visible.

Finally Pasteur decided there *must be* rabies germs in the brain and spinal cord of rabid dogs. Even if he couldn't see the germs, he felt sure they were there. So he developed a rabies vaccine. It was made from bits of dried spinal cords of dogs that had died of rabies.

Pasteur then injected the vaccine into some healthy dogs. He put these healthy dogs into kennels with rabid dogs. He found that any dog vaccinated *before* being bitten by a rabid dog did not get rabies. Also, if he could inject his vaccine into a dog shortly *after* it was bitten by a rabid animal, the vaccinated dog was safe. It did not get rabies.

Something to Do

See if you can write some headlines about Pasteur that might appear in the newspapers today. For example, MICROBES FOUND TO BE SILKWORM KILLERS or PASTEUR WINS WAR ON ANTHRAX.

A Crucial Test

Would the rabies vaccine work on people too? Or might it cause them to get the dreaded rabies? Pasteur could not be sure. And he did not dare to experiment on human beings.

Finally, a quick decision had to be made. A frantic mother brought her son to Pasteur. The boy had been bitten by a rabid dog. The mother begged Pasteur to try his rabies vaccine. With great fear, Pasteur gave a small injection of the vaccine to the boy, Joseph Meister. During the next ten days he gave the boy a series of vaccinations. At the end of the series, Joseph showed no signs of rabies. Pasteur's treatment had worked.

There was still more that Pasteur hoped to do when he died at the age of seventy-three. But he left for those who followed a great store of knowledge. Scientists who followed after him built on this knowledge. They perfected immunizations for such diseases as diphtheria, tetanus, whooping cough, yellow fever, polio, measles, and mumps.

Sum It Up

What did Pasteur learn about why food spoils?

What is pasteurization?

What was Pasteur's great discovery about the cause of certain diseases in people?

What was Pasteur's famous demonstration with sheep and an anthrax vaccine? How was this vaccine made?

How did Pasteur explain why, for some diseases, vaccination causes immunity?

How did Pasteur protect people against rabies?

Teacher's Notes

After the pupils have read this page, discuss how Pasteur succeeded in fighting rabies. Ask:

"Why did Pasteur hesitate to try his rabies vaccine on humans?"

"How do you explain how Pasteur's rabies vaccine worked?"

"How did scientists build on Pasteur's work? How are people protected against rabies today?" (Most communities have laws requiring dogs to be inoculated against rabies. There is also a rabies vaccine in case a person is bitten by a rabid dog.)

Also discuss the work of Robert Koch, described in the marginal note.

Here is the German scientist Robert Koch. He proved that a specific germ causes a specific disease. Thus, one kind of germ causes tuberculosis and only tuberculosis. Koch also discovered methods of growing microbes in test tubes in his laboratory. He devised methods of staining microbes with dyes. Then they could be seen better under a microscope.

215

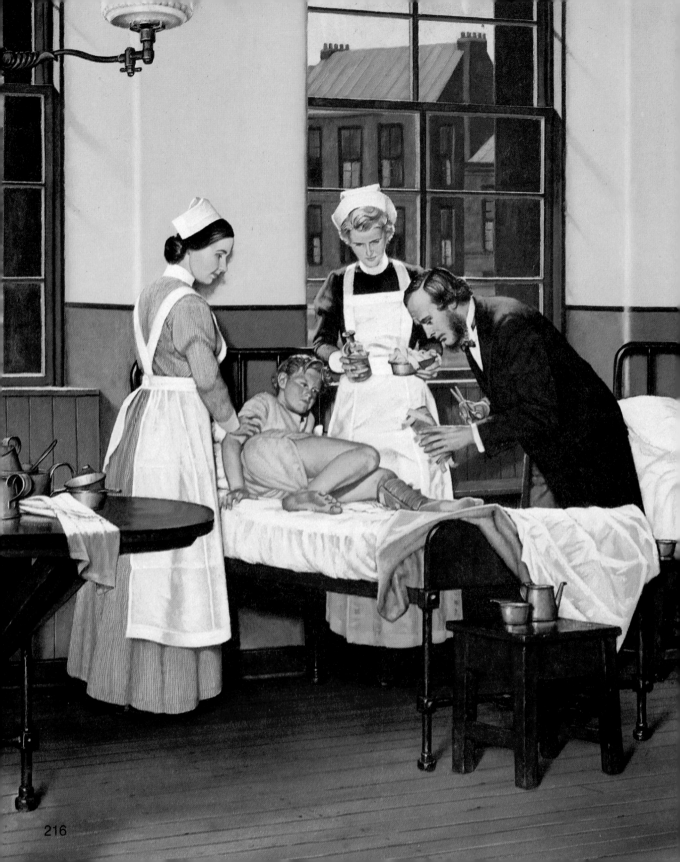

How Did Joseph Lister Fight Infections?

In Scotland, an English doctor named Joseph Lister, shown on the left, read of Pasteur's work. He thought about Pasteur's research and experiments with disease germs. Pasteur's ideas suggested to Lister that germs were causing infections in wounds.

At that time in Lister's hospital and in others, there were many deaths following surgery. The deaths were from infections in the surgical wounds. Lister began to place bandages soaked in carbolic acid over surgical wounds. He did this to kill any germs inside the wounds. And it was effective.

Lister then turned his attention to cleanliness in the operating room. He wanted everything kept as clean as possible. This cleanliness led to success in preventing infections after operations.

Within two years after starting these methods, Lister wrote to Pasteur. He said deaths among surgical cases in his hospital had been greatly reduced. Pasteur then introduced antiseptic methods in France. He urged doctors to wash their hands in soap and to sterilize their instruments before an operation.

Gradually, these antiseptic methods spread. Thus another step was taken in the war against infections.

Today the methods include steaming surgical gowns, caps, masks, gloves, and instruments. This makes them germ-free, or *sterile*. Emphasis is on keeping germs *out* of the wounds. This is instead of earlier emphasis on killing germs after they had entered the wounds.

Teacher's Notes

Students may be surprised to learn that in the 1860's and earlier, an open fracture of a bone was a very serious thing. Infection often set in the wound. The patients often died, or the fractured arm or leg had to be cut off. Similarly, surgery was a dangerous procedure because infections often developed in the wounds and the patients died.

With this background students can read how Dr. Lister fought infections and how Lister was influenced by the works of Pasteur.

Students might consider how the product *Listerine* got its name.

Glossary words: *antiseptic, sterile*

See page T37 for additional teaching suggestions.

Something to Think About

It has been said that great medical discoveries have come about as the result of the work of many scientists of many nations. What are the names and nationalities of scientists you have read about in this chapter?

Teacher's Notes

As background material, explain to the students that some diseases are spread by an agent, not by direct contact with another sick person. For example, diseases such as yellow fever and malaria are spread by a mosquito. The mosquito carries the germs from a sick person to a well person. When it bites the well person, it infects him or her with the disease germs. In the days of Dr. Walter Reed, information of this kind was suspected but had not been proven. Dr. Reed proved that yellow fever was carried by a specific type of mosquito.

After the students have read this page, discuss how Dr. Reed conducted the experiments to prove his theory.

Glossary word: *contaminate*

See page T37 for additional teaching suggestions.

How Did Walter Reed Help Conquer Yellow Fever?

Even after people knew what caused communicable diseases, more information was needed. People still didn't know all the ways in which these diseases are spread. An American doctor added to the knowledge of how one disease is spread. This disease is yellow fever, or "yellow jack."

In 1900, an epidemic of yellow fever broke out among American troops in Cuba. A commission, headed by Dr. Walter Reed, was sent to find out how this disease was spread.

Dr. Reed wondered if the disease could be spread by mosquitoes. Some scientists had suggested this idea. But how could they find out? It was thought that animals could not get yellow fever. So they could not be used in experiments. Any experiments would have to be done with people. And that was dangerous.

Members of the commission offered themselves as subjects for an experiment. So did some soldiers. The men agreed to be bitten by mosquitoes that had first bitten yellow fever patients. As a result, three volunteers became ill. One, Dr. Jesse Lazear, died.

But more proof was needed. So for three weeks volunteer soldiers were shut in a hut. It was protected by mosquito netting. But the volunteers slept in pajamas of victims who had died of yellow fever. They slept on dirty linens from the beds of those who had died of the disease. Yet not one volunteer got yellow fever from the contaminated materials.

Then Dr. Reed allowed these volunteers to be bitten by mosquitoes known to have bitten yellow fever victims. The volunteers got yellow fever after these bites. Then Dr. Reed knew his theory was right. Yellow fever is caused by bites from a specific type of mosquito.

Something to Know

Once the carrier of yellow fever was known, breeding places of mosquitoes in Cuba were cleared up. The outbreak of yellow fever was then under control.

Since that time an all-out war against the yellow fever mosquitoes, *Aëdes aegypti,* has taken place. In 1937 a vaccine was developed to protect people where yellow fever is still a threat.

ENJOY IT

Walter Reed   (1851-1902)

"O, Yellow Jack's here,
With his yellow flag flying.
And everywhere, everywhere,
People are dying.
Our doctors and nurses
Work on till they fall,
But he stings us and slays us,
In spite of them all!

"He scourges the tropics
And all the warm South,
But the North has been seared
By the breath of his mouth.
What might shall withstand him?
What skill drive away
The dread yellow fever
That sickens the day?"

It was not a wizard,
With philters and charms,
It was not a champion,
A champion-at-arms,
But a lean army surgeon,
Soft-spoken and slight,
Who read the dark riddle
And broke the dark night.

He found the mosquito
That carried the pest,
He called volunteers
For a terrible test.
They walked in Death's valley,
—And one, to Death's door—
But Yellow Jack, Yellow Jack
Slaughters no more!

There is valor in battle
And statues for those
Who pepper and puncture
Our national foes—
But, if you are looking
For heroes to cheer,
You needn't look farther
Than Reed and Lazear.

What is the "Yellow Jack" mentioned in the poem?
Who was the "lean army surgeon"?
What was the "terrible test"?
Why were Reed and Lazear "heroes to cheer"?

"Walter Reed" by Stephen Vincent Benét. From *A Book of Americans* by Rosemary and Stephen
Vincent Benét. Holt, Rinehart and Winston, Inc. Copyright, 1933, by Rosemary and Stephen Vincent
Benét. Copyright renewed, 1961, by Rosemary Carr Benét. Reprinted by permission of Brandt &
Brandt.

How Are Disease Germs Spread?

Over the years scientists have added to our knowledge of how disease germs are spread. Below and on the next three pages you can learn about some of these various ways.

By Water

The germs of some communicable diseases are *waterborne.* This means that the germs live in water and may be carried for long distances in water.

Typhoid fever is caused by waterborne germs. Typhoid fever germs live in the intestines of people with typhoid fever. When typhoid germs are discharged in bowel movements from the sick person, the germs get into the sewage. If untreated sewage with typhoid germs is sent into lakes, rivers, or other sources of drinking water, the disease can be spread. Of course, there will be no danger if the contaminated water is treated properly at a water-treatment plant.

Another waterborne disease is *cholera.* Today it occurs most frequently in Asia. Untreated sewage in some places in Asia is still dumped into drinking water sources.

Dysentery also is caused by disease germs that may be spread by contaminated water. There are two kinds of dysentery. One is caused by bacteria. The other is due to an infection by an amoeba. An amoeba is a one-celled animal. Amoebic dysentery is the disease that is present in the United States.

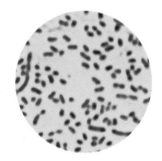

Typhoid-fever germs

Cholera germs

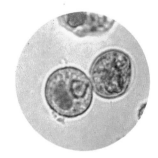

Amoebic-dysentery germs

By Air

The germs of communicable diseases such as the common cold, influenza, and chicken pox can be transmitted through the air. They are *airborne* diseases. Each of these diseases is caused by a virus.

If you have a cold and you cough and sneeze, millions of the tiny viruses go flying out on droplets of moisture from your mouth and nose. Many droplets will dry up and the germs in them will die. But some of the droplets may be breathed by a person some distance away. The person may be able to fight off the cold germs. If not, the person will soon be ill with a cold.

Through touching or kissing a sick person, you can be infected with that person's disease germs. Being close enough to breathe in droplets spread from the sick person's mouth or nose is another way germs can be passed from one person to another.

Sometimes germs are spread by indirect contact with a sick person. A person may pick up some cold germs by drinking from a glass used by a person with a cold. Or an eye infection may be passed from one person to another if both use the same washcloth or towel.

Influenza

Chickenpox

By Insects and Animals

Many creatures such as mosquitoes, houseflies, cows, rats, dogs, cats, squirrels, horses, cattle, wolves, and bats can spread disease germs.

Diseases such as malaria and yellow fever are passed by *mosquitoes* from one person to another. The *Anopheles* mosquito spreads the germs of malaria. The female *Aëdes aegypti* mosquito spreads yellow fever germs.

Houseflies are among the busiest carriers of germs. Flies breed in garbage, stables, pigpens, animal wastes, and all types of filthy places. Young flies pick up their first meals in these places. They pick up dangerous germs and carry them—on their bodies and in their stomachs—to kitchens, food stores, eating places, dairies, and water sources. The housefly carries and spreads many different kinds of disease germs.

Bubonic plague starts among *rats* who get this disease. It is spread from rat to rat by fleas that rats carry around on them. When many rats die of bubonic plague, the fleas have no home or "host." Then they bite people for food. People who are bitten by these infected fleas usually develop bubonic plague. Rats also get into foods and contaminate the food with their wastes. *Cows* can carry tuberculosis germs. People who drink milk from infected cows can get tuberculosis. That is why it is important to pasteurize milk.

Dogs, cats, squirrels, horses, cattle, wolves, and *bats* can carry rabies germs. In most communities, dogs must have rabies shots. And often such shots are required for cats as well. Then the dogs and cats cannot give people rabies through bites.

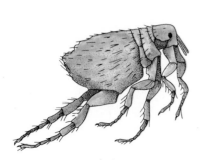

Flea (actual length indicated by line)

Rat (actual length about forty-six centimeters)

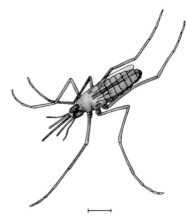

Mosquito (actual length indicated by line)

By Food

A great many disease germs are carried by food. These are the *food-borne* germs. Among them are the germs for tuberculosis, diphtheria, and septic sore throat.

Milk is a good breeding place for many bacteria. Because milk is warm when it comes from the cow, bacteria can thrive in it. Bacteria can get into milk through lack of cleanliness in handling it.

Food may be contaminated by germs if it is handled by people with unclean hands or unclean fingernails. Houseflies can contaminate food also. And food can be contaminated if it is not properly packaged and stored to prevent it from spoiling.

In past years, before sanitary control measures were put into effect, typhoid fever was sometimes spread by eating shell-fish from polluted waters.

With increased pollution of rivers and lakes, today's public health officials are alert once more for fish that are unsafe to eat. These are the fish that come from polluted waters.

Sum It Up

How did Joseph Lister fight infections?
How did Dr. Reed discover the cause of yellow fever?
What are four ways that disease germs can spread?

Milk is a good breeding place for many bacteria.

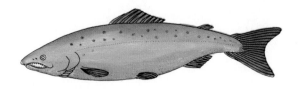

Fish from highly polluted rivers and lakes may be unsafe to eat.

HEALTH AROUND US

Teacher's Notes

"Health Around Us" is a recurring feature in this book and in this health series. It focuses on interesting and intriguing aspects of health in the world around us.

Here health pioneers are discussed. Explain to the students that there are still communicable diseases in underdeveloped countries where the means to prevent the diseases are not fully available.

See page T37 for additional teaching suggestions.

Since primitive days, drugs have been used to treat diseases. Some of the earliest drugs came from plants. More or less by chance these drugs had been found to have some value as medicines. Many drugs are still obtained from plants.

In the early 1900's a German scientist named Paul Ehrlich began a systematic search for new drugs. He wanted to find drugs that would head straight for their targets in the human body. The targets were specific germs that had invaded the body and were causing a specific disease. Ehrlich conducted careful trial-and-error tests of hundreds of chemicals. After about 600 trials, he found a drug that would destroy the germs of syphilis. Syphilis is an infectious venereal disease.

In the 1930's another important step took place in drug history. This was the development of the *sulfa drugs*. These drugs were made from dyes.

Shown here is Alexander Fleming in his laboratory where he first discovered penicillin.

Before the development of sulfa drugs, people who had streptococcus infections often died. Sulfa drugs successfully fought these infections. But some people get harmful side effects from sulfa drugs. However, some sulfa drugs are still used today.

Sulfa drugs were followed by *antibiotic drugs.* One antibiotic drug is *penicillin.* It kills or weakens certain bacteria. Penicillin is made from a mold found in the air. This drug was discovered by the British scientist, Dr. Alexander Fleming, in 1928. But it was not used widely until the 1940's.

In 1944, Dr. Selman Waksman and co-workers in the United States, developed the antibiotic called *strepto-mycin.* It is made from mold found in the soil. This antibiotic helps in the treatment of tuberculosis and typhoid fever.

From 1944 to the present, laboratory research has continued to yield antibiotic drugs. So far no drug has succeeded against diseases caused by viruses, such as colds and influenza. The search for effective disease-killing drugs will go on until all infectious diseases are conquered.

Teacher's Notes

Mention that some antibiotic drugs cause allergic reactions or other side effects. Some antibiotics are very specific and work against a limited number or types of germs. Others work against a wide spectrum of disease germs.

The FDA (Food and Drug Administration) is responsible for testing and approving all new drugs on the market. The drug is not released to the market unless the FDA is convinced that the drug has been adequately tested and is effective.

To ensure safety, new drugs being developed are tested for purity at all stages of preparation. The new drugs are tested extensively on animals before they can be used on people. The Food and Drug Administration (FDA) must approve new drugs before they can be put on the market.

Things to Do

1. Perhaps you would like to watch some microbes grow. Here is something you can do at school or at home.

Growing Microbes on Potato Slices

Equipment: A potato, 3 saucers, 3 covers for saucers, canned heat such as Sterno, a pan, a colander to set over pan.

Procedure: Wash potato and slice into pieces one quarter of an inch thick.

Steam 3 slices of potato by placing each slice, in turn, on a saucer in a colander over boiling water. Steam each slice for half an hour. Remove saucer with potato slice from colander and cover.

When potato slices are cool, uncover one by one. Then

1) Rub fingers over one slice.
2) Breathe on surface of the second slice.
3) Expose the third slice to air for an hour.

Again cover dishes and keep at room temperature for three days or so.

Keep watching for clumps of microbes. If such clumps are growing, they will probably appear as yellow or white spots. Look at these microbes under a microscope.

2. You may want to read and report on other health pioneers who aided in the battle against communicable diseases. Look in an encyclopedia for information about *Edward Trudeau* who contributed to our knowledge about tuberculosis. Or look for information about *Jonas Salk* and *Albert Sabin* who found means to protect people from polio.

3. Make a survey among your classmates. See how many have been given a measles or a polio vaccine. Make a bar graph of your findings.

4. Look in the library for books about the development of medicines to treat diseases. Here are some books you might enjoy reading:

Epstein, Samuel, and Williams, Beryl. *Medicine from Microbes: The Story of Antibiotics* (Messner).

Wright, Helen, and Rapport, Samuel. *The Amazing World of Medicine* (Harper).

5. There are also interesting stories to learn about advances in the treatment of noncommunicable diseases. For example, there is the story of the French scientist *Marie Curie* shown below. In 1903 Marie Curie and her husband won a Nobel Prize for discovering radium. This was a new chemical element. Then they showed the world how to use radium in the treatment of cancer.

You can learn more about Marie Curie in an encyclopedia. Or look for a book about Marie Curie. One easy one is *Marie Curie* by Lorraine Henriod (Putnam).

Marie Curie

Special Research

Prepare a report on how diseases such as malaria are fought today in various parts of the world. Be sure to tell what part the World Health Organization (WHO) is playing in the conquering of diseases such as malaria. One book that may help you is *Biology and World Health*, Revised Edition, by Madeleine P. Grant (Abelard-Schuman).

A man is preparing to spray mosquitoes to control malaria in Ecuador.

227

Can You Show What You Know?[1]

Teacher's Notes
Here behavioral objectives in the *cognitive* area are posed in childlike language to the students themselves. In turn, boys and girls give evidence by *observable behavior* of what they have learned.
Other hoped-for behavioral objectives lie chiefly in the less easily observed *affective* area—objectives that pertain to feelings, attitudes, and values. Some of them are:

Appreciates the long struggle to achieve the conquest of communicable diseases.

Recognizes that the work of one scientist often influences that of another.

Assumes some personal responsibility for not spreading communicable diseases through unsanitary habits.

Page numbers show you where to look back in the chapter for information, if you need it.

1. Explain what is meant by a communicable disease. (201)

2. Name five or more communicable diseases. (201)

3. Tell what is meant by *microbes,* or *microorganisms.* (201)

4. Describe some of the health conditions in communities of long ago. (201-203)

5. Tell why people who lived about 200 years ago could not fight communicable diseases effectively. (203)

6. Describe the circumstances in which microbes were first seen. (205)

7. Tell what important information Spallanzani contributed about microbes. (206)

8. Explain how Edward Jenner succeeded in inoculating against smallpox. (207-209)

9. List three important discoveries made by Louis Pasteur. (210-214)

10. Describe several procedures that Joseph Lister developed to fight infection in surgical wounds. (217)

11. Mention the medical contribution for which Walter Reed is famous. (218)

12. List four ways by which disease germs can be spread. (220-223)

13. Discuss several germ-killing drugs. (224-225)

[1]Behavioral objectives in the cognitive area are stated here directly to the students themselves.

Review It

Teacher's Notes
"Review It" is a feature that occurs at the end of each chapter in this book and in this series. It gives children a chance to think over what they have learned, to summarize, and to store away important ideas. Page references after each item make this review page a self-help one. However, group discussion can be a valuable adjunct.

Page numbers show you where to look back in the chapter for information, if you need it.

1. What were some crude ways of fighting plague long ago? Why didn't these ways work? (201-202)

2. What are microbes? (203)

3. Why didn't Leeuwenhoek's discovery solve the problem of what causes communicable diseases? (205)

4. Why are microbes "here, there, and everywhere"? (206)

5. Why do foods spoil? (211)

6. What do you think is meant by Pasteur's "germ theory" about diseases? (211-212)

7. How does a vaccination provide immunity for certain communicable diseases? (212-213)

8. Why was it important to develop a vaccine against rabies? (214)

9. What do the names of these two children suggest to you: James Phipps and Joseph Meister? (209-215)

10. How did Pasteur's work influence Joseph Lister? (217)

Copy each item from List A. After each item, write the letter and words from List B that best describe it. For example:

11. bubonic plague   b. disease spread by rats

List A

11. bubonic plague
12. epidemic
13. communicable disease
14. microbes
15. rabies
16. pasteurization
17. penicillin
18. smallpox
19. sterile
20. fermentation

List B

a. germ free
b. disease spread by rats
c. tiny living plants and animals
d. rapid spread of a disease
e. killing of harmful germs in a liquid
f. disease investigated by Jenner
g. disease spread from person to person
h. a germ-killing drug
i. disease caused by a bite from a rabid animal
j. a process which causes milk to sour

Health Test for Chapter Seven

Teacher's Notes
After students have taken the test and their papers have been scored, the test items can serve as guides for a summary discussion. Volunteers can read aloud their wording of the multiple choice statements and the rewording of the false statements. "What Do You Think?" is a special feature that offers pupils a chance to evaluate some of their newly acquired knowledge.

Copy each number on a piece of paper. After the number, write the letter that goes with the *best* answer.

1. The "tiny animals" Leeuwenhoek saw under his microscope were
   a. dirt particles   c. sheep's hairs
   b. microbes

2. Microbes in foods and liquids cause them to
   a. evaporate   c. spoil
   b. become sterile

3. The story of the conquest of smallpox is the story of
   a. Joseph Lister   c. Lazzaro
   b. Edward Jenner   Spallanzani

4. A scientist who reasoned that germs must cause communicable diseases was
   a. Edward Jenner   c. Louis Pasteur
   b. Walter Reed

5. In the process of pasteurization
   a. all germs are killed
   b. germs are weakened
   c. all harmful germs are killed

Copy each number on a piece of paper. After each number write the correct answer, *true* or *false*. Rewrite each false statement to make it true.

F 6. All microbes are harmful.
T 7. Antiseptic methods help kill germs.
F 8. Microbes multiply by laying eggs.
T 9. Antibiotics are germ-killing drugs.
T 10. Microbes grow by dividing in two.
T 11. Microbes are the cause of communicable diseases.
T 12. Dr. Reed helped conquer yellow fever.
T 13. Sterile means germ free.
T 14. Microbes in foods cause spoilage.
T 15. People with unclean hands can contaminate food they handle.
F 16. Houseflies are harmless creatures.
T 17. Squirrels can carry rabies germs.
T 18. Some disease germs live in water.
T 19. Germs can be found in the air.
T 20. Pasteur taught people much about how to immunize against diseases.

Number of Answers	20
Number Right	_____
Score (Number Right × 5)	_____

What Do You Think?

How did this chapter increase your knowledge about communicable diseases? Write your answer on a piece of paper.

SCHOOL & HOME

You have learned many things in this chapter about communicable diseases. You may want to share some of this information at home. What can you tell about how communicable diseases are caused? What can you tell about how these diseases may be spread?

There is something important you want to be sure to talk over at home. It has been said that each person can help prevent the spread of disease germs. And each person can do this by following a few very simple procedures. Here are the procedures you will want to talk about at home and to practice in daily life:

Wash your hands before you eat, set the table, or do any food preparation.

Wash your hands after you use the toilet.

Use your own towel, washcloth, comb, or brush.

Wash your hands after you play with pets.

Cover your coughs and sneezes with a tissue or handkerchief.

How will each of these procedures help?

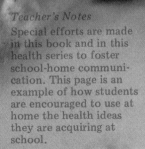

Teacher's Notes
Special efforts are made in this book and in this health series to foster school-home communication. This page is an example of how students are encouraged to use at home the health ideas they are acquiring at school.

8 A Healthy Environment

What do you think the term "environment" means?
How would you describe a "healthy environment"?
What might *you* do to make your environment a more
healthy one?

Preview It

Environment includes all that is around you. And a healthy environment contains what people need for good health. For example, people need safe water to drink, clean air to breathe, and pure food to eat. Also needed are sanitary ways to get rid of wastes and trash.

Other things contribute to a healthy environment. For instance, people need to live and work where there is not too much noise. They need places for recreation. Parks, playgrounds, and open spaces of green growing plants add to people's pleasure and sense of well-being.

It isn't easy to maintain a healthy environment. For example, people need and want cars. But cars cause much air pollution. They use gasoline for fuel, and fuel supplies are not endless. Cars can be noisy too. For a healthy environment, decisions have to be made about car use, public transportation, and so on.

There are many environmental health problems today. But there is also much thought being given to trying to solve these problems.

Look quickly through this chapter. What environmental health problems do the main titles suggest? Look for information about these problems as you read the chapter.

You will also be encouraged to do some investigations on your own. What are some things you want to learn more about?

How Can You Become Alert to Environmental Health Concerns?

Almost everyday you can read in the newspapers or magazines something about environmental health. You can find out about environmental health problems on the radio and television too. What have you read or heard about recently?

One way to keep in touch with what is going on is to keep a scrapbook. Put pictures and articles about environmental health in it.

One group at school made such a scrapbook. You can see some material from it on pages 236-241. What problems does this material refer to?

Now read the scrapbook material more carefully. What information suggests that progress *can* be made in solving environmental health problems?

What suggestions can you find about what *you* can do to improve your environment?

235

Problems of Water Pollution

These fish have been washed ashore after being killed by polluted lake waters.

A polluted stream "oiled" this duck.

Swimmers can no longer use this polluted beach.

Resuscitation is working for pollution-plagued Erie

By Ronald Kotulak
Science Editor

LAKE ERIE, ONCE so polluted that it was considered a "dead" lake, is coming back to life, according to marine biologists.

The lake is in better condition now for fishing, boating, and swimming than it has been in many years, said Rob Patten, regional marine specialist for the New York-Pennsylvania Sea Grant Advisory Service.

"While it is true that industrialization and urbanization have badly hurt the recreational resources and activities of the lake, the evidence today suggests that we should take a new look at our 'deceased' friend," he said.

LAKE ERIE, THE country's sixth largest lake, is the nation's most notorious dirty waterway. Sometimes called America's Dead Sea, its waters are pea green and lifeless in many areas.

Several years ago it was common to see six-inch carpets of algae covering the surface for 10 or 15 square miles. In biological terms, large blooms of algae is one of the vivid stages a dying lake goes thru.

The improvement in the condition of the lake, which covers more than 9,000 square miles, primarily is due to the widespread use of more efficient pollution control devices in industry, said Patten.

Stricter standards for effluent discharges and the construction of new sewage treatment plants along the lake also have had an important effect in turning the lake around.

WHAT THE MARINE scientists are especially happy about is that waterway cleanup measures can begin to show results sooner than expected. Some scientists had thought it might take 100 years to clean up the lake.

Scientists from the Sea Grant Advisory Service, a branch of the National Oceanic and Atmospheric Administration of the Department of Commerce, and the State University of New York have been measuring Erie's increasing health.

Tribune Map

237

Problems of Air Pollution

Out come the cleaned gases

Away goes the collected dust

. . . thanks to a pollution control system that can collect 150 tons of dust daily

Basic oxygen furnaces are one of the most efficient steelmaking systems in the world. But BOFs generate tremendous quantities of dust-laden gases.

How to remove the dust from the gases—and prevent it from discharging into the atmosphere?

When we installed the two BOFs at our Bethlehem, Pa. plant, we also installed electrostatic precipitators at a cost of almost $5 million. These precipitators operate at higher than 99 per cent efficiency for dust particles over a wide range of micron sizes.

Every time we make a heat of steel in one of these furnaces, the precipitator removes about 5 tons of dust from the exhaust gases. At peak operation of 30 heats a day, that can add up to some 150 tons daily . . . approximately 50,000 tons annually. The cleaned gases are discharged through a stack.

What do we do with the iron-bearing dust particles we collect? We form them into pellets and recycle them through the ironmaking process.

The Problem of Waste Paper

What you can do at home to save your environment

Every year, Americans junk 20 million tons of paper. Wouldn't you rather have it stay trees? Trees provide beauty, oxygen, recreation, many other good things. Use as little as possible, recycle what you do use.

● Give up the use of disposable plastic and paper products. Change to china plates and cups, metal utensils, cloth napkins.

● Recycle paper. Stack newspapers in bundles and save them for return to the paper and pulp industries.

● Use both sides of paper, re-use envelopes.

● Share your magazines with others or pass them on to hospitals or convalescent homes.

● Avoid the use of plastic wrap or aluminum foil (it wastes a vital metal) in your kitchen. Use refrigerator containers or wax paper.

● Every time you see excess packaging — in grocery stores, department stores, etc. — turn it down and tell them why.

We generate 5.3 pounds of refuse per person per day and it costs us $2.8 billion a year to get rid of it. We are rapidly coming to the end of land in which to bury it or water in which to toss it.

● Use a mesh shopping bag the way many Europeans do. You can buy them at import stores, or encourage your grocery store to sell them. The fewer extra wrappings you use, the more trees you save.

● Don't use the toilet as a trash basket. Sewage treatment plant operators say some things must be hand-sorted or they make the pumps break down. These include: rags, paper towels, disposable diapers.

Teacher's Notes

As supplement material mention that coarse screens keep the water in water pipes free of leaves, sticks, and fish. Also each city has a map of all pipelines so that repair workers know where to dig if something goes wrong. You, or a volunteer, might obtain from the library the book *Let's Look Under the City*, Revised Edition, by Herman and Nina Schneider (Young Scott). This is a basic book on community utilities.
See page T39 for additional teaching suggestions.

How Is the Water Supply Safeguarded?

All communities face the problem of supplying pure water for drinking and household uses. Many towns and cities get their water from nearby lakes and rivers. Some get it from deep-drilled wells, or *artesian* wells. Sometimes a city pipes its water from sources that are hundreds of miles away. Water from these various sources is carried to towns and cities through huge underground pipes.

The Water-Treatment Plant

Water goes through the pipelines to the community water-treatment plant. Here the water is purified and made safe to drink. Various methods can be used to do this.

After the water has been made safe for use, some of it is stored in large storage tanks, or water towers. But a continuous supply is forced into underground pipes leading to homes, stores, and other buildings.

What happens in a water-treatment plant?

242

Water on Farms and Small Villages

People on farms or in small villages have no water system to pipe in safe water. They get their water from wells in their yards. Well water should be tested often to make sure that it's safe to drink. Arrangements can be made with a state or local health department.

The Need for Water

There is a great need for water in this country. There are more people now to use water. There are more industries using water in their manufacturing. More water is used to irrigate crops. To maintain an adequate water supply, water must be reused. This is not easy to do if water sources get highly polluted.

How Water Is Polluted

How are water sources polluted? Sewage or household wastes are dumped into them. Industries may dump such wastes as chemicals, fibers, and oils into the water sources. Harmful wastes drain off fields and orchards. These wastes include pesticides and fertilizers. Some soil drains off the land and muddies the water. And some industries dump hot water used in manufacturing processes into nearby waterways. The hot water raises the temperature of the waterways. This is called *thermal pollution.* Thermal pollution can kill animal life in the water.

Health Effects of Water Pollution

Germs which cause diseases can enter waterways through sewage. Typhoid fever and dysentery are mostly under control in the United States. But there is still the danger of getting viral diseases, such as infectious hepatitis, from polluted waters.

Teacher's Notes

Some of the methods used to purify water at a water-treatment plant are to treat it with chlorine, to let it stand in big basins where most of the impurities settle out, or to filter it through layers of sand and gravel to remove dirt and solids. The filtered water is sprayed into the air to add oxygen to it. This helps remove unpleasant odors, and improves the taste. Another treatment of chlorine may also be given.

Glossary words: *pesticide, pollution*

Why might this sign be posted? What effects can polluted water have on fish? On fishing and boating? On the beauty of the area? On people's health?

Talk over how water may be polluted and what some of the health effects of polluted water are. Students may be interested to know that some communities use pumps to keep sewage moving through the pipes to the waste-treatment plant. Sewers may be flushed from time to time to clean out deposits of solid materials that collect. Sewers are ventilated to get rid of odors. To provide this ventilation, manholes are placed at spots where branches of the sewer meet. The manholes are large enough to permit a worker to go down and inspect the sewer.

Do You Know?

1. In the course of some sewage treatment, solid material settles to the bottom of great settling tanks. This is *sludge*. It can be used for landfill or fertilizer. Is any used in your community?

2. Some industries are finding ways to use various waste materials. For example, some corn product companies now use certain wastes to make cattle feed. Formerly, the wastes were dumped in waterways.

Waste-Treatment Plants for Sewage

Some communities still dump untreated sewage into nearby waterways. But for many years now most communities have had waste-treatment plants. These plants help prevent pollution of waterways by treating sewage. The sewage is treated at these plants before it is discharged into nearby bodies of water.

In towns and cities with public water systems, the sewage is carried in pipes from homes and other buildings. These pipes lead to sewer lines buried under the streets. The sewers lead to the community waste-treatment plant, or sewage-treatment plant.

Treatment of sewage differs in different plants. But the major aim is to destroy disease germs and other substances harmful to health. In this way, water is made safer to discharge into waterways.

Some waste-treatment plants use a one-stage, or *primary*, sewage treatment. More effective is the second-stage, or *secondary* treatment which many communities use. Today it is recommended that communities work toward a third-stage, or *tertiary,* sewage treatment. This tertiary treatment involves a whole series of processes to remove pollutants.

To help keep polluting materials out of the waterways, many industries are finding ways to remove these materials *before* they discharge their wastes. There are laws that require this in many cases. And more efforts will be needed in the years to come. Why do you think this is so?

Sum It Up

How is water made safe to drink in towns and cities?
What are three causes of water pollution?
What is the function of waste-treatment plants?
What is being done about industrial wastes?

INVESTIGATE IT

There are many things you can do to investigate how water is supplied and safeguarded in your community. Here are some things you can try to find out.

1. From where does your community get its water?

2. Where is the community water-treatment plant? Is it possible for your group to visit it?

3. Where is the water tower, or water storage tank, in your community?

4. Does your community have a sewage-treatment or waste-treatment plant? Where is it? Is it possible for your group to visit it?

5. What kind of sewage treatment is given in your community waste-treatment plant? Is there someone from the plant who could come to talk to your group?

6. What industries in your community dump wastes into nearby waterways? Do these industries treat their wastes first? How might you find out?

7. If there is a lake, river, or stream within walking distance of your school, take a trip there. Look for signs of pollution such as these things:

sewage	oil slicks, dyes
trash	odors
dead animals	algae

Make a record of what you see. Tell what you think might be done about any pollution you see. Who would you notify if you saw pollution?

Teacher's Notes
After reading this page, ask:
"What does burning have to do with air pollution?"
"When is air considered to be polluted?"
"Is air pollution a new problem? Why do you think it is becoming worse as the years go by?"
"Would you expect air pollution problems to be worse in cities or in the country?"
Glossary word: *photochemical smog*
See page T39 for additional teaching suggestions.

What Is Known About Air Pollution?

Air can be polluted just as water and food can be. Air is polluted when it has enough impurities in it to interfere with people's comfort, safety, or health. Air is also considered to be polluted when it damages things in the environment.

What Causes Air Pollution?

The process of burning, or combustion, sends pollution into the air. Whenever wood, coal, natural gas, oil, gasoline, or trash are burned, some wastes are produced. These wastes escape into the air. They are in the form of smoke, dirt, or gases. We call them *pollutants*.

Air pollution is not a new problem. This old engraving shows an industrial region in Germany. People used to think that pollution was a sign of industrial progress. Today efforts are being made to stop air pollution.

246

Some of the sources of air pollution in a community are the furnaces in homes, factories, and other buildings. Burning leaves or trash can bring about air pollution too.

Today many pollutants are added to the air by new industrial methods and materials. Thus, industries may send into the air such wastes as gases, chemicals, sand, clay dust, and other tiny particles of one sort or another. Sometimes harmful gases that are invisible are released into the air. Pesticides that are sprayed into the air can cause pollution also.

Much of the pollution in cities is caused by motor vehicles and jet planes. The air pollution is due to the incompletely burned gases from vehicle exhaust pipes. What is more, a chemical change can happen when sunlight shines on these gases. The result is a *photo-chemical smog*. The sun can be seen through such smogs. Yet the air will be hazy.

How long these wastes and harmful gases stay in the air varies from community to community. The time varies with the amount of wind on a given day. It varies according to location too. A city surrounded by hills may have more trouble than a city on a plain. This is because the hills trap the polluted air and keep it from blowing away.

But polluted air can be trapped in any community at a time when there is an upper layer of warm air to hold it down and very little wind. Then the smog gets thicker. Eyes may water. Driving may be slowed down because people can't see well. Planes may be grounded. People may feel tired. They may cough or sneeze a lot or have trouble breathing normally.

Do You Know?

Most people breathe about thirteen kilograms of air each day. People can live for weeks without food. People can live for a few days without water. But people can live only a few minutes without air. People cannot avoid breathing air, no matter how polluted it is.

Teacher's Notes
Discuss the harmful effects of air
pollution on human health, on crops,
on property, on animals. Ask:
"Why are bushes, trees, and grass
often planted along busy
expressways? (These plants improve
the quality of air; they absorb some of
the gases and fumes from car
exhausts.)
Use the "scrapbook" on the following
pages to guide a discussion on what
people can do to reduce air pollution.
Ask students what their own families
can do to reduce air pollution.
Glossary words: *cancer, emphysema,
bronchitis, allergy*

Air Pollution and Health

You have just read some of the ways in which air pollution can make people uncomfortable. Beyond those symptoms, air pollution can have even more serious effects on health.

Polluted air makes many diseases worse. Such diseases as chronic bronchitis, heart trouble, pneumonia, and emphysema can be aggravated by air pollution. The condition of people with certain allergies may become worse.

Today scientists are studying the long-term effects of air pollution on people who breathe polluted air year after year. There is evidence that air pollution may be a factor in causing lung cancer. However, this has not definitely been proved.

Other Effects of Air Pollution

Air pollution can stunt the growth of fruits, vegetables, and flowers. It can cause damage to fruit trees and crops. It can make cattle sick. Polluted air rots and soils people's clothes. It discolors paints on houses and rusts metals. Surfaces on public buildings and many famous monuments all over the world are being damaged by air pollution.

What Can Be Done About Air Pollution?

On pages 249-252 you can see some material that one group of students prepared. They looked in newspapers, books, and magazines for material about ways to reduce air pollution. Then they put the material in a class scrapbook. What ideas does this material give? What ones can you add?

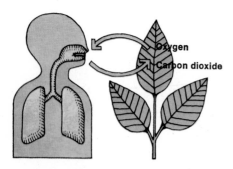

Oxygen

Carbon dioxide

Human beings inhale air to obtain oxygen needed by the body. They exhale carbon dioxide. Plants, on the other hand, take in carbon dioxide and give off oxygen to the atmosphere. What does this suggest about something people can often do to improve the quality of the air in their surroundings?

Ways to Reduce Air Pollution

What Boys and Girls Can Do!

- Don't ride in a car some place if you can WALK there.

- Drive a bicycle instead of riding in a car if you can.

- Remember that a car not used is a car that is not polluting the air.

- If you and your friends must go some place in a car, use a car pool.

- Remember that a small car gives out less pollution than a large car. Talk with your family about the advantages of having a small car.

Use and Improve Public Transportation

Many cities are trying hard to get people to leave their cars at home and ride trains or buses to work.

Here you see a new type of "bending bus." This larger bus uses the same amount of gas as other buses. But it can carry many more people. One long bus like this uses much less gas and thus saves energy.

Suppose 75 or more people ride this bus each day. That one bus could replace some 50 or more cars that the riders might otherwise use. Fewer cars on the streets mean less air pollution.

Keep Pollutants Out of the Air

Don't burn leaves. Use them for a compost pile. Or use them as mulch for the garden.

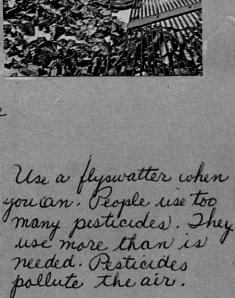

Check to see if your community still dumps garbage and wastes in a dump and burns it. This causes much air pollution.

Communities can work to have better ways of getting rid of garbage and trash.

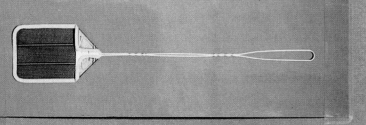

Use a flyswatter when you can. People use too many pesticides. They use more than is needed. Pesticides pollute the air.

Clean the Air!

BEFORE

AFTER

Industries must keep working on ways to clean dirty air before it is sent out of smokestacks. There are scrubbers and many other new methods that can be used to clean the air.

Car manufacturers must keep on working to produce "cleaner cars." Cleaner cars will not give off so much pollution. There are laws now to see that new cars meet certain standards about pollution. The laws should be enforced.

EXHAUST

Dirty air is being trapped here. Later it will be checked to see what kinds of pollutants are in it.

Communities can monitor the quality of the air. They can find out how polluted it is. They can find out where the pollution came from and take steps to get it stopped.

Most large cities have "smog alerts" at times. If the pollution is too bad, certain factories that cause pollution are shut down at these times. Traffic is reduced, too.

INVESTIGATE IT

Identifying Air Pollutants

1. Cut a piece of waxed paper into 6 centimeter squares. Staple to heavy cardboard.

2. Coat the waxed paper with a thin layer of Vaseline.

3. Place the papers in various locations where they can remain undisturbed for a week. The classroom, cafeteria, a backyard, the bumper of a car might be possible locations.

4. At the end of the week collect all papers. Examine them with a magnifying glass to see which received the most pollution.

5. Try to identify dust, ash, soil, and other particles.

6. Which was the most common type?

7. Which location attracted the most particles? Why do you think this was so?

8. Organize all data into a chart showing date placed, date collected, location, amount of accumulation, possible cause of pollution, and reasons for the different amounts.

9. Display the chart.

U. S.
INSPECTED
AND PASSED BY
DEPARTMENT OF
AGRICULTURE
EST. 38

Do You Know?

1. Are there any licenses posted in your community food stores or restaurants? What is the meaning of these licenses?

2. Have you noticed the round federal inspection stamp on meats you buy? What is the meaning of this stamp?

3. How are unwrapped foods in groceries and bakeries protected from contamination by dust and flies?

4. If you have a school lunchroom, investigate how food is stored and handled there to keep it safe.

What Is Known About Food Pollution?

Most bacteria grow best in moist places. They usually live in warm, but not hot places. Bacteria stop growing or grow very slowly in cold temperatures. High temperatures usually kill bacteria. So does direct sunlight.

This information helps us understand how to keep food from being polluted in our homes, in stores, and in restaurants. Your community health department cooperates with state agencies to ensure sanitary methods of handling food. The Food and Drug Department of the state Department of Public Health aids in supervising eating places in communities. The state Department of Public Health has regulations about food handling. Local and state inspectors see that these regulations are followed.

What Sanitarians Look For

When they inspect a food factory or restaurant, health workers called *sanitarians* first look to see if the workers are clean. Next they look to see if the surroundings and equipment are clean. Then they check to see if the food is properly stored or refrigerated.

If there are toilets on the premises, the sanitarians check their cleanliness too. They look to see if there are soap and clean towels. If there are things that need to be corrected, the sanitarians point out these things. Later they return to see that the necessary corrections have been made.

254

Guides for Food-Handlers

Sanitarians check to see that food-handlers use the guides shown below. From your knowledge of how bacteria grow and spread, explain the reason for each rule. Remember, too, that these same rules should be applied in your home.

1. Wash hands thoroughly with soap and water and dry them on a clean towel before you handle any food.

2. Wash your hands thoroughly after going to the toilet.

3. Be sure your fingers do not touch the insides of clean cups and glasses or the bowls of spoons, prongs of forks, or blades of knives.

4. Avoid preparing or handling food when you have a sore throat, cold, or other illness. Do not touch food if you have discharging sores on your hands, arms, or face.

5. Wash dishes, glasses, and all utensils in plenty of hot, soapy water. Change dishwater often. Rinse dishes with boiling water.

6. Keep all foods that spoil easily on the coldest shelf in the refrigerator. These foods include potato salad, baked beans, cream soups, milk, cooked spaghetti and macaroni, custards, sandwich fillings, mayonnaise, and creamed dishes. Bacteria grow well in these foods. Do not let these foods stand around unrefrigerated.

Sum It Up

What is the harm in air pollution?

What causes air pollution? What can be done about it?

In what ways can food be polluted?

How can food pollution be prevented?

Something to Know

Be careful with picnic lunches and brown-bag lunches. Here are some food safety guides.

Freeze sandwiches ahead of time. They will thaw and be just right at lunchtime.

Use dried meats like salami, pepperoni, and dried beef for sandwiches.

Carry potato salad, baked beans, deviled eggs, and fried chicken in thermos containers.

HEALTH AROUND US

Great care is taken to see that milk is safeguarded from pollution. On large dairy farms, for example, milking machines are used. The milk goes from the machines directly to cooling tanks. It is not touched nor is it exposed to air.

In large cities, milk often comes from dairy farms many miles away. It is sent in sanitized tank trucks or in tank cars on express trains. The tank cars keep the milk at a very cool temperature.

At the dairy, harmful bacteria in the milk are destroyed by *pasteurization*. That is, the milk is heated to a high enough temperature to destroy all harmful bacteria. Pasteurization makes the milk safe to drink. But it does not change the composition or the taste of the milk. You can see some pasteurizing equipment below.

Machines at the dairy are also designed to keep the milk free of harmful bacteria. The machines fill and seal sterilized bottles or cartons without help from human hands. How does this method keep the milk pure?

Teacher's Notes

"Health Around Us" is a recurring feature in this book and in this health series. It focuses on interesting and intriguing aspects of health in the world around us. This page explains the need for pasteurization of milk. Some of the germs that thrive in milk are those of tuberculosis, scarlet fever, hepatitis, septic sore throat, and diphtheria. Therefore, it is essential to keep out these disease germs from milk.

Glossary word: *pasteurization*

See page T39 for additional teaching suggestions.

What Should Be Done with Garbage and Trash?

Teacher's Notes
Discuss with students the kinds of things that go into their garbage and trash at home.
Students can read this page and the next to learn three ways that communities dispose of solid wastes (garbage and trash).
Glossary word: *sanitary landfill*

Trash and garbage are among things known as *solid wastes.* And every community faces the problem of getting rid of these wastes.

Dumping

One method that is used is *open dumping.* The garbage and trash is taken by garbage trucks to dump yards and just dumped. These dump yards are usually on the outskirts of the community. Dumping is an easy way to get rid of wastes. But it is a very unhealthy way. The dumps have a bad odor. They offer breeding places for rats and for disease-carrying insects. The dumps are unpleasant places to look at. Because burning is often done to reduce the amount of wastes, there is an air pollution problem.

Although dumping wastes in open dumps is still a widely used method, many communities are working hard to get better ways.

Sanitary Landfills

A method of disposal used in some communities is the *sanitary landfill.* If properly carried out, this is a satisfactory method. With this method, communities bury their solid wastes. Garbage trucks take the wastes to the landfill area. A bulldozer compacts or pushes down the wastes. Then a special machine thoroughly covers the wastes with plenty of earth each day.

With the sanitary landfill, there are no unpleasant-looking dump piles. There is no garbage to attract rats, mice, or flies. There are no bad odors. Also the landfill builds up low-lying areas. Often these areas, when filled, are used for parks and playgrounds.

A problem with the sanitary landfill is that many communities—especially large cities—are running out of usable land for them.

Do You Know?

Not all solid wastes get to dumps, landfills, or incinerators. Have you ever seen a river or stream that was full of wastes that careless people had put there? Where else have you seen such trash as old chairs, tires, and the like? What do you think of such sights?

Incinerating

Many large cities have city-owned incinerators where garbage brought by garbage trucks can be burned. A drawback in this method is that smoke from incinerator smokestacks pollutes the air.

In recent years devices have been developed to cut down on such air pollution. Also new types of incinerators have been developed. Many such incinerators first separate out materials that can be recycled and reused instead of burned. Among such materials are glass, iron, and certain other metals. The burnable material is then incinerated at high temperatures. This leaves only a small amount of leftover material to be buried.

Some modern incinerator plants are also being designed to produce heat and electricity. The heat and electricity are produced from the burning. Then the heat and electricity are used to heat or light buildings in the community.

Cutting Down on Wastes

The problem of waste disposal could be greatly helped if each family would throw away less. Suppose, for example, that every family saved old newspapers, cans, and glass containers. These materials could be taken to collection centers. Next the materials could go to special plants. There they would be changed into forms that could be used again. This is called *recycling.* And the know-how to use recycled material is available.

What effects do you think widespread recycling would have on garbage trucks needed and on space for landfills? What effects would it have on making available needed materials? How might a community profit from its recycling efforts?

Do You Know?

1. How is garbage collected from your home? Who pays for the service? What is done with the garbage after it leaves your home?

2. If you live in a large apartment house, this building may have its own incinerator. Check to see if this is true in your building.

3. Investigate and make a report on compactors that some people use for their garbage. What is the purpose of compactors?

A landfill

A dump yard

An incinerator building

Sum It Up

Which ways of solid waste disposal are shown above?

What are the advantages and disadvantages of each method of disposal?

What can be done to reduce solid wastes?

What do you and your family do to cut down on solid wastes?

TELL IT

These boys and girls have been investigating recycling. They have also investigated ways to cut down on solid wastes. What interesting information have they found?

Teacher's Notes

Discuss with the students what is being done in their community about setting up collection centers for newspapers, glass, and cans. From these collection centers, materials are taken to be recycled into usable materials.

Do you know that recycling a stack of newspapers only one meter high can save one tree? So, save your newspapers. Take them to the recycling centers.

We should recycle as much paper as we can. It causes less air and water pollution to recycle than to make new paper. Also it takes less water and electricity to recycle paper than to make new paper.

We ought to stop using throw-away bottles and use returnable ones instead. Do you know that a typical returnable bottle can be used fourteen to twenty times before it is broken?

Tom

Brenda

Carmela

Teacher's Notes
Ask:
"Why do you think the cone in an ice-cream cone is an ideal container?"
Ask a volunteer to obtain from the library *About Garbage and Stuff* by Ann Zane Shanks (Viking). It has excellent photographs on the recycling of waste materials.

I found out about something that could be very interesting. I read that there is research being done on making the kind of containers that could be *eaten.* For example, you might get a soft drink in a bottle made of pretzels. Or you might buy things that come in nutritious containers that dissolve in water while the things are cooking. This would really cut down on throwaway containers.

I read about an interesting piece of equipment called the *hydra-pulper.* It was developed by a company in Middletown, Ohio. It takes unsorted trash and changes it to pulp for recycled paper. At the same time, the equipment sorts out metal, glass, plastics, and fibers. All these reclaimed materials can be used again.

Charles

Duane

My dad told me that some cities such as Atlanta, Georgia, have magnetic separating machines. The magnetic separating machines can recover about 99% of all steel cans from garbage. This steel can be re-sold to be used again.

Maxine

261

Things to Do

Teacher's Notes
Some other bad effects of noise are annoyance, loss of some hearing, muscle tension, and constriction of the blood vessels.
See page T39 for additional teaching suggestions.

1. Finish this partial list of how too much noise can affect people's health. If you need help, look in books such as *Our Noisy World* by John Navarra (Doubleday).

Noise and Health

Too much noise makes people nervous.

Noise can disturb people's sleep.

Noise can make people feel tired.

2. List five things that can be done to reduce the noise in your home.

3. A volunteer might write for some pamphlets on noise to Citizens for a Quieter City, 150 Amsterdam Avenue, New York, New York 10023.

4. Discuss what people's *values* have to do with how they feel about their environment. For example, what values might lead people in a community to work for laws banning throwaway bottles?

5. Discuss how people's values might affect the kind of car they buy and the frequency with which they use the car.

6. Look at the picture on this page. This kind of pollution is sometimes called *visual pollution*. You know another name for it too. What is it?

7. Write a paragraph on the topic "Why People Shouldn't Litter." Discuss some things you think a community could do to encourage people not to litter.

8. Write a few paragraphs on one of these topics:

What Should a Person Know Who Handles Food?

What's Wrong with an Open Dump?

Why Should Paper Be Saved and Recycled?

9. Tell some things that you and your family do at home to prevent food pollution.

10. The cities of Venice, Florence, and Rome in Italy contain a wealth of ancient, world-famous buildings and statues. In recent years there has been damage to the outsides of some of these buildings and to many of the statues. Discuss why you think this is so.

11. Discuss why you think air pollution is worse now than it was one hundred years ago.

12. Rats are filthy disease-carriers that threaten health. They spread disease germs, destroy food, and bite people. Discuss what families can do to help eliminate rats.

Also investigate what your community health department will do to help get rid of rats.

Special Research

1. Make a report on flies and why they are a health menace. You might look in an encyclopedia for information. Include ways to control the spread of flies.

2. Water pollution is not the only problem some communities have. They may be troubled by a *lack* of water. Find out what is being done to help solve the problem of water scarcity. Be sure to include in your report material on desalination plants which remove the salt from seawater.

3. Make a report on how families can save water and not waste it.

Can You Show What You Know?[1]

Teacher's Notes

Here behavioral objectives in the *cognitive* area are posed in childlike language to the students themselves. In turn, boys and girls give evidence by *observable behavior* of what they have learned.

Other hoped-for behavioral objectives lie chiefly in the less easily observed *affective* area—objectives that pertain to feelings, attitudes, and values. Some of them are:

Shows interest and concern in matters of environmental health.

Takes part in activities designed to improve community health such as picking up litter and recycling.

Is willing to help reduce air pollution by walking or by driving a bicycle instead of being driven in a car.

Page numbers show you where to look back in the chapter for information, if you need it.

1. Describe what is meant by a healthy environment. (234)
2. Tell the purpose of a water-treatment plant. (242)
3. List three ways that bodies of water can become polluted. (243)
4. Mention the main purpose of a community waste-treatment plant. (244)
5. Suggest one thing industries are doing to keep from dumping polluted wastes into waterways. (244)
6. Describe what is meant by polluted air. (246)
7. List three ways in which air can become polluted. (246-247)
8. List three harmful effects of air pollution on health. (247-248)
9. Suggest three ways in which air pollution can be reduced. (249-252)
10. Suggest four sanitary guides for food-handlers. (255)
11. Evaluate three ways by which communities may dispose of solid wastes. (257-259)
12. Suggest one thing families can do to cut down on their solid wastes. (258)

1 Behavioral objectives in the cognitive area are stated here directly to the students themselves.

Review It

Teacher's Notes

"Review It" is a feature that occurs at the end of each chapter in this book and in this series. It gives the pupils a chance to think over what they have learned, to summarize, and to store away important ideas. Page references after each item make this review page a self-help one. However, group discussion can be a valuable adjunct.

Page numbers show you where to look back in the chapter for information, if you need it.

1. How can people become acquainted with environmental health problems? (235)

2. What makes you think that with some effort environmental problems can be solved or at least reduced? (237,239, 241-243, 249-252, 255-256, 258)

3. From where do communities get their drinking water? (242, 243)

4. What kinds of treatment may be given to sewage at a waste-treatment plant? Which is most desirable? (244)

5. What is meant by the term "photochemical smog"? (247)

6. What might cause polluted air to linger over a community for too long a time? (247)

7. In what ways is air pollution an expense to communities? (248)

8. What is a sanitarian? (254)

9. What foods spoil easily? (255)

10. How can valuable material be reclaimed from solid wastes? (258, 260-261)

Copy each numbered item from List A. After each item, write the letter and words from List B that best describe it. For example:

11. combustion h. burning

List A

11. combustion
12. environment
13. incinerator
14. pasteurize
15. pollute
16. recycle
17. sanitarian
18. sewage
19. tertiary

List B

a. health worker
b. furnace
c. use again
d. contaminate
e. third stage
f. household wastes
g. that which is around you
h. burning
i. kill all harmful germs

Health Test for Chapter Eight

Teacher's Notes
After students have taken the test and their papers have been scored, the test items can serve as guides for a summary discussion. Volunteers can read aloud their wording of the completion statements and the rewording of the false statements. "What Do You Think?" is a special feature that offers pupils a chance to evaluate some of their newly acquired knowledge.

Copy each sentence and fill in the missing word or words.

1. In cities, water comes into homes through underground pipes____.

2. Household wastes are called sewage_____.

3. Sewage is treated at waste—____ treatment plants.

4. Air pollution from cars comes out of the exhaust____ pipes.

5. Moist foods provide a good place for bacteria____ to grow.

Copy each number on a piece of paper. After each number write the correct answer, *true* or *false.* Rewrite each false statement to make it true.

T 6. In holding clean spoons, take them by the handle.

T 7. Most bacteria grow best in warm, moist places.

F 8. The purpose of pasteurization is to make milk taste better.

F 9. Water is purified in water towers.

T 10. Whenever things are burned, pollution goes into the air.

T 11. A city surrounded by hills may have serious air pollution at times.

F 12. Burning leaves improves the quality of the air.

T 13. Auto fumes cause air pollution.

T 14. Some health workers who help a community have clean food are called sanitarians.

T 15. You should wash your hands well after you go to the toilet.

F 16. The most sanitary way to dispose of garbage and trash is to dump it into city dumps.

T 17. By recycling paper we save trees.

F 18. One way to reduce solid wastes is for families to throw away more things.

F 19. There is nothing industries can do about air pollution.

F 20. Polluted water may be unpleasant to drink but it is quite safe.

Number of Answers	20
Number Right	_____
Score (Number Right x 5)	_____

What Do You Think?

What have you learned in this chapter that can help you make your environment better? Write your answer on a piece of paper.

SCHOOL & HOME

In this chapter you learned some things that are involved in making a healthy environment. You found out some things you can do too. Many of these things you and your family will want to do.

Here is a list of suggestions you may want to copy and take home. Talk over the ideas with other family members.

Small Steps in the Right Direction[1]

(Some Things You Can Do to Improve the Environment)

1. Keep the land free from litter.
2. Use scrap paper. It has two sides, you know.
3. Organize a cleanup campaign for your neighborhood, park, school, or recreation areas—anywhere it is needed.
4. Use local recycling centers. If there are none, work for their establishment.
5. Grow a plant or plant a tree. Green plants improve the air that you breathe.

"Small Steps in the Right Direction" (Some Things You Can Do to Improve the Environment). From Information Sheet 1, Johnny Horizon Environmental Problem, U.S. Department of the Interior, Washington, D.C. 20240.

Do You Use What You Know?[1]

Teacher's Notes
This is an end-of-book review *with special emphasis on how children are applying their health and safety knowledge in daily life.* A notable feature of this review is the provision for children to look back to pages in the book that can tell them things they need to know, in case they have forgotten. The review should facilitate a transfer of important health and safety ideas from the book to everyday life.

Page numbers after items tell where to look back in the book and find information if you need it.

1. What interesting thing can you tell about yourself? (13-15)

2. What friendly thing have you done recently? (21-22)

3. Have you made any mistakes lately? What did you do about them? (24-25)

4. Has anything made you feel angry recently? What did you do about your angry feelings? (25-26)

5. Has there been a time lately when you or someone you know felt afraid? What did you do about it? (27-28)

6. Can you think of a person or an experience recently that helped you build or strengthen your values? What happened? (29-30)

7. Have you had occasion to observe someone lately that you admire? What qualities impressed you? (30)

8. Has there been a time recently when you had contact with a handicapped person? What have you learned that helped you in this situation? (31-32)

9. Have you had occasion to disagree with someone? How did you do it? (36)

10. Has your brain sent messages to your muscles this very day? What was one of the messages? (46)

11. Suppose someone asked you what is wonderful about your body. What would you say? (56)

12. Have you noticed that a friend is growing tall at a faster rate than you are? How do you explain it? (71-73)

13. Have you noticed that your feet or hands or arms now seem a little out of proportion to your body? How do you explain it? (72)

14. Have you noticed any particular trait that you seem to have inherited? What is it? (84-88)

15. Have you been emotionally upset for one reason or another lately? What body change, if any, did you notice? (101-103)

16. How much sleep did you get in the past few nights? What makes you think it is or isn't enough for you? (105)

17. What have you done in the last day or so to keep physically fit? (108-111)

---

[1] This is an end-of-book review with emphasis on application of health and safety ideas in daily life. Numbers refer to pages where ideas being reviewed are presented.

18. Did you floss and brush your teeth last night or this morning? How did you do it? (114-115)

19. Do you use a toothpaste with an approved fluoride in it? How do you know? (116)

20. Try to remember everything you ate yesterday at meals and for snacks. Jot down what you ate. Did you have an adequate diet? How will you check to find out? (124-125)

21. Did you have breakfast this morning? If so, how can that help you during the morning? (126-127)

22. Have you bought any grocery items lately for the family? Did you look at the nutrition labels? What did you learn? (128)

23. Have you had a health checkup lately? Why did the doctor do what she or he did? (130-140)

24. What would you do if someone was choking? Felt faint? Had a breathing stoppage? Was severely bleeding? (152-157)

25. Have you had occasion to give any first-aid treatment? What treatment did you give? (158)

26. How do you keep safe when you go swimming? (162)

27. What do you do at home to help prevent falls? (164)

28. What do you do to be a safe pedestrian? (164-165)

29. Have you had occasion to use any medicine lately? What precautions did you follow? (174-177)

30. Suppose someone suggested that you experiment with a drug. What precautions might come to your mind? (178)

31. What have you learned about the legality of using marijuana? (181)

32. Suppose someone told you that there is nothing that can be done for an alcoholic. What would you say to that person? (185)

33. Have you done any thinking lately about the effects of smoking on health? What did you think about? (186-188)

34. What have you done lately to keep from spreading disease germs? (220-223)

35. What have you done lately to help improve your home, school, or community environment? (267)

Books for Boys and Girls[1]

Books of Information

American National Red Cross. *Basic First Aid: Books 1, 2, 3, 4* (Doubleday).

Gabel, Margaret. *Sparrows Don't Drop Candy Wrappers* (Dodd).

Grant, Madeleine P. *Biology and World Health,* Rev. Ed. (Abelard).

Gregg, Walter H. *Physical Fitness Through Sports and Nutrition* (Scribner).

Hall, Elizabeth. *Why We Do What We Do: A Look at Psychology* (Houghton).

Knight, David C. *Your Body's Defenses* (McGraw-Hill).

LeShan, Eda J. *What Makes Me Feel This Way? Growing Up with Human Emotions* (Macmillan).

Madison, Arnold. *Drugs and You* (Messner).

_____. *Smoking and You* (Messner).

Paul, Aileen. *Kids Cooking Complete Meals* (Doubleday).

Ravielli, Anthony. *Wonders of the Human Body* (Viking).

Scheinfeld, Amran. *Why You Are You: The Story of Heredity and Environment* (Association).

Silverstein, Alvin, M.D. and Virginia. *Sleep and Dreams* (Lippincott).

Books to "Grow On"

Calhoun, Mary. *Honestly, Katie John!* (Harper). This third book about Katie tells of her experiences in sixth grade.

Cleaver, Vera and Bill. *Grover* (Lippincott). Grover faces the reality of trouble and death in the family.

Gray, Genevieve. *Sore Loser* (Houghton). A story told through correspondence of Loren Ramsey, telling his former friend what it's like in the new classroom.

Konigsburg, E. L. *Altogether, One at a Time* (Atheneum). Four stories that deal with young people's minds and emotions.

Lathan, Jean Lee. *Rachel Carson* (Garrard). Biography of a famous marine biologist who was one of the first to stir people to care about saving their environment.

Malone, Mary. *Annie Sullivan* (Putnam). True story of the teacher of Helen Keller, a girl who could not see or hear.

Witheridge, Elizabeth. *Just One Indian Boy* (Atheneum). Andy learns that an Indian boy can't succeed without school.

Wolf, Bernard. *Don't Feel Sorry for Paul* (Lippincott). A book to acquaint readers with the problems of the handicapped.

[1]See also page T40 for additional books.

Metric Chart

METRIC MEASURES

CUSTOMARY MEASURES

LENGTH

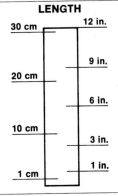

10 millimeters (mm) = 1 centimeter (cm)
100 centimeters = 1 meter (m)
1000 meters = 1 kilometer (km)

12 inches (in.) = 1 foot (ft.)
3 feet = 1 yard (yd.)
5280 feet = 1 mile (mi.)

MASS (WEIGHT)

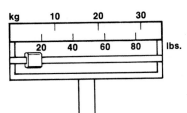

1000 milligrams (mg) = 1 gram (g)
1000 grams = 1 kilogram (kg)
1000 kilograms = 1 metric ton (t)

16 ounces (oz.) = 1 pound (lb.)
2000 pounds = 1 ton (t.)

VOLUME

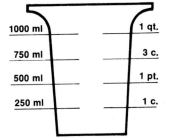

1000 milliliters (ml) = 1 liter (l)
1000 liters = 1 kiloliter (kl)

8 fluid ounces (fl. oz.) = 1 cup (c.)
2 cups = 1 pint (pt.)
2 pints = 1 quart (qt.)
4 quarts = 1 gallon (gal.)

TEMPERATURE

CELSIUS

FAHRENHEIT

Water boils 100° ———— 212° Water boils

Body temperature 37° ———— 98.6° Body temperature

Water freezes 0° ———— 32° Water freezes

Glossary

Full Pronunciation Key

The pronunciation of each word is shown just after the word, in this way: **ab bre vi ate** (ə brē′vē āt). The letters and signs used are pronounced as in the words at the right. The mark ′ is placed after a syllable with primary or heavy accent, as in the example above. The mark ″ after a syllable shows a secondary or lighter accent, as in **ab bre vi a tion** (ə brē′vē ā″shən).

Foreign Sound: H as in German ach. Pronounce k without closing the breath passage.

a	hat, cap	p	paper, cup
ā	age, face	r	run, try
ä	father, far	s	say, yes
		sh	she, rush
b	bad, rob	t	tell, it
ch	child, much	th	thin, both
d	did, red	ᴛʜ	then, smooth
e	let, best	u	cup, butter
ē	equal, be	u̇	full, put
ėr	term, learn	ü	rule, move
f	fat, if	v	very, save
g	go, bag	w	will, woman
h	he, how	y	young, yet
i	it, pin	z	zero, breeze
ī	ice, five	zh	measure, seizure
j	jam, enjoy	ə	represents:
k	kind, seek		a in about
l	land, coal		e in taken
m	me, am		i in pencil
n	no, in		o in lemon
ng	long, bring		u in circus
o	hot, rock	ər	represents:
ō	open, go		er in mother
ô	order, all		ur in pursuit
oi	oil, voice		
ou	house, out		

This pronunciation key is adapted from the *Thorndike-Barnhart Intermediate Dictionary.*

ad re nal gland (ə drē′nl gland′), either of the two endocrine glands, one on the upper part of each kidney. The adrenal glands secrete adrenaline, cortisone, and certain other hormones.

a dren al ine (ə dren′l ən), a hormone secreted by the adrenal glands.

ac id (as′id), a sour chemical substance. The acids caused by fermentation of sweet foods in the mouth can cause cavities. The foods can be removed by brushing the teeth.

A ë des ae gyp ti (ā ē′dēz ē jip′ti), mosquito that transmits the virus causing yellow fever.

al co hol (al′kə hal), the colorless liquid in gin, whiskey, wine, beer, and so on that makes them intoxicating.

al gae (al′jē), group of water plants that can make their own food. Algae contain chlorophyll, but lack true stems, roots, or leaves. Scum on rocks and seaweed are forms of algae.

al ler gy (al′ər jē), pl. **al ler gies,** unusual sensitiveness to certain substances, such as a particular kind of pollen, food, hair, or cloth. Hay fever, asthma, headaches, or hives are common signs of allergy.

a moe ba (ə mē′bə), pl. **a moe bas,** one-celled water animal, so small that it can be seen only with a microscope.

am phet a mine (am fet′ə mēn″ or am fet′ə min), drug used medically to increase the activity of the brain or some other part of the body.

a ne mi a (ə nē′mē ə), lack of blood; not enough red cells or hemoglobin in the blood. Anemia causes weakness.

A noph e les (ə nof′ə lēz), kind of mosquito that transmits malaria to man.

an ti bi ot ic (an″ti bī ot′ik), substance produced by certain microorganisms that can destroy or weaken other microorganisms. Penicillin is an antibiotic.

an ti bod y (an′ti bod″ē), pl. **an ti bod ies,** substance produced in the blood or tissues of the body. It can destroy or weaken bacteria. Or it can make ineffective the poisons produced by bacteria.

an ti sep tic (an″tə sep′tik), substance used to slow up or prevent growth of micro-organisms, especially on living tissue.

a or ta (ā ôr′tə), pl. **a or tas,** main artery of the body, leading out of the left side of the heart to smaller arteries all over the body, except for the lungs.

ar ter y (är′tər ē), pl. **ar ter ies,** one of the many blood vessels that carry blood away from the heart to all parts of the body.

a scor bic ac id (ə skôr′bik as′id), chemical name for vitamin C, found in such foods as citrus fruits and tomatoes. The lack of ascorbic acid in the diet causes scurvy.

bac ter i a (bak tir′ē ə), tiny living plants that can usually be seen only through a microscope. Some harmful bacteria cause disease or tooth decay. Some helpful bacteria turn milk into cheese or cider into vinegar.

bar bit ur ate (bär bich′ər it or bär bich′ə-rāt″), drug used for relaxation and sleep. When misused it can cause drug dependence.

ber i ber i (ber′ē ber′ē), deficiency disease affecting the nerves, accompanied by weakness and extreme loss of weight. It occurs especially in tropical areas and is caused by lack of thiamin.

blood (blud), red liquid in the blood vessels such as veins and arteries; the red liquid that flows from a cut.

blood count (blud′ kount′), count of the number of red and white cells in a sample of blood to see if blood is normal.

blood pres sure (blud′ presh′ər), pressure exerted by the blood on the walls of the blood vessels, especially the arteries.

blood ves sel (blud′ ves′əl), any tube in the body through which the blood circulates. An artery, vein, or capillary is a blood vessel.

bone (bōn), the hard substance forming the skeleton of the body.

brain (brān), mass of nerve cells inside the skull or head of a person or animal. The brain controls almost all of the functions of the body. It enables us to learn, think, and remember.

bron chi tis (brong kī′tis), inflammation of the mucous membrane that lines the bronchial tubes in the lungs. Bronchitis is usually accompanied by a deep cough.

caf feine or **caf fein** (kaf′ēn), a stimulating drug present in coffee and tea.

cal cu lus (kal′kyə ləs), *see* **tartar.**

can cer (kan′sər), a very harmful growth in the body that tends to spread and destroy healthy tissues and organs; malignant tumor. There are many different kinds of cancer.

cap il lar y (kap′ə ler″ē), *pl.* **cap il lar ies,** a blood vessel with a slender, hairlike opening. Capillaries join the end of an artery to the beginning of a vein.

car bo hy drate (kär″bō hī′drāt), substance made from carbon dioxide and water by green plants in sunlight, composed of carbon, oxygen, and hydrogen. Carbohydrates in food furnish heat and energy for the body. Sugar and starch are carbohydrates.

car bon di ox ide (kär′bən dī ok′sīd), colorless, odorless gas present in air. It is a waste product formed by the body. You breathe out, or exhale, carbon dioxide that is in your lungs.

car bon mon ox ide (kär′bən mo nok′sīd), a colorless, odorless, very poisonous gas. It is part of car exhaust and tobacco smoke.

chem i cal (kem′ə kəl), any simple substance that is used to cause changes in other substances. Sulfuric acid, chlorine, and borax are chemicals.

chro mo some (krō′mə sōm), any of the microscopic threadlike particles that appear in the cell nucleus during cell division. They contain genes that determine heredity.

co caine (kō kān′), stimulant drug once used to deaden pain.

co deine (kō′dēn), a narcotic derived from opium and prescribed medically for relief of pain.

con tam i nate (kən tam′ə nāt), defile; pollute; taint; corrupt: *Flies contaminate food.*

cor ti sone (kôr′tə zōn), hormone obtained from the cortex of the adrenal glands or produced synthetically.

den tal car ies (den′tl ker′ēz *or* kar′ēz), decay of dental tissues; tooth decay; cavity.

de pres sant (di pres′ənt), drug that quiets the nerves, relieves worries, and sometimes encourages sleep.

der ma tol o gist (dėr mə tol′ə jist), a doctor who specializes in treating the skin and its diseases.

de sal i na tion (dē sal″ə nā′shən), the process of changing salt water into drinking water.

di ges tion (də jes′chən *or* dī jes′chən), the changing or breaking down of food in the mouth, stomach, and intestines so that the body can use it.

DNA *(de ox y ri bo nu cle ic ac id)* (dē ok″sə-rī″bō nü klē′ik as′id), complicated molecules, present in most chromosomes, which control the growth and heredity of the cell.

drug (drug), substance used as a medicine or in preparing medicines. Drugs are obtained from plants, molds, minerals, and so on, and are often made from chemicals. Aspirin is a drug.

egg cell (eg′ sel′), the female reproductive cell. A new plant or animal develops from a fertilized egg cell.

e lec tro car di o graph (i lek″trō kär′dē ə-graf), instrument that detects and records the electrical impulses produced by the action of the heart with each beat. It is used to diagnose diseases of the heart.

e lec tro en ceph a lo graph (i lek″trō en-sef′ə lə graf), instrument that measures and records the brain's electrical activity.

em phy se ma (em″fə se′mə), respiratory disease in which the air sacs of the lungs become enlarged. The air sacs are less able to supply oxygen to the blood and remove carbon dioxide from it.

en do crine gland (en′dō krən *or* en′dō krīn gland′), any of various glands, such as the thyroid gland, that produce secretions which pass directly into the bloodstream or lymph instead of into a duct.

ep i dem ic (ep″ə dem′ik), the rapid spreading of a disease so that many people or animals have it at the same time.

e soph a gus (ē sof′ə gəs), tube for the passage of food from the mouth to the stomach.

fats (fats), a class of nutrients essential in our diet; they build fatty tissues and serve as a source of energy.

fer ment (fər ment′), undergo or produce a gradual change in which bacteria, yeast, and so on, change sugar into alcohol and produce carbon dioxide.

fer ti li za tion (fėr″tl ə zā′shən), union of male and female reproductive cells to form a cell that will develop into a new individual.

flu o ride (flü′ə rīd″), substance that can help prevent tooth decay. It can be added to toothpaste, or it can be put directly on a person's teeth by a dentist.

---

a hat, **ā** age, **ä** far; **e** let, **ē** be, **ėr** term; **i** it, **ī** ice; **o** hot, **ō** go, **ô** order; **oi** oil, **ou** out; **u** cup, **ů** put, **ü** rule; **ch** child; **ng** long; **sh** she; **th** thin; **ŦH** then; **zh** measure; **ə** taken, mother

gall blad der (gôl′ blad′ər), pear-shaped sac attached to the liver in which bile is stored until needed for digestion.

gas tric juice (gas′trik jüs′), the digestive fluid secreted by glands in the lining of the stomach. It helps break down foods, particularly proteins.

gene (jēn), unit of heredity found in the chromosomes. Each gene influences the inheritance and development of some characteristic.

germ (jėrm), a microscopic animal or plant, especially one which causes disease.

hal lu cin o gen (hə lü′sən ə jən), drug that produces altered sensations, or the seeing or hearing of things that do not exist.

he red i ty (hə red′ə tē), the transmission of genetic physical or mental traits from parent to child.

her o in (her′ō ən), dangerous, habit-forming drug made from opium.

hor mone (hôr′mōn), chemical substance formed in the endocrine glands. It enters the bloodstream and affects or controls the activity of some organ or tissue. Adrenaline and insulin are hormones.

im mune (i myün′), protected from disease, poison, and so on: *Vaccination makes a person practically immune to polio.*

in oc u late (in ok′yə lāt), give a person or animal a preparation made from killed or weakened germs of a particular disease. The preparation will protect the body against that disease.

in su lin (in′sə lən), hormone produced by special cells in the pancreas that helps control the burning of sugar in our bodies.

in tox i cate (in tok′sə kāt), make drunk: *Too much wine intoxicates people.*

in vol un tar y (in vol′ən ter″ē), not controlled by the will: *Breathing is mainly involuntary.*

kid ney (kid′nē), one of the pair of organs in the body that takes liquid wastes and excess water out of the blood. The kidneys then pass on these wastes to the urinary bladder.

large in tes tine (lärj′ in tes′tən), lower part of the intestines where water is absorbed and wastes are eliminated.

lar ynx (lar′ingks), upper end of the windpipe, where the vocal cords are and where the voice is produced.

liv er (liv′ər), large body organ that makes a digestive juice and helps the body use food. The liver also changes sugar into a different form and stores it.

LSD (*ly ser gic ac id di eth yl am ide*) (lī ser′-jik as′id dī eth″ə lam′īd), hallucinogenic compound of lysergic acid that has highly dangerous properties.

lung (lung), one of a pair of saclike, spongy body organs located in the chest. When you breathe in, the lungs take oxygen from the air. When you breathe out, they release carbon dioxide into the air.

mar i jua na (mar″ə wä′nə), the dried flowering tops and leaves of the Indian hemp plant. It is commonly called "pot."

276

mem brane (mem′brān), a thin, flexible layer of tissue or other living material which lines or covers cells, organs, and other parts of the body.

mi cro or gan ism (mī″krō ôr′gə niz əm), animal or vegetable organism too small to be seen except with a microscope.

mi cro scope (mī′krə skōp), instrument with one or more lenses that makes small things look larger.

min er al (min′ər əl), any substance that is neither plant nor animal, but which often occurs in tiny amounts in foods such as meats and vegetables.

mor phine (môr′fēn″), narcotic made from opium, used medically to lessen pain and cause sleep.

mo tor nerve (mo′tər nėrv′), bundle of nerve fibers that carry messages from the brain or spinal cord to the muscles.

mus cle (mus′əl), tissue that can be tightened or loosened to make a part of the body move.

nar cot ic (när kot′ik), drug that is capable of causing drowsiness, sleep, unconsciousness, or stupor. Such drugs blunt the senses.

nerve (nėrv), fiber or bundle of fibers that carry messages between the brain or spinal cord and other parts of the body.

ni a cin (nī′ə sən), chemical name for one of the group of B vitamins, found in such foods as lean meat, wheat germ, and eggs.

nic o tine (nik′ə tēn″), poison contained in the leaves, roots, and seeds of tobacco.

nu cle us (nü′klē əs *or* nyü′klē əs), mass of specialized protoplasm found in most plant and animal cells without which the cell cannot grow and divide.

nu tri ent (nü′trē ənt *or* nyü′trē ənt), nourishing substance found in foods, having specific functions in maintaining the body.

nu tri tion (nü trish′ən *or* nyü trish′ən), series of processes by which food is used by animals and plants for growth, energy, and so on.

oph thal mo scope (of thal′mə skōp), instrument for examining the interior of the eye.

o pi um (ō′pē əm), a narcotic obtained from the opium poppy and from which various other narcotics are extracted.

or tho pe dist (ôr″thə pē′dist), surgeon who specializes in treating deformities and diseases of bones and joints.

os si fy (os′ə fī), to change into bone.

o tol o gist (ō tol′ə jist), doctor who deals with the ear and its diseases.

o to scope (ō′tə skōp), instrument for examining the auditory canal and the eardrum.

o var y (ō′vər ē), the organ of a female in which eggs are produced.

o vum (ō′vəm), *pl.* **o va** (o′və), *see* **egg cell.**

ox y gen (ok′sə jən), colorless, odorless gas that forms about one-fifth of the air.

---

a hat, **ā** age, **ä** far; **e** let, **ē** be, **ėr** term; **i** it, **ī** ice; **o** hot, **ō** go, **ȯ** order; **oi** oil, **ou** out; **u** cup, **u̇** put, **ü** rule; **ch** child; **ng** long; **sh** she; **th** thin; **ŦH** then; **zh** measure; **ə** taken, mother

pan cre as (pan'krē əs), gland near the stomach that empties several secretions into the small intestine to aid digestion.

pas teur i za tion (pas"chər ə zā'shən), process of heating a substance to a high enough temperature to destroy harmful bacteria.

pe di a tri cian (pē"dē ə trish'ən), doctor who specializes in dealing with children's diseases and the care of children.

pen i cil lin (pen"ə sil'ən), antibiotic that is made from mold.

per i o don tal dis ease (per"ē ə don'tl də-zēz'), condition in which the gums, bones, and tissues supporting the teeth are affected and the teeth become loose.

pes ti cide (pes'tə sīd), any of the various substances used to kill harmful insects, fungi, vermin, or other living organisms that destroy or inhibit plant growth, carry disease, and so on.

pho to chem i cal smog (fō"tō kem'ə kəl smog'), smog caused by the action of sunlight on the incompletely burned gases from car exhausts.

pi tu i tar y gland (pə tü'ə ter"ē *or* pə tyü'-ə ter"ē gland'), small, oval endocrine gland situated beneath the brain. It produces several hormones necessary to life.

plaque (plak), thin film composed of saliva, bacteria, and food debris. It is constantly being formed on the surfaces of the teeth.

pol lu tion (pə lü'shən), polluting; defiling; uncleanness; for example, air pollution.

pro por tion (prə pôr'shən), a size, number, or amount compared to another.

pro tein (prō'tēn), one of the substances containing nitrogen which are a necessary part of the cells of animals and plants. Meat, milk, cheese, eggs, nuts, fish, and beans contain protein.

pro to plasm (prō'tə plaz"əm), essential, living, colorless, jellylikel material of which every plant and animal cell is composed.

pro to zo an (prō"tə zō'ən), *pl.* **protozoans,** microscopic animal that consists of a single cell.

psy chi a trist (sī kī'ə trist), doctor trained in prevention and treatment of mental disorders.

pu ber ty (pyü'bər tē), period during which the physical changes which lead to manhood or womanhood take place.

red blood cells (red' blud' selz'), cells that with the white blood cells form a large part of blood. Red blood cells contain hemoglobin, which gives them their color. They carry oxygen from the lungs to various parts of the body.

re flex (rē'fleks), an involuntary action in direct response to a stimulation of some nerve cells. Sneezing, vomiting, and shivering are reflexes.

REM (*rap id eye move ment*) **per i od** (rap'id ī' muv'mənt pir'e əd), stage of sleep during which most dreaming takes place.

re pro duc tion (rē"prə duk'shən), process by which animals and plants reproduce others like themselves.

ret i na (ret'n ə), layer of cells at the back of the eyeball that is sensitive to light. It receives images of things looked at.

rick ets (rik′its), disease of childhood caused by a vitamin D and calcium deficiency and resulting in softening, and sometimes bending, of the bones.

san i tar i an (san″ə ter′ē ən), person who plans and conducts environmental health programs, enforces government regulations on environmental health, and so on.

seal ant (sē′lənt), compound used for sealing.

sed a tive (sed′ə tiv), *see* **depressant.**

sen sor y nerve (sen′sər ē nerv′), nerve fibers that carry messages from the sense organs to the brain or spinal cord.

skel e tal mus cle (skel′ə təl mus′əl), any of the more than 600 muscles that are attached to and cover the skeleton.

skel e ton (skel′ə tən), the bones of a body, fitted together.

small in tes tine (smôl′ in tes′tən), slender part of the intestines, extending from the stomach to the large intestine.

smog (smog), combination of smoke and fog in the air.

sol vent (sol′vənt), substance, usually a liquid, that can dissolve other substances.

sperm (spėrm), one of the cells produced by the male reproductive organs.

spi nal cord (spī′nl kôrd′), thick, whitish cord of nerve tissue in the human back. It reaches from the brain down through most of the backbone. Nerves go from the spinal cord to different parts of the body.

ster ile (ster′əl), free from living germs.

steth o scope (steth′ə skōp), instrument used by doctors to hear the sounds produced in the lungs, heart, and so forth.

stim u lant (stim′yə lənt), food or drug that temporarily increases the activity of the brain or some other part of the body.

stom ach (stum′ək), the large muscular bag in the body which receives, mixes the food, and digests some of it before passing it on.

strep to my cin (strep″tō mī′sn), powerful antibiotic effective against tuberculosis, typhoid fever, and other bacterial infections.

sul fa drugs (sul′fə drugz′), any of several drugs made from dyes and used to combat various bacterial infections.

syn the size (sin′thə sīz), to make artificially.

ter ti ar y treat ment (tėr′shē er″ē trēt′-mənt), third step in which wastes and harmful substances are removed from sewage.

tes ti cle (tes′tə kəl), gland in a male animal that produces sperm; testis.

ther mal pol lu tion (ther′məl pə lü′shən), contamination resulting from the discharge of excess heated water into a waterway.

thi a min or **thi a mine** (thī′ə mən), chemical name for vitamin B₁ which is found in such foods as green vegetables and cereals.

thy roid gland (thī′roid gland′), endocrine gland in the neck which secretes a substance that helps regulate the rate at which the body uses its store of energy.

---

a hat, ā age, ä far; e let, ē be, ėr term; i it, ī ice; o hot, ō go, ȯ order; oi oil, ou out; u cup, u̇ put, ü rule; ch child; ng long; sh she; th thin; ᴛʜ then; zh measure; ə taken, mother

tra che a (trā′kē ə), see **windpipe**.

tran quil iz er (trang′kwə lī″zər), a drug that may be prescribed by doctors to relieve tension or lower blood pressure.

trans plant (tran splant′), transfer (skin, an organ, and so on) from one person, animal, or part of the body to another.

u re ter (yu̇ rē′tər), duct that carries urine from a kidney to the bladder.

u ri nal y sis (yu̇r″ə nal′ə sis), analysis of a sample of urine.

ur i nar y blad der (yu̇r′ə ner″ē blad′ər), soft, thin sac in the body that receives urine from the kidneys. The bladder stores and later discharges urine.

ur ine (yu̇r′ən), the fluid that is excreted from the kidneys as a waste product of the body. Urine goes to the urinary bladder and is then discharged from the body.

u rol o gist (yu̇ rol′ə jist), an expert in dealing with the urogenital tract in the male or the urinary tract in the female and their diseases.

vac ci na tion (vak″sə nā′shən), inoculating a person to protect him or her from a communicable disease.

vac cine (vak′sēn″), substance containing weakened or killed virus or the killed bacteria of a particular disease. A vaccine can be injected, or taken orally, to stimulate the body to produce antibodies.

vein (vān), one of the blood vessels or tubes that carries blood to the heart from all parts of the body.

vil li (vil′ī), tiny hairlike parts growing out of the lining of the small intestine. The villi absorb certain substances.

vi rus (vī′rəs), any of a group of disease-producing organisms that reproduce only in living cells. They can be seen with an electron microscope.

vi ta min (vī′tə min), any of certain special substances required for the normal growth and nourishment of the body.

vol un tar y (vol′ən ter″ē), deliberately intended; done on purpose: *Talking is voluntary; breathing is only partly so.*

white blood cells (hwīt′ blud′ selz′), colorless cells that float in the blood and lymph. Some of them destroy disease germs.

wind pipe (wind′ pīp″), passage by which air is carried from the throat to the lungs; the trachea.

X ray (eks′ rā′), 1. ray which penetrates substances that light cannot penetrate. X rays are used to locate breaks in bones and cavities in teeth and to diagnose and treat certain diseases. 2. picture made by means of X rays.

---

a hat, **ā** age, **a** far; **e** let, **ē** be, **ėr** term; **i** it, **ī** ice; **o** hot, **ō** go, **ȯ** order; **oi** oil, **ou** out; **u** cup, **u̇** put, **ü** rule, **ch** child; **ng** long; **sh** she; **th** thin; **ᴛʜ** then; **zh** measure; **ə** taken, mother

About the Book

This book is especially designed to meet the health and safety needs, interests, and concerns of students of ages eleven to twelve or so.

First and foremost, these boys and girls want to know more about themselves. They wonder what makes them think and feel and act as they do. They would like to be better liked by others. They ask, "How can I learn to understand others better?" Ample material on these common mental health and human relations concerns is included in this book.

Interest in the workings of the human body is still pronounced. So a chapter is presented that features a script on this topic from a well-known health center.

The query "Am I growing normally?" is answered in a chapter on "Growth." Growth patterns of girls and of boys in the preteen and early teen years are considered. A simple explanation of heredity is provided as well.

A chapter on "Health Questions Answered" gives essential information about sleep, physical fitness, care of the teeth, nutrition, and the importance of the health checkup.

Age-appropriate material is given about drugs. Girls and boys learn about prescription drugs, over-the-counter drugs, sedatives, stimulants, tranquilizers, hallucinogens, narcotics, sprays and solvents that may be used improperly, alcohol, and tobacco.

Basic information on emergency care and on safety are given in the chapter "First Aid and Safety."

To satisfy curiosity about what causes communicable diseases and how scientists have made progress over the years in controlling them, there is a chapter on the history of public health. Against this background, a follow-up chapter on community and environmental health problems of today takes on added meaning. Such timely topics as water pollution, air pollution, food pollution, and proper disposal of solid wastes are featured in the final chapter called "A Healthy Environment."

Interspersed throughout each chapter are special features such as health-related poems and works of art and students' own writings on pertinent health topics.

Tests and quick reviews abound and help students check their own progress. And a notable feature of each chapter ending is the "School-Home" page which motivates sharing health information at home and applying it in daily living.

Marginal notes to students and "Things to Do" sections at chapter endings also offer a variety of activities.

Teaching tips appear throughout the *Teacher's Edition* which includes "Teacher's Notes" overprinted in blue on the students' pages and a special "Teacher's Supplement."

To facilitate sucessful use of this book by the students for whom it is particularly intended, much attention has been given to making the text highly readable. Classroom tryouts prior to publication indicated that this book can easily be read by youngsters of the age for which it was designed. Readability scores are as follows:

Dale-Chall Readability Formula	Grade 6
Fry Readability Formula	Grade 6

Acknowledgments

For illustrations and photographs on these pages:
Cover—Ralph Cowan. 33—Department of Vocational Rehabilitation. 34-35—Courtesy of Shiro Fukurai from *How Can I Make What I Cannot See?* published by Van Nostrand Reinhold. 46, 47, 49 (Left)—Copyright © 1971, 1974 by Scott, Foresman and Company. 50—Copyright © 1972, 1974 by Scott, Foresman and Company. 52, 57-61—Copyright © 1971, 1974 by Scott, Foresman and Company. 62—EMI Medical Inc., Northbrook, Illinois. 72, 74, 75—Copyright © 1971, 1974 by Scott, Foresman and Company. 77—Yale Journal of Biology and Medicine, Volume 22, page 595, © 1950. 81, 86 (Top)—Copyright © 1971, 1974 by Scott, Foresman and Company. 86 (Bottom), 87—Photographs from Janet Rowley, M.D., Department of Medicine, The Pritzker School of Medicine, The University of Chicago and the Argonne Cancer Research Hospital operated by The University of Chicago for the U.S. Atomic Energy Commission. 88—Copyright © 1971, 1974 by Scott, Foresman and Company. 89—Copyright © 1972, 1974 by Scott, Foresman and Company. 90 (Bottom Two Rows)—Photographs from Federal Bureau of Investigation, U.S. Department of Justice, Washington, D.C. 90 (Top Two Rows), 91, 93—Copyright © 1971, 1974 by Scott, Foresman and Company. 97—Forty-fifth Annual Thanksgiving Day Dinner by Bill Owens. 101—Copyright © 1971, 1974 by Scott, Foresman and Company. 106—Courtesy of University of Chicago Sleep Laboratory under the direction of Dr. Allan Rechtschaffen, Director. 107, 109—Copyright © 1972, 1974 by Scott, Foresman and Company. 114-115—Copyright by the American Dental Association. Reprinted by permission. 120—Copyright © 1971, 1974 by Scott, Foresman and Company. 124, 125, 126, 131, 132—Copyright © 1971, 1974 by Scott, Foresman and Company. 133—Photographs from Maurice F. Rabb, M.D., Department of Ophthalmology, University of Illinois at the Medical Center, Chicago, Illinois. 134—Photographs from Richard A. Buckingham, M.D., Department of Otolaryngology, University of Illinois at the Medical Center, Chicago, Illinois. 135 (Top Left, Bottom Left, Bottom Right)—Photographs from R. Stuart Weeks, M.D., Department of Otolaryngology, The University of Chicago, Chicago, Illinois. 135 (Top Right)—Photograph from Paul H. Holinger, M.D., Department of Otolaryngology, University of Illinois at the Medical Center, Chicago, Illinois. 138—Photograph by Steven O. Schwartz, M.D. 139—Copyright © 1971, 1974 by Scott, Foresman and Company. 143—Courtesy fo Del Monte Corporation. 153, 157, 159, 161—Copyright © 1971, 1974 by Scott, Foresman and Company. 163—Courtesy WMAQ, News 5, Chicago, Illinois. 164-165—Courtesy of National Safety Council. 184—Copyright © 1971, 1974 by Scott, Foresman and Company. 189—Photograph by Leo Stashin. 190-191—Courtesy of American Cancer Society. 193—From *Smoking and You* by Arnold Madison, published by Julian Messner, A Division of Simon and Schuster, Inc. Copyright 1975 by Arnold Madison. 201 (Left)—Copyright © 1971, 1974 by Scott, Foresman and Company. 201 (Right), 202—Photographs from National Library of Medicine, Bethesda, Maryland. 203—Copyright © 1971, 1974 by Scott, Foresman and Company. 204—Copyright © 1959 Parke, Davis & Company. 205—Photograph from The Bettmann Archive, Inc. 206—Copyright © 1971, 1974 by Scott, Foresman and Company. 208—Copyright © 1960 by Parke, Davis & Company. 210—Copyright © 1962 by Parke, Davis & Company. 212, 213—Copyright © 1971, 1974 by Scott, Foresman and Company. 215—Photograph from The Bettmann Archive, Inc. 216—Copyright © 1962 by Parke, Davis & Company. 220 (Right—Courtesy of Dr. Dieter H. Sussdorf. 220 (Center)—Photograph from National Medical Audiovisual Center. 220 (Left)—Courtesy S. Stanley Schneirson, M.D., and Abbott Laboratories. 221 (Left)—Microphotograph courtesy of Virus Laboratory, University of California, Berkeley, California. 221 (Right)—Microphotograph courtesy of American Society for Microbiology. 222—Copyright © 1971, 1974 by Scott, Foresman and Company. 224—Photograph from The Bettmann Archive, Inc. 227 (Left)—Courtesy Wide World. 227 (Right)—Center for Disease Control, Atlanta, Georgia. 236—Photographs from Federal Water Pollution Control Administration. 237—Article: Abridged from "Resuscitaiton Is Working for Pollution-plagued Erie" by Ronald Kotulak from *Chicago Tribune,* June 1, 1975. Reprinted, courtesy of the Chicago Tribune. Map: Tribune Map. 238—Copyright © 1974 by Scott, Foresman and Company. 239—Courtesy Bethlehem Steel Corporation. 240—Copyright © 1971, 1974 by Scott, Foresman and Company. 241—"What You Can Do at Home to Save Your Environment" from "If You Want to Save Your Environment . . . START AT HOME!!" by Carroll Harrington, et al. Published by Palo Alto branch of American Association of University Women and Hawthorn Books. © 1970 by Palo Alto branch of American Association of University Women. Reprinted by permission. 242—Courtesy of the Fort Worth Water Department. 246—Engravings from The Bettmann Archive, Inc. 248—Copyright © 1972, 1974 by Scott, Foresman and Company. 250—Courtesy of AB Volvo, Gothenburg, Sweden. 251 (Left)—Copyright © 1972, 1974 by Scott, Foresman and Company. 251 (Right)—Copyright © 1971, 1974 by Scott, Foresman and Company. 252 (Top)—Photographs from *Fortune Magazine.* 252 (Center)—Courtesy Environmental Protection Agency. 252 (Bottom)—Copyright 1971, 1974 by Scott, Foresman and Company. 254—Courtesy U.S. Department of Agriculture. 256, 259 (Center)—Copyright © 1971, 1974 by Scott, Foresman and Company. 262—Photograph by Tom Meyers from Photo Researchers.